1866 · 1991

125th

ANNIVERSARY

FROM THE
GROUND UP

FROM THE

GROUND UP

THE · BUSINESS · OF BUILDING · IN · THE AGE · OF · MONEY

DOUGLAS FRANTZ

HENRY HOLT AND COMPANY NEW YORK

Published by Henry Holt and Company, Inc.,
115 West 18th Street, New York, New York 10011.
Published in Canada by Fitzhenry & Whiteside Limited,
195 Allstate Parkway, Markham, Ontario L3R 4T8.

Library of Congress Cataloging-in-Publication Data
Frantz, Douglas.
From the ground up : the business of building in the age of money / by
Douglas Frantz. — 1st ed.
p. cm.
Includes bibliographical references and index.
ISBN 0-8050-0996-5
1. Rincon Center (San Francisco, Calif.) 2. Real estate
development—California—San Francisco—Case studies.
3. Construction industry—California—San Francisco—Case studies.
I. Title.
HD268.S4F73 1991
333.77'15'0979461—dc20   91-9150
CIP

Henry Holt books are available at special discounts
for bulk purchases for sales promotions, premiums,
fund-raising, or educational use. Special editions
or book excerpts can also be created to specification.
For details contact:
Special Sales Director, Henry Holt and Company, Inc.,
115 West 18th Street, New York, New York 10011.

First Edition

DESIGNED BY KATY RIEGEL
MAP BY JEFFREY WARD

GRATEFUL ACKNOWLEDGMENT
IS MADE TO JOHNSON, FAIN & PEREIRA ASSOCIATES
AND TO PERINI CORPORATION FOR SUPPLYING
MANY OF THE ILLUSTRATIONS USED IN THIS BOOK

Printed in the United States of America
Recognizing the importance of preserving
the written word, Henry Holt and Company, Inc.,
by policy, prints all of its first editions
on acid-free paper. ∞

1 3 5 7 9 10 8 6 4 2

FOR CATHERINE

"Was he, Thomas Buddenbrook, a man of action, a business man—or was he a finicking dreamer? Yes, that was the question. . . . For the first time in his career he had fully and personally experienced the ruthless brutality of business life and seen how all better, gentler, and kindlier sentiments creep away and hide themselves before the one raw, naked, dominating instinct of self-preservation."

—Thomas Mann, *Buddenbrooks*

CONTENTS

An illustration section follows page 146

FROM THE GROUND UP

1

RINCON AT MORN

The view from the 20th-floor apartment is postcard-perfect. Early-morning fog tumbles out of the hills above Sausalito. Alcatraz is wrapped in a misty blanket. Patches of San Francisco Bay are visible beneath the fog, a solitary sailboat bobbing in and out of sight. Treasure Island, the navy base in the bay, has disappeared in the gray swirls.

Closer to the apartment, on the right, the waterfront terminal is quiet. The commuter ferries will begin to dock in an hour or so, bringing lawyers, bankers, and secretaries from Marin County to toil in the office towers of San Francisco. As they shuffle out of the terminal, the commuters will pass beneath the elevated, double-decked Embarcadero Freeway, its huge concrete columns buttressed with wooden supports since the earthquake in October 1989 threatened to send the highway crashing down.

Visible off to the left are the tall buildings of the financial district, headquarters of the Wells Fargo Bank, Citicorp Center, Pacific Stock Exchange, and Bank of America. Peeking above those skyscrapers is the sharp tip of San Francisco's tallest building, the forty-eight-story Transamerica pyramid. Once the city's most radical structure, the pyramid is now an icon in its skyline. Also off to the left is Nob Hill, with its elegant hotels, steep streets, and quaint cable car tracks. Partially visible in the distance is the rust-red span of the Golden Gate Bridge.

Much closer now, twenty stories below the window, a solitary man in a business suit sits on a gray-green metal bench in the building's courtyard. Steam rises into the morning chill from his Styrofoam cup as he snatches a moment's peace before heading off for the day's battles. The courtyard satisfies the need for a sense of security in a public place; as the day goes on, and the hustle of the urban landscape commences, the courtyard will continue to hold out a promise of relief, a place where a person can sit or stand without getting in the way of anyone else. Its granite planters brim with pink begonias and purple impatiens, and its graceful benches are sited carefully on the granite floor beneath outdoor lamps. Near the center of the courtyard, an obelisk tapers to a height of ten feet, its white, brown, and blue ceramic surface highlighted by diving dolphins.

The tower that contains this apartment 200 feet above the courtyard is the twin of one a few feet away. Both are made of concrete and glass in shades of gray. The towers are curved, so that they cradle the courtyard below. They are eighteen stories tall, topped by identical twenty-four-foot spires, and sit on a shared six-story base that houses professional offices and retail space. The total structure reaches twenty-four stories into the air, or 240 feet, not counting the spires. The top two floors of each tower are used for mechanical systems, such as the heating and air-conditioning units.

The six-story office base creates the southern border for the courtyard below the high-rise towers. The base also forms the courtyard's sides on the east and west. The east and west extensions will eventually contain stores, but for now their large glass windows are covered with off-white paper as they await tenants.

From above, the overall configuration is that of a square-bottomed U.

At the open end of the U, the plaza's north side, a five-story archway frames a huge window on the rear facade of a five-story, older building. The older building is made of white concrete. Its top two floors are new and, except here at the back, they are recessed from its edge fifteen feet so they are not visible from the street. Below the arch, three sets of wide glass doors stand open and a colonnade, with a patterned marble floor, leads into the smaller building. A woman emerges from one of the apartment buildings, briefcase in one hand and newspaper tucked under an arm. She strides across the courtyard and disappears into the smaller building. Minutes later, a couple comes out of the apartments and follows the same path.

Two men, deep in conversation, walk into the courtyard through one of the two glass-canopied entrances on opposite sides of the plaza at midblock and also disappear into the smaller building. The canopies span the twenty-seven-foot gap between the older building and its new neighbor. The link between the old and new is tenuous, partly for obvious architectural reasons and partly for hidden engineering ones. The old building, built five decades ago, is more rigid than its new neighbors and would sway less in an earthquake. The results, if the buildings were tied together in any significant manner, would be disastrous.

By now, it is nearly seven o'clock on the morning of June 18, 1990. The sun has come up over the bay and soon the fog will burn off to unveil a glorious, cool summer day in San Francisco. Within the next hour, this multiple-use development, known as Rincon Center, will awaken fully as more of its residents leave for jobs and workers arrive to labor in its offices and to search for food among the restaurants beneath its 200-foot skylight. Tourists and other pleasure seekers will begin to arrive to marvel at its unique free-form waterfall, which plunges five tall stories from ceiling to floor and fills the older building with the joyful sounds of a summer rainstorm.

This is the story of Rincon Center, a mixed-use project in San Francisco that includes apartments, offices, shops, and restaurants. It also is the story of the men who shaped and built Rincon Center, the dreamers who seek riches and immortality by launching great buildings onto today's urban landscapes. They are modern-day gamblers who have learned to exploit every loophole possible in pursuit of maximum profit. In boom years, they amass enormous profits and pray that they can stave off bankruptcy in the lean ones. Only the smart developers survive these boom-and-bust cycles.

The full range of human emotions were as much a part of erecting this complex development as the steel, concrete, and glass that give it tangible form. Those who build tall buildings would prefer that it not be so. Plans and schedules and budgets are meant to order the process and eliminate such unnecessary items as emotion. As Rincon Center neared completion in 1989, its construction manager, John Costello, observed: "In our business, we don't like drama. But this building had plenty."

What are the fruits of that five-year drama? Stunning views from a 20th-floor apartment. An elegant rain column and a new stop on the Grayline tour. A dozen restaurants in a dozen flavors for hungry office workers. Office space for 1,500 or so people, and 320 apartments in a city desperate for urban housing. Survival for an outdated but historic post office. Another notch of fame for a rising young star in the world of architecture. A development team battered by millions of dollars in cost overruns. And money, in various denominations, from large to larger, flowing in various directions.

Yet in the end, when the drama has been played out, what is left on which to judge whether the effort was worthwhile, whether the mark that remains from all this labor is sterile and ugly or uplifting and golden, whether a dysfunctional neighborhood has been put on the road to health? The building, of course. Long after the owners have collected their profit or lost their shirts and the architects, engineers, and laborers have moved on to other projects, a million square feet of concrete, glass, and marble on a full city block remain as testament to their labors.

Rincon Center is bounded on the north by Mission Street and on the south by Howard Street. The eastern border, closest to the bay, is Steuart Street, and the western one is Spear Street. Four lanes of ugliness, the Embarcadero Freeway, curve around the southern edge of the site. Not long after the 1989 earthquake, one of Rincon's owners said he wished the entire freeway had fallen down; it would have cleared the views of the bay from the lower floors of the development. Uptown is west from Rincon, and three blocks in that direction is the busy Transbay Terminal for public buses. The ferry terminal is two blocks north and slightly east, on the waterfront. North and slightly west is the Embarcadero stop on the Bay Area Rapid Transit.

The entire site is situated in an area known as "South of Market," regarded in recent years as fertile territory for urban pioneers. Market Street has long been the boundary in downtown San Francisco between premium developments and the rest. The financial district, Fisherman's Wharf, and the huge Embarcadero Center are north of Market; warehouses and transient hotels dominate to the south.

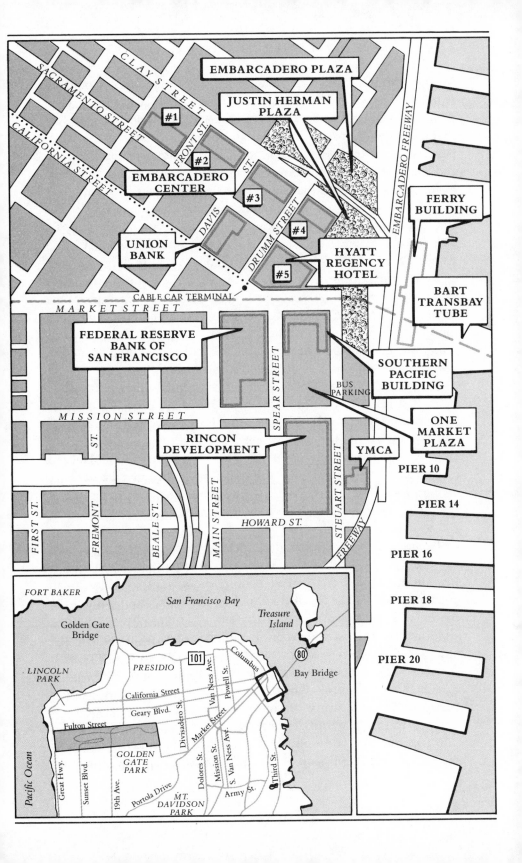

Once, this location was under ten feet of bay water. Countless wooden ships were abandoned here in the late 1840s and 1850s, when their crews ran off to seek their fortunes in the gold rush. As San Francisco grew into the financial and business capital of the West, portions of the bay were filled in to accommodate the expanding city and the area became home to Chinese laundries, saloons, brothels, hotels, and chandleries that served the shipping trade.

In 1940, the federal government completed a postal facility on the site. Covering almost half a block, the structure was built on 3,800 wooden pilings sunk in the bay and the mud. It was called the Rincon Annex Post Office. Gilbert Stanley Underwood, an architect who enjoyed a small measure of fame on the West Coast during the 1920s and 1930s, designed it: the post office is a three-story example of the Streamline Moderne school of architecture. It is a compact and symmetrical structure, with clean lines that are graced by two-story windows and punctuated by nautical devices, such as dolphins, portholes, and railings, in recognition of the location's heritage.

Today, the exterior of the post office is little changed on three sides. Cut into black granite above the two small entrances on Mission Street are the words "United States Post Office Rincon Annex." But the rear facade has been ripped away and replaced by the giant archway and glass window. And the interior bears no resemblance to the warren of offices and long tables for sorting mail that did not have enough historical or architectural importance to warrant preservation. The two new floors that have been added are topped with the 200-foot-long skylight.

Beneath the lightly tinted glass of the skylight, a five-story atrium has been carved out of the center of the building. The project's structural engineer compared creating the atrium to using a can opener to pry off the lid of the building and then scooping out the contents. The ground floor of the atrium is ringed by restaurants, tables and chairs clustered in common dining areas, an art gallery, and other small shops. The upper stories house offices, with large windows and balconies overlooking the atrium. Its design and detailing were the focus of a prolonged battle among the architects, the developers, and a small army of consultants that in many ways was a microcosm for the entire development process at Rincon Center.

Most people enter the old post office through one of three original entrances, two on Mission Street and one on Spear. The two-story lobby retains the feel of the post office. The floor is government green granite. Twenty-seven bold murals line the 400-foot lobby. They depict the history of California, from the early Indians to the founding of the United Nations in San Francisco, and are the work of the late Anton Refregier. They have been painstakingly restored by a team of experts. Metal grates still cover the service windows and above them are plastic signs: PARCEL POST, STAMPS, LETTER DROPS, FIRM MAILING, LOCK BOXES. But behind the grates are displays for the shops in the atrium. There is no longer a place to mail a letter in the old building. The new post office is in the second building at the other end of the block. Still, the question most often asked of the security guard at the information podium in the historic lobby is, "Where can I mail this letter?"

Falling water is the first thing one hears upon entering Rincon Center through the post office lobby. It is less than a roar, louder than a trickle. A visitor who follows his ears through the lobby to the atrium soon finds the source: some eighty-five feet above, barely visible against the skylight, is a square Plexiglas plate measuring eight feet on each side and perforated by 4,000 precisely drilled holes. Every minute, a recirculating pumping system sends a steady fifty-five gallons of water swirling onto the plate. The water pours continuously through the holes and falls straight into a pool flush with the floor. Think of it as a giant but elegant shower.

Every first-time visitor instantly and automatically looks straight up on entering the atrium. When the building first opened, visitors were so mesmerized that some walked right into the pool while staring at the ceiling. Several slipped and fell in the shallow water, causing the building's owners untold worries about possible lawsuits. The inelegant solution devised by the owners over the objections of the architect and the artist was potted plants at critical spots along the perimeter of the pool.

Small metal tables with laquered wooden tops and matching metal chairs surround the atrium. The chairs are half-price knockoffs of an Italian design that would have cost $600 each. In the mornings, they are usually about one-quarter full as workers grab a quick breakfast or cup of coffee. At the start of the day, the atrium is in shade. As the sun rises and the light filters in, the aluminum mullions supporting the skylight break the sunshine into patterned shadows that creep down the west interior wall. The wall was designed to evoke the warmth and grandeur of sandstone, but that is one of many illusions necessitated by budget limitations on Rincon Center. The atrium walls are gypsum board, also known as drywall, that have been artfully painted and cut to look like sandstone. Similarly, some of the round columns defining the eating area in the atrium appear to be red granite but are merely hollow columns with a *faux* finish applied by a team of painters. Small screened openings in their bases help ventilate the atrium.

By mid-morning, the sun has moved down the walls as far as the new murals that line the perimeter of the atrium. Designed specifically for the space by New York painter Richard Haas, they depict the modern history of San Francisco in panels of beige, blue-gray, and pink. The murals seem faded and washed out compared with the Refregier works in the old lobby.

A few minutes before eleven o'clock, a young man in a tuxedo pulls the cover off a Steinway grand piano a few feet from the rain pool and begins to play, moving from Broadway show tunes to classical as the lunch crowd trickles in. Rincon's developers stole this idea from the Trump Tower in New York City.

Traffic in the atrium picks up about eleven-thirty as the lunchtime crowd begins to arrive in earnest. By shortly after noon no tables are left, and men and women in business dress vie with workers from nearby construction sites for spots on the two-tiered platforms that, curving around the perimeter of the atrium, offer additional seating. On their laps, they balance trays from restaurants with such names as the Tampico Taqueria, What a Deli, Arabia, and All Stars. The buzz of a hundred conversations is muffled by the constant sound of falling water. This is a scene that is repeated every weekday in the atrium, which has already become far and away the most popular lunchtime gathering spot in the neighborhood.

By two o'clock, only a few stragglers remain and the after-work crowd does not materialize on this Monday as it often does on Thursdays and Fridays. Only a few people meet for a quick soda or cookie before moving on. At night, most of the people who come into the atrium head for Wu Kong, a fancy and highly rated Chinese restaurant, or Asta, which serves American cuisine and was named for the dog in the movie *The Thin Man*.

Outside, at the far end of the courtyard, sit the two apartment towers. The sun has dropped below the skyline, leaving the courtyard shaded and cool. In truth, the courtyard is chilly and shaded much of the day because the towers block out the sun, except between eleven o'clock in the morning and one in the afternoon. The shadows are unavoidable, given the density of the two towers at the south end of the site. Numerous sun and shade studies were conducted during the design process in an attempt to ensure that sun reaches the plaza at least during the noon hour. People still use the space during periods of shade, but it is rarely as packed as some of San Francisco's other outdoor areas.

The few people who work in the six floors of offices in the new portion of the project use a small lobby and elevators off the back end of the plaza. This space is still almost entirely empty, costing the developers thousands of dollars a day in lost rent. In a conscious attempt to separate the work and living portions of the complex and maintain the two different security levels, the office workers are cut off from the more elegant lobby on the Howard Street side of the building that serves the apartments. There, a concierge is on duty behind a large custom-made wooden desk. The walls are covered with fine woods and the lights are brass. Unlike the relatively unrestricted access to the commercial space, all visitors to the residential portion of the building are stopped and identified.

The first apartments were available early in the summer of 1989. On this June day almost a year later, a leasing agent named Jill Dilley says the towers are 96 percent occupied. The choicest apartments, those on the east and south sides of the towers, have panoramic views of the Bay Bridge and Oakland. Many of them were snapped up even before the building opened. The early customers included local architects who admired the project, people who work in the area and had followed the structure's progress, and corporations looking for a convenient pied-à-terre for visiting executives. Scattered throughout the building are the below-market "affordable" units, occupied mostly by young singles who fall within the income guidelines set by the city.

All that Dilley has to show a prospective tenant is a two-bedroom, two-bath apartment on the 20th floor with a northern view of the city and the bay. It is the same spot from which the visitor watched the sunrise earlier that morning, courtesy of a friendly security guard. The apartment has a small, well-appointed kitchen and a medium-size living room. Both bedrooms are small and one is chopped into a strange configuration to accommodate the intersection of two structural girders. Another girder curves around the exterior, dropping the ceiling about eight more inches right at the windows. But any sense of claustrophobia is relieved by the panorama beyond the huge windows. This particular apartment is 1,000 square feet and the rent is $2,100 a month, on the high end for San Francisco. Better take it fast, because it's the only big one available, warns Dilley.

"This building has been a big success since before it opened," brags Dilley.

Perhaps that is true. But it is not the whole truth. Not by a long shot.

2

THE RISKS OF
THE GAME

Real estate developers assemble pieces of land, arrange financing, secure government approvals, and hire architects and engineers to design and build big projects. It can be a long and complicated process, requiring creativity and persistence. But real estate developers are not business people in the traditional sense. In their hearts, they are gamblers. The smart ones gamble with other people's money, raising their stakes from banks, syndicates, and big-time investors. They hedge their bets by exploiting the potpourri of tax breaks and subsidies offered by Uncle Sam. And even in this era of equal opportunity, real estate development remains a man's field or, more accurately, a boy's game.

Through the late 1970s and early 1980s, real estate development was a lot like sex: when it was good, it was really great and when it was bad, it was still pretty good. Fueled by generous tax laws and big banks, and small savings and loans burning to lend money to hordes of borrowers of sometimes dubious repute, an unprecedented building boom transformed downtowns across America. So it's no surprise that, by 1984, many areas around the country were suffering from an overbuilding that was beginning to send tremors through the nation's banking community. Some developers would try to grow their way out of the problem, taking out bigger and bigger loans and putting up more buildings in a variation of the old Ponzi scheme. Those who had not stretched their finances so thin could afford to pull back and wait until the market shook out. It ran in cycles anyway, as they all knew.

Randy Verrue is a real estate developer whose instincts told him 1984 was a time to proceed cautiously. The San Francisco market, where he works, had gone through a feverish period in which office buildings and condominiums seemed to sprout overnight on every corner of downtown. Between 1979 and 1984, San Francisco had added 10 million square feet of office space, a fifth of the total built in the previous 100 years. More than sixty new office buildings had been constructed downtown and *California* magazine worried about the effect on San Francisco: "This city, once mythologized as Baghdad by the Bay, might now be better christened Houston by the Pacific."

Verrue feared that the results of the building boom were about to be felt in increasing vacancy rates and stagnant or even declining rents, both bad news for developers. His company was already feeling the pinch: the twenty-three-story Ecker Square, the first new high-rise office condominium built in San Francisco, had been completed in 1983 and sales were lagging. And Verrue expected it to get worse before it got better.

So that spring, when word spread that a full city block near the waterfront was going to be opened up for development, Verrue's interest was tempered by his anticipation of the market's coming problems. Still, because the site was the last substantial open space between the financial district and the waterfront in San Francisco, he was intrigued. But there were problems with the location and restrictions in the way it could be developed. As he sat in his office in the Alcoa Building and rolled the idea around in his mind, analyzing the risks and potential benefits, Verrue came to the conclusion that he did not want to sink the company's money into developing the Rincon Annex Post Office.

Randy Verrue earned his living making such decisions. He was the western division manager of Perini Land & Development Company, the real estate development subsidiary of Perini Corporation. Based in Framingham, Massachusetts, just outside Boston, Perini was the nation's fifth-largest construction company in 1984. Real estate development traditionally is a regional business, and there are few national powerhouses. Although it has always been best known as a construction company, Perini usually is counted among the national development firms. In the mid-1980s, the firm and its development arm were involved in projects across the country, from Boston to Florida to Northern California.

Verrue's primary job was to scout out and secure promising development deals up and down the West Coast and then oversee them to completion. In five years with Perini, he had put together a series of transactions that had either made substantial amounts of money or appeared destined to once they were finished. In one of the most complicated, he had untangled a twelve-year-old zoning dispute over a Lake Tahoe luxury-home development that had threatened to cost Perini millions of dollars.

Earlier in 1984, Verrue pulled off a deal that grabbed everyone's attention back in Framingham. The owner of a small San Francisco office building called the Ice House was in financial trouble, facing foreclosure. Verrue offered him a bargain-basement price, just enough to enable him to avoid a total loss. Before the deal was even closed, Verrue had arranged to resell the property overnight at a profit of $2.25 million. He had a $1 million deposit from the new buyer. He had set up this second deal without the knowledge of the building's hard-pressed owner. The only problem was that Verrue had to close his purchase within a week if his turnaround sale was to hold up. As the deadline approached, the building's owner threw in a final demand. He insisted on free rent and two parking spaces in the Ice House for a year for his personal business.

"It was nine-thirty or ten at night and we were trying desperately to close the deal," said Verrue, a sturdy man with the build of a football fullback, thinning strawberry blond hair, and a thick layer of confidence. "But when he said there was just one more thing and then brought up the parking spaces and free rent, I closed my notebook and walked out. Our attorney was flabbergasted. He knew about the turnaround sale and the money we'd make off it. I knew that if I gave in on the free rent, something else would pop up. At midnight I got a call at home saying to show up at nine A.M. and close the deal."

The thrills of real estate development are not all in the money, although there can be plenty of that. More intangible is the sense of conquest. In the Ice House deal, the building's owner had blinked first. The amounts involved in that transaction may have been small by the standards of major developers, but it was the kind of deal that even the big boys really like. The Ice House deal brought Verrue to the attention of the corporate family. The quick profit was appreciated. But it was the story of how Verrue had literally walked away from the bargaining table that evoked the real admiration in Perini's home office.

Perini Corporation was founded in 1900 by Bonfiglio Perini. At that time, the small construction company was known as B. Perini & Sons. The name was changed to Perini Corporation in 1954. Although Perini went public in 1961 and sold stock to investors as part of an aggressive expansion, the business has never lost its original family flavor. David Perini, the grandson of the firm's founder, is the chairman and chief executive, and its employees are treated as part of the family.

With his star rising at Perini, Verrue was not inclined to risk a blot on his career by making the wrong decision on the development of the site known as the Rincon Annex. Five years before, he'd seen firsthand what one decision could do for a career. In 1979, Verrue was an administrator with the city of Long Beach. One of his jobs was leading the city's attempt to shed its image as "Iowa by the Sea." In that capacity, he was overseeing plans for a waterfront convention center and adjoining hotel. Among the bidders for the hotel portion was Perini Land & Development, which had put together its proposal in association with Sheraton. There were other bidders and, as the deadline approached, Perini's arrangement with Sheraton fell through. Perini president Thomas Steele asked Verrue for an extension to line up another hotel partner. Verrue refused and immediately awarded the contract to a competing group aligned with the Pritzker family and their chain of Hyatt hotels.

Tom Steele had been impressed by Verrue's decisiveness and later that year, when Perini was eyeing an expansion on the West Coast, he telephoned and asked if Verrue would be interested in the new post of western division chief in San Francisco. The timing was right, and Verrue moved north.

Which is where he was when, in the spring of 1984, he sat down and summarized for himself the possible risks and rewards associated with the proposed Rincon Annex development. He would see if reality matched his initial reaction. At the top of the risk list was the fact that the old three-story Rincon Annex Post Office had to be retained as part of the new development. The U.S. Postal Service, which owned the land and was soliciting development proposals, had so stipulated. In Verrue's mind, the old building was of marginal historical value and appeared to be a real obstacle to full-scale commercial development on the site.

Although the post office was less than fifty years old, both the building and the striking murals in its lobby were on the National Register of Historic Places. Their inclusion on the register had been a strategic maneuver by city preservationists faced with the Postal Service's announcement in 1979 that it wanted to vacate the spot and sell it. A number of San Francisco's historic structures had fallen to the wrecking ball in recent years, and the preservationists were determined that Rincon Annex would not share that fate, even if the facility only dated back to 1940. So when the Postal Service announced that Rincon Annex was outdated and the government planned to sell the building, the preservationists rose up to object.

The building, which had been put up by the Works Project Administration, was deemed worth saving as a classic example of the Streamline Moderne style popular among architects for government buildings in the 1920s and 1930s. Sentiment was also strong that Anton Refregier's twenty-seven bold murals, which lined its 400-foot lobby, had to be preserved. A Russian immigrant, Refregier had won the commission for the murals in a national competition and he had painted them in watercolors on the lobby walls between 1941 and 1948. Many of the city's artists had watched Refregier's progress, and some had assisted him.

An earlier attempt to get rid of the murals had demonstrated the depth of feeling for them. At the height of Senator Joseph McCarthy's reign of terror, a conservative California congressman named Hubert Scudder demanded that the murals be removed from the public space. He was particularly incensed by a panel that re-created San Francisco's bloody waterfront strike of 1934. But artists and longshoremen banded together to save the murals.

Though of recent vintage, Rincon Annex Post Office and the art that graced its lobby were as much an urban heirloom as countless older buildings. Its fitness for preservation rested not so much on age as on its place in the history of the city and its residents. The National Park Service, which decides what goes on the historic list, agreed.

After the building and its art were placed on the National Register, the Postal Service backed down on the proposed sale. For a period, there were discussions with the city, which eyed the site as the location for a new hotel to anchor redevelopment of the district. But then another spot was found for that and the Postal Service ultimately decided it would negotiate a long-term lease with a developer. Of course, any new development would still have to preserve Rincon Annex and the Refregier murals. A fine victory for the preservationists, but a black mark for the development potential from Verrue's point of view.

Verrue's list of drawbacks also included the location of the 3.47-acre parcel. It was "South of Market," the psychological dividing line for premium rents and an area that a San Francisco business magazine had recently dubbed the city's "last frontier." Verrue didn't have much stomach for becoming a pioneer, especially on the cusp of unsettling times for the commercial real estate market.

Developing the site would be complicated further by the fact that the land was to be leased from the Postal Service, not purchased. A long-term lease, which usually runs ninety-nine years, carries major liabilities. The rent is routinely based on a formula that calls for regular payments of specific amounts plus a share of the revenue generated from tenant rents paid to the building's owner. This means that the entity leasing the land, in this case the Postal Service, gets a share of the escalating revenue as a project matures and generates more and more cash. If the project is not successful, the regular rent payments must still be made.

For Verrue, a fourth negative factor was the requirement that the Rincon Annex development contain new housing and that some portions of it be subsidized for lower income tenants. This caveat had been worked out between the Postal Service and the San Francisco Redevelopment Agency, which maintained zoning control over the Rincon Annex site because it was in an area that the agency was supposed to rejuvenate. The housing component was part of the city's response to pressure from community groups worried about the demise of affordable housing in San Francisco and the exodus of people and jobs to the suburbs. But the requirement raised questions in Verrue's mind about the economics of the deal.

As with the commercial office arena, San Francisco's market for condos was glutted by years of heady building. On top of that, the location of this proposed project was marginal. Could people be enticed to rent apartments or buy condominiums in the area at the prices the developer would need to charge? Would office workers and

professionals be willing to trade the charm of the city's residential
neighborhoods or the comfort of a suburb for a home where everything closed up at night?

Any attempt to void the housing provision would be a long shot
and it would invite retaliation from an increasingly powerful organization, San Franciscans for Reasonable Growth. Led by a feisty ex-
Vietnam War protester and lawyer named Sue Hestor, the group had
mounted a series of campaigns that appealed to the city's growing
fears that developers were erasing San Francisco's heritage.

When the San Francisco Planning Commission met each Thursday, Hestor would be there to speak out against the latest proposed
office tower. She refused to take vacations because she was afraid of
what the planners would approve in her absence. At the meetings,
she'd grab the microphone during the public comment period and
spend her allotted five minutes railing against developers who destroy small businesses and low-income housing to build expensive
condominiums and sleek offices. Former commission secretary Lee
Woods once described her technique succinctly: "She intimidates,
threatens, and shocks. When she's shouting, it's almost like a beating
she administers."

When the city ignored her, Hestor and her group went to court
and filed lawsuits against every new high-rise. By 1982, Hestor had a
dozen lawsuits pending in California courts accusing the city planning department and the developers of ignoring the environmental
impact of the high-rises. Rather than examining the cumulative
effect of so much building, as Hestor believed state law required, the
buildings were judged individually and approved without concern
for their impact on existing housing stock or the overloading of the
city's public transit system brought on by so much concentrated
development in the core area. The group scored important court-
room victories and tied up projects for months. Delays cost developers money, so they began offering Hestor out-of-court
settlements. That money was used in turn to finance affordable
housing and more community-interest groups.

Mayor Dianne Feinstein, an unabashed ally of the pro-growth
forces, was paying attention, too. She ordered her planning commission chief, Dean Macris, to examine two basic scenarios for downtown: one that involved slow growth, with limits on new office
space, and another that advocated continued expansion at whatever

the market would bear (an option that Hestor derided as the "let 'er rip theory of planning"). But the promise of a study did not go far enough to placate Hestor and the segment of the public that was beginning to pay attention to her message. "All the stuff we had been warning about since 1971, they could see it was happening," said Hestor. "It was registering in the public consciousness how bad things were. Housing costs had skyrocketed and the commuter mess had gotten far worse."

In 1983, Hestor responded by getting enough signatures to put a new initiative on the ballot. It called for imposing new fees on developers to pay for improved public transportation and finance new affordable housing, and it sought additional protections for landmark buildings. In November, the initiative received 49 percent of the vote, narrowly missing passage, but was the best showing yet for the slow-growth forces. Flexing her new muscle, Hestor warned that she would launch an even tougher initiative for the next municipal election.

Feinstein and her allies in the business community recognized that they were going to have to come up with a real zoning plan for downtown. The plan that Dean Macris had begun a year earlier would have to be accelerated, with results real enough to placate Hestor and the others who didn't seem to understand the value of unfettered expansion. If the city and the business interests did not come up with a workable compromise, the cure imposed by the voters would be bitter indeed.

Randy Verrue and most other developers in San Francisco were aware of the pendulum's swing toward the slow-growth forces. And Verrue considered it as he evaluated the pros and cons of the Rincon project. It would not come for a while, but the results of this exercise in community activism would turn out to be America's toughest zoning code for a major urban area. The San Francisco Downtown Plan, for which Feinstein would receive nationwide publicity and praise, was about to be forced on her administration and the city's real estate development interests.

So there were plenty of reasons not to take on an office and residential building in a marginal area in 1984. Yet Verrue had items to write down on the positive side of the list, too. Chief among these was his belief that the current slump was uncharacteristic of San Francisco. When the city bounced back, the expansion of the financial district would reach into such marginal areas as South of Market. The city was already trying to funnel new development into the area, and the rundown residential hotels and tiny shops that gave the neighborhood its downtrodden atmosphere would not last forever. Once the area took off, the Rincon Annex site would be as good as gold.

In Verrue's opinion, Perini Land & Development had the skills to develop and operate a successful mixed-use project. In 1962, Perini had been one of the partners in the redevelopment of an area of the city known as Golden Gateway Center. One of the first major urban redevelopments in the United States, it consisted of 1,196 apartments, 58 town houses, and 60,000 square feet of retail and commercial space in four 23-story high-rises. Golden Gateway Center covered ten acres and included the renovation of a number of existing buildings. The development included the 25-story Alcoa Building, which was designed by Skidmore, Owings & Merrill, the architecture firm of choice for many of the nation's biggest developers. The Alcoa Building, one of San Francisco's first International Style structures when it was completed in 1967, is reminiscent of Skidmore's larger and more famous John Hancock Center in Chicago—but then, one of the reasons real estate developers are so fond of Skidmore is that the giant firm can be counted on to turn out high-quality, familiar buildings.

In the commercial development business, your market can be your fate. Even though Verrue's analysis turned up pluses as well as minuses on Rincon Annex, it came down to a question of when the expansion of the financial district and ancillary businesses would reach South of Market. In a business where short-term returns are almost always viewed as superior to long-range investments, and federal and state tax laws have been structured to provide real estate developers with maximum profit in minimum time, Randy Verrue did not want to gamble on the market's arrival at Rincon Annex. He decided to stick with his instincts and not submit a proposal to the city and Postal Service to develop the site.

3

ASSEMBLING
THE TEAM

Michael I. Blumenthal had watched with an envious eye as huge projects transformed San Francisco's skyline in the 1970s and early 1980s. An ambitious real estate speculator, he had often told associates that he was eager to move to the big time from his small projects on the fringes of the city. When the Postal Service requested proposals for developing the Rincon Annex site, he saw his chance.

Real estate developers are the generals who plot the strategy and recruit the soldiers—the general contractors, structural engineers, mechanical engineers, and architects. The largest among them, Trammell Crow in Dallas and Canadian-based Olympia & York, control vast amounts of land and office and residential space across the United States and employ hundreds of specialists in every area of management. Smaller developers restrict themselves to regions, cities, or even neighborhoods. But they all share the same goal: doing deals.

Blumenthal was one of the little guys, operating out of a small office on the 37th floor of one of the buildings at Embarcadero Center in San Francisco. He had a part-time bookkeeper and a receptionist. The name of his business changed over the years—Blumenthal and Associates, Welsh Common Associates, and in 1984, Interbank Corporation. What Blumenthal had was a knack for spotting deals. Typically, he would spot the opportunity and then bring in a devopment firm as a partner to actually build the project. In 1984, he was working on several small deals both in outlying areas and within San Francisco. He also was overextended financially, a precarious position in the best of times and an extremely dangerous one in the sluggish San Francisco market. A lot of businessmen confronting these problems sell off what they can and try to survive on a smaller scale. Others rely on different means.

Blumenthal had seen the Postal Service's request for proposals to develop the Rincon Annex and it sounded like a hot prospect. He would need a major partner to land this project. So he went to someone he had known for several years—Poo Quong Chin, the president of one of San Francisco's largest structural engineering firms, Chin & Hensolt Engineers.

"Mike came in and said that he'd like to go into this together," said Chin, who is known by his initials, P. Q. "I felt this was a natural site, a great location. I felt that north of Market was so overcrowded and rents were so high that this area had potential."

Chin & Hensolt had made some of San Francisco's most important buildings stand up. The firm was the structural engineer for the Transamerica pyramid in the early 1970s and before that for Candlestick Park, the windswept sports stadium on the southern outskirts of the city. Since its founding in 1957, the company had been employed as the engineer on over 3,000 projects with construction costs totaling $3 billion.

But Blumenthal's proposal was different: he wanted Chin on board as an owner as well as the structural engineer. Along with being an experienced and respected structural engineer, Chin had a streak of speculator in him. He had invested in real estate, particularly in Hawaii, and he liked to dabble in the stock market. So Blumenthal's proposal that he acquire an ownership interest was attractive.

"You see the equity partners getting the big money and as an engineer it is very, very difficult to earn the big figures," Chin says. "Normally, we don't get into the equity ownership. But I had done this in the past on smaller projects and it had worked out well. It was a good chance to get involved. There is nothing to prevent any engineer from becoming a partner as long as he has the money. John Portman is an excellent example of architects doing it. But engineers are not as innovative. We are looking for ways that things won't work, not necessarily how they will work."

But it looked to P. Q. Chin as though the Rincon Annex deal would work and so he agreed to wear two hats on the project, structural engineer and part owner. Along with the shot at more money, there was another reason. When the world examines a high-rise, credit usually is parceled out to the architect first and the developer second. Rarely does public acclaim filter down to the structural engineers. Their work is vital, but by its very nature it is hidden. Indeed, many architects and developers tend to view the engineers as little more than servants to the architect. Engineer Mario Salvadori once described his profession this way: "One of the main reasons for their employment is that, as the saying goes, an engineer is a fool who can do for one buck what any other fool can do for two." On cutting-edge work, however, experimental structural engineers have become known for their innovation and skill.

Inherent frictions exist between the structural engineer and the architect on a project. One of these is the clash between the artist and the pragmatist. A high-rise architect must be well versed in the basics of engineering so that his designs are not impossible to execute. But the most innovative and stylish architects routinely push the envelope on construction techniques to give their works an edge. When the engineer is unable to execute the design, perhaps because current theory does not exist to define the new condition, the possibility of failure tends to fall on the engineer, rather than on the overreaching architect. If the engineer is able to pull off a challenging architectural demand, the credit winds up going to the architect anyway.

So there is often a sense among engineers that they are second-class members of a development team. P. Q. Chin is a proud man. His father had come to San Francisco from southern China in the 1920s and operated a string of successful pawnshops in Chinatown. P. Q. had shown great promise as a student and eventually obtained an engineering degree from Stanford University. Over the years, P. Q. Chin had built a leading engineering firm and become a prominent citizen. Being an owner on the Rincon Annex project offered the sort of respect that he felt he and his firm deserved.

The Postal Service and the San Francisco Redevelopment Agency would be evaluating the competing proposals for the site on the basis of design and the track record of the team. So Blumenthal and Chin decided to strengthen their lineup with a general contractor as the third partner. A general contractor oversees the entire construction of a project, supervising the performance of the dozens of subcontractors hired to do the forty to fifty specialty jobs associated with a major project. Like structural engineers, they usually work for a fee and rarely are equity partners in a development.

Chin discussed the deal with several major San Francisco contractors, but no one was willing to take a chance on the project. They were more accustomed to working for fees, not taking the risks involved in ownership—particularly on a project south of Market. After half a dozen turndowns, Chin turned to Ron Tutor, the president of Tutor-Saliba Corporation, a major construction and engineering firm with its headquarters in Sylmar, about thirty miles north of Los Angeles. Chin had been involved on several jobs in which Tutor-Saliba was the general contractor. At the time, they were working together on the restoration of San Francisco's historic cable-car system.

While he was not the first choice, Ron Tutor was a natural choice. The son of the company's founder, he had always operated with a certain flair. And he lived that way, too, indulging in red Ferraris and fancy airplanes. Like Chin, Tutor had worked on dozens of major construction projects and seen the developers walk off with the lion's share of the money while he was paid fees as the general contractor. He also had seen several major construction companies creating development arms in an attempt to get a greater share of the profits. So when P. Q. Chin invited him aboard, Tutor hesitated for about thirty seconds before responding: "Yeah. I'm in."

The next step was coming up with a concept to submit to the Postal Service. To do that the new partners hired a San Francisco architect named Peter Bolles, who was a longtime friend and associate of Chin. The original design was dictated as much by the requirements of the Postal Service request for proposals as by architectural vision. Indeed, the Postal Service requirements for all competitors contained the core elements of the project that would survive long after Bolles had been replaced: the necessity for some sort of central atrium or shopping core and a division of the new construction into two buildings or towers to avoid creating too much bulk on the Howard Street end of the site.

In response to the Postal Service requirement that the project contain affordable housing as well as commercial space, the group's plan called for condominiums on the vacant half-block, with certain units set aside for low-income and moderate-income families. The condominiums would be in two new towers at the south end of the site. Splitting the bulk into two buildings fit neatly into one of the central themes emerging as part of the city's new downtown plan, which would favor slender buildings that added new shapes to the skyline and created as few shadows as possible on the streets.

There was one extra stroke that would turn out to be critical: the plan called for adding two stories of new offices to the three-story post office. Blumenthal had discovered the possibility of adding the two floors by carefully reading the documents outlining the limitations on development of the old post office. Chin believed the existing walls and foundations could be strengthened to support the new weight.

The extra floors were a good idea. Most developers cram as much rental space as possible into a project under the simple formula that more rental space equals more cash flow. Adding the two floors would increase the revenues from the project and provide a way to recoup some of the anticipated extra costs associated with renovating the post office.

The renovation costs were a big question mark. New construction costs can be estimated fairly accurately because the important factors are known—the price of steel or concrete, the amount of time to erect the building, the cost of stone versus glass for its skin. Estimating for a major renovation is far trickier because there is no way to determine ahead of time exactly what problems lie behind old walls and beneath old floors. One major question mark on the Rincon Annex, for instance, was whether the hundreds of wooden pilings supporting the old building were sound. If not, the expense of replacing them would be astronomical.

"I saw the South of Market area growing because the financial district was already only a stone's throw away," Blumenthal said later. "But there were risks. We wanted to go condo and there was a big risk in developing condos in the San Francisco market at this time. The biggest risk, though, was how much it would cost to rehab Rincon. We thought it made a lot of sense to add two more floors to the post office. It helped the economics. Other groups bidding on it did not do that."

The proposal was one of seven submitted to the Postal Service for developing the site. Within weeks, the field was narrowed to three, with the Blumenthal-Chin-Tutor group making the cut. The choice would be made by the Postal Service, and the city redevelopment experts would then work out the architectural details with the winners. Among the questions that postal officials raised was the group's lack of experience in developing a major urban project and its financial resources to complete the project if unexpected problems arose.

"We need another name. We need a deep pocket," Chin told his partners. With development fees typically running $20 million or more on a deal of this size, there would be plenty of money to share, so long as they landed the project.

Tutor-Saliba had been involved with Perini Corporation on several major construction projects in California, including the expansion of Los Angeles International Airport, a new $150 million convention center in San Diego, and numerous highway projects. In fact, Perini's western construction division was slated to get a small piece of the construction work under the original proposal for Rincon Annex. In addition, Chin had a long relationship with Jack Chiaverini, Perini's senior vice-president for western construction and a fellow engineer. So in the spring of 1984, Chin telephoned Chiaverini and asked whether the company might be interested in a much larger role in the Rincon project. Chiaverini, who was based in San Francisco, said he would talk to the bosses back in Framingham and with Randy Verrue, the executive vice-president in charge of the development subsidiary, Perini Land & Development.

Trained as a civil engineer, Jack Chiaverini had been with Perini Corporation since 1950. He had risen through the ranks on the basis of skill and hard work, supervising massive construction projects in the United States and South America. He was a heavy-construction expert, but he was also respected within the company as a canny businessman and as a friend of David Perini. So when Chiaverini showed up in Verrue's office, outlined what he had been told by P. Q. Chin, and suggested another look at the Rincon Annex project, Verrue agreed quickly.

Verrue met with Blumenthal and reviewed the package that had been put together. He liked some of what he saw, particularly the idea of adding two floors to the post office. The new floors helped focus Verrue's attention on the advantages of a far more substantial rehabilitation of the old structure, and that conjured up an enticing new angle—tax credits. In fact, in a bizarre twist of tax law, the prospect of spending more to renovate the post office could make the whole project more attractive from the point of view of economics.

In an effort to encourage developers to save historic buildings, Congress had passed a law in 1981 that provided a tax credit for money spent rehabilitating historic structures. The goal was to encourage the revitalization of older commercial areas and historic residential neighborhoods. The National Trust for Historic Preservation, a Washington-based advocacy group, and other organizations had pushed the legislation through in an attempt to reverse the wholesale destruction of city centers. They knew that the only way to stop the developers was to make it financially attractive to them to save old buildings.

The tax plan was fairly simple: For every dollar spent renovating an old building under federal guidelines, a developer would receive twenty-five cents' worth of tax credits. The credits could be used against the developer's own profits or passed along to investors in the project through limited partnerships. Transferring the credits to investors proved extremely popular among developers, because it allowed them to attract capital from wealthy investors, such as doctors, dentists, and professional athletes, looking for a tax shelter.

The historic tax credit was added to the more general investment tax credit and depreciation allowances that had existed since the 1970s. The original tax incentives had made real estate partnerships the most popular tax shelters among the wealthy from the middle 1970s on.

Under the general regulations, the investors could make relatively modest contributions to a project and the developer then borrowed the remainder of the money needed for the building in the name of the partnership. By deducting the interest on the construction loan and taking a rapid depreciation write-off, the partnership would be able to show huge paper losses in the early years of a project. This loss could then be divided among the investors and they could use it to offset other types of taxable income. These were known as "passive" losses because they occurred solely on paper and the investors were not actively engaged in the business that generated them.

Their value could be enormous for upper-bracket taxpayers in the era before tax reform. For example, an individual in the 50 percent tax bracket who invested $100,000 in a project might actually be buying "losses" of $200,000 or more, thus saving $100,000 or more in taxes. When the losses had run their course and the building was finally sold, the income the investors received would be taxed at the lower capital gains rate.

Similar tax shelters were available for investments in movies, horse breeding, oil and gas leases, and coal mines as well as other exotic ventures. But real estate partnerships were viewed as the surest bet for investors, particularly if there was the added kicker of the historic tax credit.

These real estate partnerships were popular among developers, too, and their existence revamped the economics of high-rise development in the early 1980s. Previously, most developers required either a lease with a major tenant or substantial amounts of their own money in order to obtain a construction loan from a bank for a project of $50 million or $100 million. This also meant that demand for office space had to be strong if a building was to make sense. But the creation of the real estate partnerships allowed developers to undertake projects on a much more speculative basis because they were driven by the desire for tax write-offs, rather than by a need for more office space or even by common sense.

Employing this sort of tax-based financing, known as a limited partnership, put the Rincon project in a new light for Verrue. The tax credits could attract outside investors, and the more money investors contributed, the less capital Perini Land & Development would have to put into the project. Risking other people's money was a much safer way to develop the project.

Verrue flew back east to discuss the development with Tom Steele, the chief executive of Perini Land & Development. He told Steele it looked like the Blumenthal-Chin-Tutor troika had a good chance of being designated by the city to develop the old post office site and he said that the project might be a winner, particularly based on the tax advantages. Verrue thought Perini's development credibility would tip the scales in favor of the project.

Steele, who has an MBA from Harvard, had been the chief financial officer of Perini Corporation before he became CEO of the development subsidiary. So he, too, was attracted by the numbers associated with the historic tax credits on the post office rehabilitation.

The high interest rates of the early 1980s and the soft markets in some areas had bankrupted some big developments. More and more often, companies seemed willing to walk away from a project, leaving the lender holding the bag. Perini Corporation had never walked away from a project in its eighty-four-year history. But good business sense dictated to Tom Steele that he not tie up any more of the company's money than necessary in the Rincon Annex site. If the tax incentives meant that wealthy investors could be persuaded to risk their money, the project would become much more attractive.

Simply stated, the tax credits would make the deal work. Perini Land & Development would put up as little money as possible and use the funds raised from investors to clear a chunk of profits early in the deal. The location of the project would still be marginal and the San Francisco office market would remain questionable. There were still problems to surmount regarding the lease and uncertainties associated with a major renovation and the city's new zoning restrictions looming on the horizon. But much of that risk could be passed on to investors, while the rewards would remain largely with Perini and its development partners.

"We made a judgment, based on the unique setting of the facility and the tax benefits available for the project, that it was something we should take a swing at the second time around," said Steele. "The biggest argument against the deal, in my mind, was still that it was a complex project. But we thought that we could make it work by using the tax benefits to raise the equity."

Steele and Verrue were savvy enough to recognize that the others in the deal viewed them as the deep pocket, so they were determined to gain control over the project from the start. If their money was at stake, they would be the ones with control over how it was spent.

When Verrue returned to San Francisco, he told Blumenthal, Chin, and Tutor that there were two ironclad conditions that had to be met in order for Perini Land & Development to become involved: Perini would have to exercise exclusive control over the management of the project, including selecting a new architect to design the development, and Perini would have to have an ownership share of more than 50 percent.

The others agreed readily and they formed a two-tiered partnership called Rincon Center Associates. The first tier of the organization was the general partners, who would be responsible for the active development and management of the project. Perini Land &

Development was a general partner and owned 50.1 percent of Rincon Center Associates. Michael Blumenthal was the other general partner, with a 2 percent ownership interest. The remainder was divided among the limited partners, who formed the second tier. They would receive profits according to their ownership share but would play a passive role in the management operation. The limited partners were P. Q. Chin, with 18.45 percent; Tutor-Saliba Corporation, with 13 percent; and Blumenthal with another 16.45 percent.

Once the planning got underway, a key element would be arranging to raise money from private investors through an offering coordinated by one of the country's major tax-shelter operations. But the basic relationship among the members of Rincon Center Associates was laid out by the middle of 1984.

Blumenthal received his 2 percent share as general partner in addition to his limited partnership share because he retained his role as lead negotiator with the Postal Service in the effort to win the designation. The partnership agreement also specified that he would receive a fee for $300,000 once the group got the project. While he portrayed himself to his new partners as prosperous and well-heeled, Blumenthal needed a winner to stay afloat. He got it in June of 1984, when the city and the Postal Service agreed to award the development project to Rincon Center Associates.

An enormous amount of work remained before construction could begin. The lease terms had to be negotiated with the Postal Service. The San Francisco Redevelopment Agency, the city agency with control over the neighborhood, would have to approve the final plan for developing the site. But for Michael Blumenthal, the designation marked the end of his active involvement with the development, although he wanted desperately to retain his ownership interest and association with it because of its big-time aura. That was a battle he was destined to lose, but it would turn out to be the least of his problems.

For Randy Verrue, winning the designation marked the start of the most challenging project of his career. He would have to arrange the financing, hire a management team, and find the right architect. But first, he would have to decide just what he wanted to do with a full city block in a marginal neighborhood of San Francisco.

4

THE PROGRAM

Every building performs a function. Most are constructed to enclose people in interconnected spaces and protect them from the distractions of climate while they undertake a particular activity or set of activities. There are residential buildings, office buildings, churches, stadiums, and structures for restaurants and shops. Each function requires its own structural components, demands its own architectural language; materials, roofs, walls, windows, doors, and floors vary from office to home to restaurant, as do the mechanical elements required to support each function. So a building is first defined by its function.

A mixed-use project must perform many functions simultaneously and, as a result, its definition is more complex. There may be a shop next door to a restaurant beneath an office topped by an apartment. Each activity demands unique structural and design elements. For a mixed-use project to succeed, the functions must be blended harmoniously and efficiently to assure that each activity exists both on its own and as a part of the larger whole. This task creates demands that are absent from, say, the construction of a single-use, high-rise office building, and they are felt by the architect, the contractor, and the engineers who are designing and building the mixed-use project.

The first person to tackle the complications of a mixed-use project is the developer, whose most critical task is to decide what is going to take place within the building. The developer determines how much space should be allotted to office use and how much to residential, how many restaurants the building and neighborhood can support and what types of shops might succeed in attracting the right customers. From that determination, called "the program" by most developers, the design of the project flows. And if that program is flawed, not much that comes after can really save a project from the only failure that matters to a developer—financial failure.

A 1960s-era example of how a mixed-use center can fail exists just a few blocks from the Rincon Annex site. It is the four tall office buildings of John Portman's Embarcadero Center. Poor planning left the retail stores in the complex hidden in a maze of walkways and dark shadows created by the towering high-rises. The shadows also blocked out the sunlight from the restaurants located within the project, depriving San Franciscans of one of their favorite pastimes—eating outside in the sunshine. Those were mistakes that the developers of Rincon Annex were determined not to repeat.

In the case of the Rincon site, the city and the Postal Service had established the basic parameters: the old post office would remain intact, the project would contain housing as well as commercial space, and the push for a new downtown zoning plan would limit its height and bulk. But within those parameters, the variations were countless and, as the developer and the general partner in charge, it would be up to Perini Land & Development to make the decisions.

Soon after the group received the designation to develop the site, Randy Verrue began visiting the neighborhood. It was a short walk from his office in the Alcoa Building and for several weeks he strolled over at all times of the day and evening. The post office was still operating and the streets surrounding the building reflected the tensions apparent in many urban areas undergoing dramatic change.

"The first thing is to walk around the site and begin to get the feel of the neighborhood, where the neighborhood might be going," said Verrue. "My perception was that the market was definitely moving in this direction. We were not pioneering. There were already office buildings here and, within a five- to seven-year period, the financial district would be down here."

On the north side, across Mission Street, was One Market Street, a forty-story office building. On the west, across Spear Street, was another newer office building, 100 Spear Street. To the south, across

Howard Street, was vacant land and the base of the Bay Bridge between San Francisco and Oakland. To the east, between the post office and San Francisco Bay, was a row of two- and three-story buildings that had been chandleries, laundries, and transient hotels dependent on the waterfront for their existence. There was also a YMCA. Some of the shops were still open, and the hotels housed many of the city's poor, working and nonworking.

To Verrue, the rundown hotels and struggling shops were not so much an impediment as an anachronism. Already an eight-story office building had been wrapped around the corner of Steuart and Howard streets, a signal that someone else had faith in the neighborhood's future. He knew that downtown development was moving this way and that the old buildings would be replaced one of these days, either by being transformed into chic restaurants and boutiques or obliterated to make room for another huge project. Either way, he didn't figure that they would be around much beyond the completion of his development.

One element that caught his eye had been on his original list of pluses for the site. The proximity of the Bay Area Rapid Transit station and the ferry terminal meant that thousands of workers streamed through the area daily on their way to office jobs. But what Verrue saw when he visited the neighborhood at lunchtime was another big opportunity: the workers emerging from the buildings around the Rincon site headed up Market and Mission streets toward their restaurants and delicatessens. He also noticed that there were few shops in the area that catered to upscale office workers—few bookstores and nice clothing stores.

By Verrue's rough calculations, there were 4 to 5 million square feet of office space in the neighborhood and the 75,000 or so occupants of that space could support a lot of new restaurants and some new shops, too. A good number of them, he decided, wouldn't mind living close enough to their jobs to walk to work. A few blocks to the north was a successful Hyatt Regency Hotel and, with the growth of the area, he also figured that it might support another hotel as part of the Rincon development.

From these basic observations, culled over a period of about a month, Verrue began to formulate the program for the development. In his mind, he began to apportion shares of space for the various activities that would be housed in the multipurpose building. Although consultants and market studies would later play a role, Verrue was relying on his instincts as a developer and his experience in resurrecting downtown Long Beach to determine the successful mix for Rincon Center.

While Verrue was beginning to formulate a program, a new employee in his office was working out the details of the lease with the Postal Service. This was Jay Mancini, and negotiating the lease was the opening act in what would become for him the most dramatic, wrenching, and exhilarating experience of his career. A native of the San Francisco region with an MBA from the Wharton School at the University of Pennsylvania, Mancini had been working for Campeau Corporation, the big Canadian developer, on the construction of a complex of medium-size office buildings near Candlestick Park in South San Francisco when an executive headhunter contacted him about an opening at Perini Land & Development. It was June of 1984, and Mancini was thirty-eight years old. With the Campeau project caught in the economic downturn affecting San Francisco, he happily left it and signed on as a general project manager with PL&D.

His work on the Candlestick Park project had brought Mancini into contact with the people who lived in the working-class neighborhoods of South San Francisco. Few urban developments of any size in the 1970s and 1980s could proceed without considering the relationship with the surrounding community. Cities implemented strict guidelines on how much work must be apportioned to minority-owned firms and women-owned companies. Most also designated the minimum percentage of laborers who must be local or minority-group members or both.

Mancini had negotiated with representatives of South San Francisco's black community in the early 1980s over the use of local residents as laborers and security guards for the project in exchange for political peace to allow the project to go forward. Unlike developers who fulfill such promises by employing sham minority firms or cooking the employee numbers, Mancini carried out his end of the bargain by hiring even more blacks and local residents than promised. In doing so, he won the respect of many community leaders and a measure of recognition from local politicians.

It was natural, then, for Verrue also to charge Mancini with negotiating various community issues with city officials. Mancini had been hired as Verrue's assistant, and he did not have the experience to take on a major project on his own. But the delegation of the community issues was part of a pattern that would continue until Mancini wound up with complete day-to-day control over the hugely complex project. In the middle of 1984, however, from Verrue's point of view, giving Mancini more responsibility freed Verrue for the larger task of finding the right architect to execute his program for Rincon Center.

Developers and architects often have an uneasy relationship. Neither can exist without the other, at least not where huge urban projects are involved. Developers need the architects to create the designs that implement their visions. Architects need the developers to finance the projects that embody their designs. Yet neither cares to give too much credit to the other.

For developers, architects and their designs tend to be one means to an end, the end being a financially successful project. Some developers have grown rich without giving a damn about what their buildings look like. Trammell Crow, principal owner of the biggest development company in the United States, has said that he has not even seen half the buildings his company has built. For these developers, the architect's job is to stay within budget and deliver on time.

Architects have always relied on patrons. As the primary patrons have changed in recent decades, going from governments and public projects to developers with private projects, so too has the role of the architect. The vision that bricks and mortar could help make a better city and that architects were part of a social movement flourished in the 1930s and was revived in the 1960s. Since then, it has pretty much languished. Paul Byard, a lawyer-turned-architect in New York City, offered an extreme view of the state of modern architecture to a New York Architectural League's symposium in 1989: "For architects, these are disquieting times. We have nothing of any moral or social importance to design or build. No one is asking us to design new schools, new housing, new public buildings or anything like them."

In today's environment, an architect confronts the reality that, since most work is being commissioned by private developers, certain de facto moral and social dramas must be played out in their arena. This does not mean, however, that the public is no longer represented. Indeed, without their own buildings to supervise, public agencies have assumed a far more active role in the design and execution of buildings erected by private developers. The result is a complicated dance in which public agencies attempt to exert as much control as possible and the average private builder becomes evermore secretive and conservative in protecting his financial objectives.

Another recent trend has increased the architect's reliance on private developers as patrons. A handful of corporations, most notably International Business Machines, Volvo, and Procter & Gamble, have made architecture a part of their image and have invested knowingly in design. But throughout the 1980s, as long-term strategy was replaced by a concentration on short-term profits, fewer and fewer corporations were willing to devote capital to building their own structures. Instead, they leased space in speculative skyscrapers put up by developers.

Along the way, some more enlightened developers learned that good design sells well to corporations in search of prestigious headquarters locations. Design became a way for developers to compete for the big corporate tenants who ensure a project's success when they lease numerous floors and who themselves bring an aura of prestige. This broader notion of good design also became a defensive tool for developers facing demands from city agencies and increasingly influential community groups. To win approval for a project, developers needed to choose architects with reputations for producing buildings that harmonize with a neighborhood or bring glory to a skyline. This in turn increased the stature of architects.

This development also meant that architects had to change in the 1980s. Propriety had to figure in the equation for a new design. Did the structure fit with the surrounding buildings, the landscaping, the neighborhood, the city itself? No longer would it be enough to design a spectacular building and plop it down without regard to context. The design had to fit into the architectural fabric of its surroundings. And the architect had to be prepared to defend the design articulately before city planning commissions and organizations of laypeople who were playing a bigger role in deciding which projects got built and which did not.

The architect as tweedy, pipe-smoking academic was replaced by a new reality: the architect as showman. This role came with a new set of demands. The developers perceived the architect as part of their public relations apparatus, a sort of "convincer" in dealing with public agencies and community groups. The architect confronted a narrow line here, balancing his relationship with the developer and his sense of propriety when it came to the design and value of the project itself. The architect, too, realized that there were risks in future dealings with government agencies if he sided solely with the developer in these disputes. Few of the major names in architecture, however, were shy about stepping into the limelight as showmen and, as a result of this willingness, architecture in the 1980s became a more popular art than at any time in U.S. history.

This new relationship between developers and architects is not without its unfortunate side effects. They are best exemplified by the buildings erected by Donald Trump, a shrewd salesman who also proved to be an able manipulator of architecture itself. Buildings such as Trump Tower in New York City demonstrate the willingness of some architects to place their profession squarely in line with a developer's single-minded desire to maximize profits by appealing solely to the wealthy and privileged.

Randy Verrue was at best minimally conscious of this interplay when he set out to find the new architect for Rincon Center. Verrue said that the original plan by Peter Bolles was not grand enough and that the delineation between the office and residential spaces was not clear enough. But what really bothered him was that Bolles wasn't a big enough deal. Architects had become names and Verrue wanted a name.

His first choice was Skidmore, Owings & Merrill. The firm had a solid reputation among developers and it had designed the Alcoa Building for Perini two decades before. It also had a large San Francisco office, with seventy design architects alone and a strong support staff to handle any complex project. It was also a simple matter logistically, since both SOM and Verrue had their offices in the Alcoa Building.

Jay Mancini participated in the discussions with SOM and he felt it was a mismatch from the start. "We didn't see eye to eye from the first interview," he said. "They had a little of an attitude that they would design the building and we would stay out of the way. They seemed to be saying, 'We'll design your building for you. You just get out of the way. You just pay the bills and shut up.' Well, we wanted a team, with an architect who would be directed by us." Mancini's perception that the owners direct the architects would later play a central role in his clashes with the architect eventually chosen for Rincon Center.

Verrue wound up rejecting SOM, but his reasoning was a little different from Mancini's. The architectural firm had insisted on responsibility for construction costs. This, they said, would enable them to monitor the progress and try to keep the work on time and on budget. The practice varies from project to project and firm to firm, but it is not unusual for the architects to be responsible for costs, particularly on a project of the complexity of Rincon. In cases where the architect is not responsible for monitoring the costs, it is done by the developer.

But this was a point on which Verrue could not budge, not because he wanted to keep his own finger on the pulse of the costs— that would have been a worthwhile reason—but because of the unique nature of the partnership agreement with Tutor-Saliba. In addition to serving as general contractor, Tutor-Saliba was going to monitor the construction costs on the project. Verrue and Tom Steele had reasoned that this was a cost-efficient arrangement: they would not have to pay an architect the additional fee and Tutor-Saliba, as one of the owners of the project, would have a strong incentive to keep costs down and increase the profits that the partners would share in the end. Verrue also assumed that Chin & Hensolt, with P. Q. Chin as an owner, would have the same incentive for keeping a lid on costs.

"In a normal situation, we might have given cost-control authority to the architect or employed a complete staff on our side to monitor costs and payments," said Verrue. "Either way, you keep the general contractor at arm's length. That is the way it normally happens. But here our partners are the structural engineer and the general contractor. We thought they would keep us out of trouble because they were equity partners. I presumed they were going to keep a sharp eye on costs. We thought they could simply do the job."

Later, some members of the project staff argued that Verrue was trying to cut administrative costs and enhance his reputation for producing high profits by not hiring at least an accountant and construction consultant to watch over costs. Verrue rejects that claim. Regardless of the reason, his decision was a mistake that would ultimately prove the adage "Penny wise, pound foolish."

The second choice as architects was another large firm, St. Louis–based Hellmuth Obata & Kassabaum Inc. Perini Corporation had also worked with HOK's large San Francisco office in the past, but that former association proved to be a sticking point. HOK had designed the Alameda County Jail across the bay in Oakland several years before and Perini Corporation had done much of the construction work. The project had used a new type of concrete to form the walls and, several years after its completion, the concrete was falling off the building. The county had filed a lawsuit against the concrete manufacturer and virtually everyone else associated with the project, including HOK and Perini. As a result, Perini's lawyers advised Verrue that he should not undertake another project with HOK until the legal matter in Oakland was resolved.

With what Verrue considered to be the two top architectural firms in San Francisco eliminated, he began to think about firms outside the city. Many firms across the country were large enough to handle a project the size of Rincon. But Verrue wanted a San Francisco connection, and he could think of only one outside firm that had designed a building there that had achieved the status he sought for Rincon Center. The firm was William L. Pereira Associates in Los Angeles.

At the time, Bill Pereira was a legendary if diminishing figure in California architecture and urban planning. His master plan for Irvine, California, in the sprawling agricultural land south of Los Angeles had landed him on the cover of *Time* magazine in 1963. He had designed structures as diverse as the rocket-launching installations at Cape Canaveral and the spindly-legged theme restaurant at Los Angeles International Airport.

The firm had recently completed an elegant forty-one-story office building at the corner of Sansome and Sutter streets in San Francisco, Citicorp Center, just a few blocks uptown from the Rincon Annex site. Verrue had walked past the building many times and admired the outdoor atrium that joined the building to the street. There were small metal tables and chairs in a marble courtyard surrounded by classical pillars. The building itself was glass and white granite, with sleekly rounded corners. These features were similar to the atmosphere of elegance and openness that Verrue hoped to create at Rincon.

But it was Pereira's Transamerica building on the edge of San Francisco's financial district that was foremost in Randy Verrue's mind as he considered the architect's work.

Completed in 1973, the Transamerica building had shocked the staid residents of San Francisco even before construction began. Public reaction had forced Transamerica to agree to trim the height of the building by several stories, a move that Pereira later complained robbed the structure of the inherent elegance he had designed into it. The resulting forty-eight-story tower, rising to a sharp point above the skyline, was dubbed "the dunce cap" by some angry residents.

The real crime of the Transamerica building, as pointed out years later by *New York Times* architectural critic Paul Goldberger, was that "it dared to be different, it celebrated the flamboyant side of San Francisco's personality while ignoring the city's underlying desire to be conventional." It took several years, but eventually San Franciscans softened their view of the building, recognizing that its slim, pointed shape intrudes on the city's skyline far less than many conventional skyscrapers. Gradually it became a cultural and corporate symbol both for the city and for its owners, the Transamerica Corporation, which features the pyramid prominently in its international marketing.

Verrue was less interested in flamboyance than in the symbolic value of the pyramid from a business perspective, the image it conveyed for Transamerica Corporation. He wanted a building that would, in his words, "be grand, make a statement, invite people to take another look." So in early July of 1984, Verrue telephoned Pereira's headquarters in Los Angeles and asked if the company would be interested in discussing a project in San Francisco.

The following day, Jay Mancini was tidying his desk in preparation for a three-week vacation in Europe. He knew that he would have little free time once the Rincon project got underway, so he wanted to be thoroughly rested. Verrue came in and mentioned that he had called the Pereira firm. Mancini was aware of Bill Pereira's reputation. He did not expect a decision to be made before he returned. Indeed, he left behind a memo for Verrue describing the qualities he thought were necessary in an architect and expressing his hopes that they could settle the matter soon after he got back.

When Mancini returned from his vacation, Verrue greeted him by saying, "By the way, I've hired Pereira."

"Why did you hire Pereira?" asked Mancini.

"Well, I interviewed this new design guy of theirs, Scott Johnson, and he appears to be a pretty bright guy who could work with us."

Mancini is a compact man. Short and trim, he bristles with self-control. He had been a Marine lieutenant in Vietnam and peppers his conversations with military phrases. He describes his reaction to the selection of the architect in his absence as that of "a soldier following orders." But, when pressed, he acknowledges that he was hurt not to have been consulted on the critical decision. Some people believe that slight colored his relations with Scott Johnson throughout the project. In any event, his response to the news was direct and characteristically proper: "Great," said Mancini. "Get him up here and we'll get going."

5

SNOW WHITE AND THE SEVEN DWARFS

It was fitting that the cover of *Time* magazine on September 6, 1963, identified William Pereira as a planner, not an architect. Pereira excelled at orchestrating vast areas of empty land into cities, villages, and university campuses to serve the needs of people. His plans for carving a new community out of 93,000 acres of open land on the southern edge of Los Angeles constituted the largest private development project in the world and it had landed him the coveted *Time* cover.

Pereira had designed a community in which economic and environmental forces would be harnessed to a plan for orderly growth. There were community buildings and the Irvine campus of the University of California and a new city along the Pacific Ocean. Only part of his vision was realized before the ravenous real estate market overtook orderliness and transformed Irvine and surrounding Orange County into a far more ordinary place.

Born in Chicago in 1909, Pereira said often that he could not remember a time when he did not want to be an architect. As a boy, he routinely carried a sketchbook with him and his first part-time job, at the age of twelve, was painting signs. He worked his way through the University of Illinois painting scenery and performing other odd artwork jobs. He graduated, with a degree in architecture, in 1930.

His first architectural job was with the Chicago firm of Holabird and Root, which had designed some of the city's important downtown buildings. There, Pereira helped lay out plans for the 1933 Chicago World's Fair. But he made his early mark designing theaters for a Midwestern chain controlled by Paramount. Among his theaters was the Esquire, a landmark on Chicago's State Street.

When his wife, Margaret, was offered a contract as a studio actress, he went along to Hollywood, where the popularity of his theater designs brought him a commission to design a new studio for Paramount and temporarily diverted him from his profession. Before he was done with the studio design, Pereira was named Paramount's art director and in 1942 he shared an Oscar for his trick photography in *Reap the Wild Wind*, a Cecil B. deMille film. He went on to produce two of his own films before returning to architecture.

In 1950, Pereira formed his own architectural firm in Los Angeles with Charles Luckman, a classmate from the University of Illinois, who had just left his job as president of Lever Bros. While Luckman's later designs would never be acclaimed critically, just before he lost his job he had performed a lasting service for modern architecture: he had commissioned Gordon Bunshaft of Skidmore, Owings & Merrill to design a headquarters building in New York for Lever Bros. It was SOM's first major skyscraper, a vertical box of glass and steel atop a horizontal one, all set on columns over an open first floor. The result was a light, airy abstraction of a building and an open plaza that contrasted sharply with its dark granite neighbors. It was to influence the course of American architecture for the next two decades.

The firm of Pereira and Luckman flourished, going from fifteen employees to about 400 within five years and designing a wide range of projects, such as CBS Television City in Hollywood, the rocket-launching installations at Cape Canaveral, military bases in Spain, the Santa Barbara campus of the University of California, and Los Angeles International Airport, the first new airport for the jet age.

But Pereira grew unhappy with the pressures of grinding out so much work. "It was like working in a factory," he said in an interview in the early 1960s. "Everybody was standing in line with projects for us to do. I don't say we were doing inferior work; I just know I wasn't doing my best."

In establishing William L. Pereira Associates in 1958, he took about half the staff with him to a new, three-story building on

Wilshire Boulevard. From that smaller base, he designed many major buildings in California, including the Hollywood Film Museum and the Los Angeles County Museum of Art, a building that was much heralded when it opened but was later subjected to severe criticism. His concept for the Transamerica pyramid was first conceived as the headquarters for ABC in New York, but that building was never built. He also continued designing college campuses, including Utah's Brigham Young University, the University of Missouri, Occidental College in Los Angeles, and the striking Malibu campus of Pepperdine University.

When *Time* featured him on its cover for his regional plan for Orange County, Pereira was at the height of his power, a commercial success and an influential member of the city's cultural scene. He was fifty-four years old and the man pictured on the front of the magazine was exceptionally handsome, with iron-gray hair and chiseled good looks. He drove a Bentley and lived in a modern mansion he had designed in the city's affluent Hancock Park neighborhood, a few minutes' walk from his bustling office on Wilshire. When the *Time* reporter visited Pereira's office, he found "a deluxe garret with a skylight in the peaked ceiling, black leather chairs, white marble coffee table, and a king-sized desk awash with reports, sketches and papers."

Throughout the 1960s and early 1970s, Pereira's skills as a planner and architect brought in a steady stream of architectural and planning assignments. The firm undertook many projects in the oil-rich nations of the Middle East and, in 1979, won a big share of a massive $700 million plan to expand his original design of Los Angeles International Airport. But there were also setbacks and disappointments. By the late 1970s, Pereira's Modernist architectural style had fallen out of fashion and he had failed to keep up with the changes in taste. Perhaps the most severe blow came when the board of the Los Angeles County Art Museum decided to add a new gallery and face to the complex. Pereira, who had designed the original in 1963, was not even invited to submit a design and he grumbled to a friend, "I wish they'd just cover that damn thing up."

In 1979, Pereira was seventy years old and had health problems. A hip injury, suffered when someone forced his car off the road the previous year, had never healed and it left him aching and limping. Over the years, he had tried to develop a young successor to take the helm of the firm, but Pereira's ego never allowed him to give anyone the room to establish himself. Glenwood Garvey, a bright young designer, had seemed to be in line for the spot when he was named president of the firm in the mid-1970s while still in his thirties. But he grew dissatisfied and left to form his own firm a few years later. He was soon replaced as heir apparent by Arthur Golding, another accomplished young architect.

As Pereira's health declined and he faced financial pressure from a divorce, he decided to sell his interest in the firm to the seven senior executives, most of whom had been with him for a decade or more. "Bill was getting on in years and had been looking for some time at the most appropriate form of ownership transition to see that the firm continued," recalled Golding. "We hired a management consultant and he designed the plan for a transition from essentially one-man ownership to a broader base."

The buyout was started in 1980 and the transition was structured to take about two years. In the meantime, Pereira assumed the title of chairman and was supposed to turn over the daily operations to the others. But he was unable to divorce himself from the day-to-day decisions of the office and the arrangement soon became known within the office as "Snow White and the Seven Dwarfs."

Pereira Associates had always been Bill Pereira. The management and ownership changes had been an attempt to pass the mantle smoothly. But with Pereira unable to let go and partners either unable or unwilling to take charge, the people who hand out the big-ticket architectural jobs were uncertain about the firm's direction. In fact, after the buyout began, one of the first major management initiatives was locating some outside blood to invigorate the planning side of the operation. Bill Pereira assumed the lead role in finding the right person.

A year earlier, he had interviewed a young architect and planner who was working in Washington, D.C., and was interested in returning to his native Los Angeles. The man's enthusiasm for planning had stuck in Bill Pereira's mind. The interview had also made a strong impression on the younger architect, William H. Fain, Jr.

"We had spent four wonderful hours in his office on Wilshire Boulevard in the summer of 1979 and we really got into discussions about building cities and that kind of thing," said Fain some years later. "It was a fabulous discussion. He absolutely understood the dynamics and complexities of dealing with very big problems. When you deal with most architects, you find a person whose experience is very narrowly defined. He is doing curtain walls and that is all he does. He won't have this ability to understand and be interested in the problems of the world. But that is where Pereira's interest was and that is where mine was."

The meeting had started shortly before four o'clock in the afternoon and about eight o'clock that evening, Pereira's striking blond second wife, Bronya, swept into the office with an entourage in tow en route to the theater. Pereira stood up and walked over to a closet, pulled out a black cape, draped it over his shoulders and strode out the door. The stunned Fain sat in the office for several minutes before he got up and left.

During the course of the day, Fain had been introduced to the senior figures in the office of 125 employees. He had met four or five of the other partners, but none left any lasting impression. Perhaps it was only that they were simply overshadowed by the larger-than-life Pereira, Fain thought. In any case, Fain decided against joining the firm and he returned to his job as a planner with a government-backed organization called New Communities Development Corporation and his part-time teaching position at Harvard's Graduate School of Design.

A year later, Pereira was on the telephone inviting Fain to return to Los Angeles for another look at the firm. The weakness in the supporting cast was still apparent to Fain, but this time he felt that Pereira's role would be diminishing. The resulting vacuum could provide Fain with an opportunity to get hold of major projects fast. He took the job.

Bill Fain was an interesting choice for the Pereira firm. He is the son of a Los Angeles businessman and a member of an affluent family. He had graduated as valedictorian of the architecture school at the University of California in Berkeley in 1968, worked for a small architecture firm, and spent two years as an urban designer for the city of New York. In 1973, he entered Harvard to get a master's degree in architecture. While there, he met another California refugee and Berkeley graduate, Scott Johnson. The two worked together on plans for a special zoning district in neighboring Boston and in two studio workshops in architectural design, where students display their creative work for the often-brutal judgments of their peers and professors. Fain and Johnson began to develop a friendship, based in part on the complementary nature of their interests and talents and in part on their shared sense of being outsiders at the elite eastern institution.

The Boston zoning study grew out of a class on transportation and urban design in which the overall assignment was to develop an understanding of the way transportation patterns affect neighborhood development and design. As the class progressed, the professor, an adjunct faculty member named Joseph Passoneau, parceled out specific sections of the city to groups within the course. Fain and Johnson wound up working on a redesign for part of Boston's downtown, and Johnson fell naturally to work on the design elements while Fain studied the broader implications of the effects of architecture on transportation flow.

"I don't want to say that we understood where we wanted to go from there, because you never do, but it was a very good association because Scott's design talents and my interest in the larger picture worked well together," said Fain.

After completing his graduate work, Fain took a job with the Boston Redevelopment Authority, then later moved to the New Communities Development Corporation, a government-backed agency in Washington that had been set up in the late 1960s to help develop planned new communities across the country with a combination of public and private financing. The best-known and most successful example of its work was Columbia, Maryland. By the time Fain arrived in 1976, the program was winding down and the biggest chore was determining which projects were doomed and which, with adjustments, might succeed.

One of the things Bill Fain found when he started work at the Pereira office was an operation pretty evenly divided in two halves: one side was architectural, producing the designs and working drawings for buildings; the other was planning, coming up with plans to transform bare sites into residential and commercial developments. Atop the division sat Bill Pereira, with a hand in both the architectural and planning domains.

Fain soon found himself crossing the imaginary line between departments. His earlier experience with city government in New York meant he was familiar with zoning codes, the pliable regulations by which cities try to orchestrate their growth. Fain's expertise could be as useful to the designers in designing buildings as it was to planners in designing new urban areas.

Working in both areas gave Fain a good view of the entire office, and what he saw was disturbing. All of the senior partners had migrated to administrative positions, leaving almost no one below them who knew anything about doing buildings. They had simply spent too long in Bill Pereira's shadow, relying on him to do it all. And Pereira's health was deteriorating as he struggled against cancer, so he had far less time and will to bring in new business. Fain began to worry that the company would not survive much longer. Yet Pereira refused to let go of the firm, and when he would not yield the top design authority to Golding in the summer of 1983, Golding quit to teach and form his own successful architecture firm.

By that time, the firm had undergone a series of layoffs. Golding's departure sent a spasm of anxiety through the remaining partners and the seventy-five or so other employees. Pereira tried to calm their fears, promising to conduct a nationwide search for a new design chief who would see Pereira Associates to the end of the decade and beyond. The six remaining partners, led by longtime Pereira associate Roy Schmidt, conducted the actual search, interviewing more than fifty young designers from around the country. Fain, who was not a partner, played no role in the search. But a few weeks after the search began, he got a letter from Scott Johnson, who said that he had been contacted by the partners at Pereira Associates about the job of chief of design. What was it like there? asked Johnson, who was then a top designer in the New York office of the renowned architect Philip Johnson.

Fain quickly telephoned his old friend and laid out for him the problems and the potential at the firm. He was blunt: there were serious troubles with senior guys, they were not carrying their weight in terms of bringing in new business and executing the work that was in the firm. Pereira was fighting cancer and there was a risk that the place would go under when he died. But there was the possibility that Fain and Johnson, eager young men in their thirties, could combine their talents, take over the firm, and rebuild it in their own image.

The two men talked secretly over several days that summer. Then one day, Schmidt came into Fain's small office and asked if he knew an architect named Scott Johnson from his days at Harvard. Fain said he certainly did.

"Well, what's he like?" asked Schmidt. "We're thinking of him as the new design chief and we've gotten it down to three finalists."

"Oh, he's terrific," said Fain. "Hire him."

So R. Scott Johnson came to join his former classmate at the troubled firm of William L. Pereira Associates.

6

ARCHITECT ARISING

When Scott Johnson was born in 1951, his parents lived in Spreckels, California, a company town founded by Claude Spreckels, the sugar beet king. There was an aging factory, two rows of houses surrounding a central park, and vast fields of sugar beets beyond. The Johnsons lived in one of the houses on the park, paying $17 a month rent. Johnson's father was a plant geneticist with a doctoral degree who worked for the Spreckels Sugar Company. In two greenhouses and a small laboratory next to the factory, he supervised efforts to coax more sugar out of the beets and developed a broad range of field and laboratory experiments to improve disease resistance.

As a child, Scott Johnson was not interested in the science of his father's job, but rather in the visual imagery, the geometry of agriculture: the greenhouses, with row after row of flats containing beets in various stages of growth, the quality of the light that filtered through the limed glass windows, the flatness of the fields spreading across the Salinas Valley.

When Scott was in the first grade, the family moved to the town of Salinas. Five years later, Russell Johnson became director of research at the Spreckels headquarters in San Francisco and they moved to Hillsborough, one of the nation's wealthiest communities.

From his earliest memories, Johnson was interested in art. When he got in trouble for drawing on a wall at home, he began to sketch his cowboys and Indians on the underside of chairs and tables so that they would go undetected by adults. At gatherings of their large Mormon family, Scott painted the scenery and created the masks that the children used to entertain themselves. In high school, his interest in art turned to architecture. He took an independent course in architectural readings. In his sophomore year, he read all of Frank Lloyd Wright's monographs and Ayn Rand's novel *The Fountainhead*. Scott Johnson began to think seriously about a career in architecture.

Vietnam was a distraction for Johnson, though not in the same way as it was for many of his classmates. He was a freshman architecture student at Stanford University in 1969 and opposition to the war was at its height. The subject of every class discussion seemed somehow to revolve around the conflict across the Pacific. "I didn't want to go to a product design class and talk about Vietnam," he said. "That was fine for the street or dorm. I was active in the moratorium. I was just ambitious by this point in my life to learn about the tools for doing physical design."

Indeed, Scott Johnson didn't have time for distractions. He did not intend to be just any old sort of architect. He thought he would do nothing less than design skyscrapers, the most monumental and complex structures. That would demand that he be exposed to the most advanced knowledge available.

Johnson spent his sophomore year in Italy, where he experienced European architecture for the first time and developed a love for classical design and art that would influence all of his later work. Johnson's preparation for architecture as a youngster had been through art and already as a college student he drew beautifully, so his affinity was natural.

There is an informal but definite division in the architecture profession between architects who consider themselves engineers and those who are inclined to view themselves as artists. Johnson is clearly aligned with the latter group, and he offers this explanation and defense: "Architecture for me is art. It has more to do with art than with physics or mechanical engineering. Often architects with this philosophy are put down by competitors as just artists. Prospective clients are warned that the artists can't create truly lasting, functional buildings, that they are too self-indulgent and unable to design a workable structure. That is nonsense. The mind is not divisive. You need to know material to know what it can do. In a sense, an artist must be more knowledgeable about mechanics and materials because he is testing them, pushing their limits, creating new and revolutionary designs, rather than relying on what has been accomplished a hundred times before by the cookie cutter school of architecture."

When Johnson returned from Europe, he transferred to Berkeley in search of an architecture program he felt was more serious. He plowed through Berkeley in a year and a half, emerging in the summer of 1972 with a degree in architecture. His first job as an architect was in the small office of a San Francisco architect named Al Seyranian. There were four or five architects in the office and their main staple was designing small bank branches and little warehouses. Johnson spent a year there, experiencing the sort of mundane world that befalls the vast majority of architects, while waiting to apply to graduate school.

In the fall of 1973, he entered the Harvard Graduate School of Design. The school offered a master's degree in two and a half years for graduates of architecture schools, but Johnson wanted to move faster. He persuaded the faculty to let him finish the program in eighteen months, with extra credit for his previous work experience. But a catch was added: he had to pass his first design class.

Design studios are the crucibles of architecture school. Each student is given the same design assignment for the ten-week class and at the end of the course their work is spread around the room for critiquing by their fellow students and the professors. These final reviews are preceded by all-day, all-night preparation sessions known as *charettes*, the French word for the cart that is wheeled through the studios to collect drawings from the students for final review at the École Nationale des Beaux-Arts in Paris. At Harvard, *charettes* are renowned for their brutal toughness and competitiveness.

"You are saying, 'This is my creative thinking. This is me.' Since creativity is the thing for which life exists, this is really all of you out there on the line and sometimes the results can be tough," said Johnson.

For instance, the assignment for one workshop was to design a plan for student housing. One student's concept called for an open-ended system of poles and cubes; residents could select a living cube and place it anywhere they wanted on any pole they chose within the complex. There was no master plan, and therefore no master. The plan was anarchical, totally antithetical to Harvard's design program, which at the time revered Le Corbusier and his insistence on composition, a mission, and naturally a master. The design was ridiculed by professors and students alike. One senior faculty member informed the young student, "I wouldn't give an F to a basket weaver for this." The hapless student left school a short time later.

Johnson fared better in his crucial first design class. The project on which Johnson's extra credit hinged was the design of a beach house. At the conclusion of the ten weeks, everyone tacked his or her drawing to the studio walls. Johnson had the sense that his classmates were looking for a sign of weakness in the tall, blond cigar smoker from California. His project was the last one reviewed by the professor, Urs Gauchat. He studied it carefully before telling the class: "Everyone should come over and look at this project. This is the best project I have seen. I want you all to study it."

Johnson gained instant credibility, and instant credit for his work experience. "The review caused most teachers and students to back off, to feel I had a certain level of talent, and to be open-minded to the experimental projects that I would do in the classes to follow," he said. He still has the drawing of the beach house.

To support himself, Johnson had a part-time job in a small architecture firm on Harvard Square. The work was pleasant and undemanding, consisting mostly of using his drawing skill to do design sketches for the partners. Years later, Johnson's clearest memories of the place were of its collegiality, the interaction between people of commensurate abilities who respected the ideas of their fellow workers. All partners had equal standing and they reasoned together in a democratic collaboration. That was a lesson Johnson absorbed and would one day reject.

In 1975, Johnson returned to California and married his high school sweetheart, Meg Bates, who was finishing medical school in Los Angeles. Johnson again felt like an outsider. He was a Northern Californian in Southern California, a Harvard-educated architect in a city where the profession was dominated by graduates of the University of Southern California and UCLA. After interviews with several of the big architecture firms, he wound up working for Skidmore, Owings & Merrill. SOM had a large San Francisco office, but California's economic center was shifting to Los Angeles and the firm wanted to grab a share. Dick Ciceri, a senior partner in the San

Francisco office, had been dispatched south to open a new practice. He hired Johnson to help him.

Ciceri's job was to sell the firm to L.A.'s big developers and Johnson's job was to do the design work. Daily, Ciceri trudged from corporation to corporation, carrying SOM's proposals for a new building at Universal Studios or a new hotel in Orange County. People were always willing to hear him out, but nothing that Johnson designed that first year out of Harvard was built.

This is not unusual for architects. Developers often seek proposals from several different firms. Local governments customarily hold competitions for new public buildings and architects submit not only drawings but lavish and expensive models. The process can be costly, since designing the simplest building to the point where it can be rendered as a drawing can easily require 100 hours or more of work. Nonetheless, SOM viewed the Los Angeles effort as an investment in the future, since the future of California was so clearly in Los Angeles.

But for an ambitious young architect, it was a frustrating year of turning out what are known in the trade as "paper projects," works that exist only on paper, like the big fish that got away. "They were interesting lessons in how to get told no," said Johnson. "Dick Ciceri would go out day after day and present plans and never get discouraged and never take it personally. He was remarkable."

At the end of the year, Johnson asked to move to the firm's established San Francisco office. "I need to work on something that gets built," he explained. So he moved to San Francisco and to the long, rectangular room on the 16th floor of the Alcoa Building where sixty designers sat in straight rows at identical desks turning out their portions of SOM's projects. An assembly line version of creativity.

Here was where theory and reality came together and the coupling, from Johnson's perspective, was uninspiring. The organization of the office was exemplary, each phase of the design and technical work planned and executed with precision. The senior partners brought in the commissions and developed the overall scheme for a project. The execution of the design was parceled out to the junior architects at the drafting tables in the large room. These architects designed their portion of the whole, and these were fused into the completed design.

Another set of architects would use the design drawings to develop the technical drawings, called the working documents. These are extremely detailed documents that provide the ultimate blueprint, which the general contractor and subcontractors on the job follow to build the actual structure. There were architects at SOM who spent their careers deciding where to place toilets in office buildings, determining the optimum distance between the toilet and the elevator. Others produced the details and specifications for attaching the glass or granite or concrete skin of a building to its steel frame.

Each of these tasks was repeated over and over on a single project, as successive generations of drawings reflected revisions to the building and accumulated details. Every floor has its own drawing, containing enough detail to estimate the amount of material needed for that part of the project, the number of doors required, the position and number of electrical outlets, and the heating and ventilating and air-conditioning connections. The detailed picture of the building and the calculations of its cost emerge from these working drawings.

The entire process had evolved into a science at Skidmore. The designs were executed smoothly and efficiently, the working documents were generally clear and precise. The path from concept to construction was the same for every project and, to Johnson's critical eye, the results were generally as uniform as the process itself.

This uniformity raised a concern in Johnson's mind: if all the clients were different, if all the sites were different, and if the problems that each project was trying to address were different, why then were all the buildings so similar?

Watch a four-year-old play with blocks and you understand the fascination of architecture for most architects. Design is fun, which explains a lot about why architects are willing to work long hours at low pay in insecure jobs. At its best, the outcome of the process is unpredictable and exciting, each structure a new challenge. If those elements are missing, so is much of the challenge itself.

For a year and a half, Johnson worked at his desk near a window. Most of his time was spent designing parts of casinos, hotels, and exhibition spaces that were all part of an extraordinary auto museum planned by Nevada gambling tycoon Bill Harrah. One hotel contained an extraordinarily lavish suite that the SOM crew referred to as "the Bobbie Gentry suite," in honor of the aging Harrah's current girlfriend, singer Bobbie Gentry. The joke was what passed for fun at Skidmore, Owings & Merrill in those days.

In the spring of 1978, Johnson and his wife Meg took a holiday in Europe, visiting Spain, France, and Italy. The return to Italy, where his year as a student had so shaped his view of architecture, was nostalgic and something of a revelation. On the plane trip home, he said to Meg: "I'm not doing what I want to be doing. I don't think I'm doing what I should be doing, either."

One lunch hour soon after his return, Johnson walked through the large design room at SOM. He studied the drawings on each desk, pieces of the seventeen projects underway in the office. Some were major skyscrapers, others were less important buildings. After the impromptu tour, Johnson asked himself: "Do I like any of these projects? Would I be pleased to have my name on any of them?" He answered his own questions: "No, I really wouldn't be happy about this work."

The design studio had a bulletin board a few feet from Johnson's desk; news clippings on architectural events and in-house notices were posted on it. A few days after his walk through the office, he watched as a noisy group of architects gathered at the bulletin board. He got up from his desk and walked over to see what was causing the commotion. On the board was a clipping from the front page of the *New York Times*—a story about Philip Johnson's design for a new AT&T headquarters in New York and a rendering of the building. The dramatic structure rose straight up thirty-seven stories, with an immense broken pediment at the top that was reminiscent of nothing less than a Chippendale highboy. The young corporate architects were shocked by the radical design. Johnson listened as they derided Philip Johnson, saying that he had finally and unequivocally gone off the deep end.

Scott Johnson's response was different: "I thought it was pretty interesting. It was conceptually interesting. And I was bothered by the consensus among my colleagues at SOM. It was not clear to me that this design was terrible. I was left with a vague sense of its rightness at the time, its energy, and the facility of its designer. There was much I didn't understand about it, but it provoked me to want to know more."

One element that Johnson knew he liked was the design's use of historical ideas, the decisive pediment at the top, the undulating rhythm of the vertical window wall, and a series of Renaissance-inspired arches at the bottom of the building. There was a parallel with the project on which Johnson was working at SOM that day, the facade for a new bank in San Francisco's financial district. The general partner in charge of the design, Chuck Bassett, had toyed with using, as an homage to history, figurines of old walruses from the historic building that now occupied the site. It was an unusual move that caused a controversy within the office, although the figurines were used in the end.

Soon after the commotion subsided at the bulletin board, Johnson walked into the office of Mark Goldstein, the design partner who was his boss. He said he had to leave. He met with John Merrill, the senior managing partner in the office, and told him the same thing. Johnson could not give them a concrete reason. He was unhappy. He appreciated the experience at SOM, but he wanted a new challenge. Both men asked why he was leaving. Was it money? Was it personalities? They got no answer beyond the fact that it was time to move on.

After he arrived home that day, a colleague at the office telephoned. Bill Harrah had just died. Suddenly it was unlikely that Harrah's cherished auto museum would be built. Another paper project.

Meg Bates was fed up with her husband's inability to settle down. When he came home that evening, they argued over what she perceived as his pattern of dissatisfaction. The dissatisfaction had also infected their marriage and, though neither said the words, divorce seemed to be a possibility.

Bates was also dissatisfied with her job. She was in the midst of a grueling ob-gyn internship. She found the twenty-four-hour days unnecessarily demanding and brutal. She questioned whether the process was in the best interests of the patient or the physician.

"I'm going to quit my internship," she said, her unhappiness fueled by anger with her husband.

"Well, I'm going to New York to look for a new job," said Johnson.

"Well, I'll ride with you to New York."

Two weeks later, in the summer of 1978, they packed the car and headed east. Meg had arranged to work for a federal program to increase the number of physicians in rural areas and she got out of the car in Cortland, New York, about 200 miles north of New York City. Scott helped her get settled in a small rented house next to a river. Then he headed for New York.

He found a small apartment in the West Village and began looking for work. He had interviews at a number of the major architecture firms and a few small ones. There was really only one choice for Scott Johnson and, after three weeks of tough negotiations over salary, he signed on as a designer at Johnson and Burgee, the home of Philip Johnson.

The contrast to Skidmore, Owings & Merrill was as sharp within the firm as it was in the architecture they produced. There were no memos at Johnson and Burgee, no documents delineating the corporate hierarchy and the reporting lines. Scott Johnson soon realized the office operated this way by design; it allowed Philip to intervene in any project he chose, at any level of progress.

The office was in the Seagram Building, the first major corporate skyscraper designed by Mies van der Rohe and done in conjunction with Philip Johnson. The thirty-eight-story tower of glass and bronze on Park Avenue, completed in 1958, is regarded by many critics as the triumphant example of the decade's movement toward Modernism in architecture. It became the model not only for Mies's later buildings but for a generation of architects who admired the serenity and clarity of its design.

The offices of Johnson and Burgee on its 36th floor were far from serene. The outer office and Philip's office, which were the firm's public face, were plush and filled with modern art by the likes of Frank Stella and Jasper Johns. The door to the drafting room opened on a far more Spartan place: the floor was vinyl tile and the room had an industrial feel as recent graduates of architecture schools hunched over drafting tables.

Arriving his first day, Johnson was handed a sheaf by Philip. It contained the conceptual drawings for the Dade County Cultural Center in Miami, Florida, a giant project encompassing a full city block. Execute it, he was told. Take a trip to Miami if he felt he needed to look over the location. Walking away, Philip added casually, "Oh, yes, by the way, the local AIA is suing us."

The AIA is the American Institute of Architects, guardian of the profession's reputation and would-be arbiter of its standards. Johnson soon discovered that he had been dropped into the middle of a political maelstrom, precisely the type of controversy that seemed to follow his new boss everywhere he built a building in those days.

In this case, architects in Miami were designing the same slick, Modernist glass silos and boxes that their colleagues around the country were putting up. But Philip Johnson had moved beyond Modernism. His AT&T building had been the first major commercial building to indulge in Postmodernism and capture the public's attention. The complex that he had designed for the cultural center was done in an Italianate Revival style, a romantic historicism also emerging in different forms from the studios of Cesar Pelli, Michael Graves, and other well-known practitioners.

In what was destined to become the pattern of their relationship for five years, Scott Johnson refined the details of the cultural center design and shuttled back and forth to Miami to calm the natives.

As had happened in the small Cambridge firm during his Harvard years, Johnson found himself drawing many of his mentor's concepts for buildings. The two men would often sit in Philip's office and the elder architect would discuss his concept for a particular building, perhaps sketching his ideas. Johnson would return to the drafting room and draw out the building that Philip had described and return with it to the boss for more discussion and refinements. Over the course of many days or weeks, the final sketches would emerge.

In a sense, Scott Johnson could see his future at the firm: it was John Manley. A long-time associate of Philip's, Manley had helped work on the Seagram Building years before. Manley was known within the office as "Philip Johnson's hands." Scott soon joined Manley in executing the master's concepts. He was involved in some way with almost every major skyscraper that came out of the New York office during those years. Unlike Manley, however, Scott Johnson would not be content to remain in the background.

By 1983, Philip Johnson was seventy-seven years old and he and Burgee, who was fifty years old, began to consider ways to ensure the future of the firm. The first choice was to begin allocating some design credit to Burgee. Get him out of the shadows and into the limelight. The firm's name was changed to John Burgee with Philip Johnson. Another part of the plan was to name Scott Johnson, who was then just thirty-one years old, the design partner and bring in two others as principals in the new organization. The structure would fill the vacuum left by the easing of Philip's control as he reduced his work.

Scott Johnson loved living in New York. His marriage had been repaired and he and Meg were alternating weekends between Manhattan and upstate. His job was ideal in some ways: if a client objected to a design change or wanted to cut back a budget, he could call on Philip, who would bring his eminence to bear on the situation. The tedious work of preparing working drawings was left to others, or farmed out to another firm. But Scott Johnson had begun to weary of being in the great man's shadow.

"I was designing, but it was always important to work in support of Philip," Johnson remembered. "I had my own ideas by then. It was becoming important for me to be known as Scott Johnson and for people to know me for my own thinking. I'd been operating in support of Philip Johnson and now it looked like I would play a similar role for John Burgee. John wanted to be known for design, so my little shadow was going to get eclipsed again. Now it was time for me to do my own thinking and accept full responsibility."

Although always in the elder man's shadow, Scott Johnson had built a reputation of his own within the profession. He had been contacted by executive recruiters and representatives of other firms, so he was aware that he had accumulated some value in the marketplace. Perhaps he should strike out on his own.

During this period, Johnson received a telephone call from Bill Pereira in Los Angeles. He wanted to know if Johnson would be interested in a design job. A few days after the initial call, he spoke with Roy Schmidt, the president of Pereira Associates, who described the opening for a new design chief. Johnson was intrigued at the prospect of receiving recognition for his design work, but there were risks. It would mean leaving behind the reputation he had built in New York and the safety of working for one of the preeminent firms in the country. He viewed the growth of Los Angeles as nothing short of cancerous and worried about the city's historical failure to support innovative architecture on a grand scale. He did not even admire many of the buildings designed by Bill Pereira. And he learned from his old Harvard pal, Bill Fain, that the office was old and tired.

But the job was a chance to escape the shadow of Philip Johnson and take over the design reins at an established firm. So he flew out to Los Angeles to listen to the offer. Since he had the sort of mixed feelings that would allow him to walk away from the position if it was not structured exactly to his liking, he was able to negotiate an arrangement that gave him complete control over the design process at the firm and the promise of a partnership in the near future. He took the job.

The architect who arrived for work at Pereira Associates in August of 1983 was in his early thirties and quite handsome. He was slender and slightly over six feet tall, with his blond hair swept back the way Michael Douglas would later style his in the movie *Wall Street*. Meeting him that first day, his new colleagues found a smiling, polite young professional who could be engaged easily in an enlightened conversation about a broad range of matters.

But the situation Scott Johnson encountered at Pereira Associates was more unsettling than he had anticipated. Things had grown worse since he had spoken with his friend Fain. Bill Pereira's health had deteriorated sharply, yet no one had stepped in to assume control of the firm. It was floundering in the hands of the Seven Dwarfs and the question in Johnson's mind was whether it would stay afloat long enough to give him a chance to salvage the operation.

One evening soon after he started, he laid out what he saw in a conversation with Fain. "The perception of the firm on the street is very bad," he said. "I had thought the name of the firm would help get clients. I had expected a base on which to build business. I thought that once I got control of the design process at a big firm, my troubles were over. Boy, Bill, was I wrong."

There was one bright spot. The month before he started, the firm had signed a deal to design a building to be called Fox Plaza for Marvin Davis, the wealthy oilman who owned 20th Century-Fox at the time. Maybe it was the first step on the road to salvation for the firm and fulfillment for its new design chief.

7

MAN CREATING

Whenever anyone asked how he produced his designs so quickly, Frank Lloyd Wright would respond, "I simply shake them out of my sleeve." While his tongue was partly in his cheek, Wright did possess an uncanny ability to sketch his works with a speed that amazed clients and colleagues alike. Edgar Tafel, Wright's longtime associate, described how Wright designed what many critics regard as his masterpiece, the house for Edgar J. Kaufmann on Bear Run in Pennsylvania.

Kaufmann had hired Wright several months before and, having heard nothing about the progress, one day telephoned the architect's office and asked to visit so that he could see the design work for his house. Permission was granted and Wright, with his assistants watching, sat down with the plot plan for the site, which he had visited just once. He began to draw. He sketched the first-floor plan, then the second floor. The elevation was drawn, the side sketches of details. A bridge leading from the house, over the water and into the woods. He kept up a running commentary to his assistants, describing his work and his reasoning. Pencils were worn down, broke, were replaced. Sheets of paper were filled and flipped aside. Then, in a final flourish, the title of the house was scrawled across the bottom: Fallingwater. The entire process took two hours.

An architectural masterpiece, as with any work of art, is part mystery. In architecture, however, much of the process is recorded through the various stages of drawings. So, if the wellspring of inspiration remains hidden, a method of execution is available for study. In drawing the sketches for Fallingwater, Wright was following the traditional path of architects by beginning with pencil and paper.

Drawings, of course, are the two-dimensional representations of the architect's imagination, and their primary use is to test various ideas during the design process. Nothing shows the effect of forms and shapes literally like a three-dimensional physical model. So the real beginnings of today's complex high-rises are often found in museum board, a form of heavy-duty cardboard that comes in many colors. Museum board can be cut into shapes and glued into three-dimensional models. In the beginning, these models are hardly more sophisticated than children's building blocks. They show the mass of the building and permit the architect and client to evaluate the balance and flow of the design in relation to the site. As the work evolves, the models grow more detailed, eventually giving way to more complete schematic drawings as the design is refined. This process can take weeks and even months in high-rises and other complex projects as the architect's vision is molded by the requirements of the client, the site, and his own aesthetic sense.

The next phase is the schematic drawings, which are based on the architect's finalized drawings and define the main components of the structural system—the material, steel or concrete, the types of floors, and the placements of the columns and bracing. Based on the schematics, estimates can be made of the amount of material and labor required. These drawings also form the basis on which the contractor and subcontractors will bid for the job.

Schematics are followed by another, still more detailed set of plans known as the design development drawings. Here, the schematic drawings are detailed further to show all of the visual aspects of the building, such as the pattern of the exterior skin or the articulation of a balcony. These drawings also identify the specific finishes that will be used and integrate the engineering and mechanical systems into the actual design.

Next come construction documents, also called working drawings. The construction documents, which are prepared under the direction of the structural engineer, provide the sufficient technical detail for the workers actually to build the building. They are so detailed that a plumber can see where to hang the toilets. It is these documents that are finally presented to the city building departments so that they can determine whether the structure will meet the safety and design requirements of the jurisdiction.

These design steps follow logically and, as would be demonstrated during the development of Rincon Center, the interruption of one stage will cause a logjam on an entire project.

It used to be that work on a project would not begin until the final city approvals were in place and the final bids from subcontractors had been evaluated and accepted by the developer. But, with few exceptions, high-rises today are built by what is called a fast-track method, which involves starting the construction before the final design is completed. The impetus is solely economic: waiting for approvals and final bids would mean delays of a year or more while the developer must pay the mortgage on the land and postpone receiving income from the completed project. In addition, completing drawing sets on parts of the building allows the owner to buy major materials earlier, usually at lower prices. Over the cost of an entire building, this can amount to a tremendous savings. So, with fast tracking, the foundation for a project may be underway before the design is finished for the upper floors, or the structural steel can be ordered before the final exterior material is determined.

There are risks. Approvals may be delayed. Bids on various components, based on uncompleted drawings, may turn out to be off by a wide margin, sending the final cost soaring. An unexpected design problem or a structural difficulty can throw off the schedule. Successful fast tracking requires a sophisticated understanding of the project by those doing the budgeting and a cushion against potential cost increases. Rincon Center was destined to have too little of both.

By late July of 1984, Rincon Center Associates, which had been incorporated that month by Perini Land & Development Corporation, Tutor-Saliba, P. Q. Chin, and Michael Blumenthal as the partnership responsible for construction of the project, had signed an architectural contract with Pereira Associates.

Once the legalese and obfuscations are pared away, there are two main elements in a contract between an architect and a developer—fees and responsibility for the budget. In the matter of fees, there are two basic options. One calls for the architect to be paid a flat fee or lump sum to design a project and see it to completion. The fee is often based on a multiple of the square footage of the project and may include any special design complexities that require extra effort by the architect. The flat fee is preferred by most developers because it provides the most accurate figure possible for architectural fees, which run into the millions of dollars on major projects.

The other primary method pays the architect a fee pegged to a specified percentage of the total construction cost of the project. It's like a taxi meter—the more miles you ride, the more it costs. Only with architects, the meter counts the number of hours spent on a project by the firm's designers and other personnel, who charge at varying rates that are tied to experience and rank. So, from the architect's viewpoint, it stands to reason that his pay should be tied to the cost of construction, since the more construction involved in a project, the more work he will have to execute. It also means that the architect has an incentive to stick with a project beset with overruns that might drive off someone who had negotiated a flat fee.

There are many other payment methods, such as hourly rates and multiples of salary expenses. But lump sums are used in about one-third of all contracts and a percentage of construction costs is used about one-fifth of the time. Both of the preferred methods typically provide for additional fees when work has to be redesigned because of changes initiated by the developer or because of unforeseen circumstances after the basic design is completed.

Some developers feel that basing an architect's fee on a percentage of the construction cost represents an inherent conflict of interest for the architect. As the costs mount, so does the architect's fee—and the architect exercises considerable control over costs.

Pereira's negotiators on the Rincon Center contract, Roy Schmidt and Bill Fain, insisted that the firm's pay be a percentage of total construction costs. Their main argument was that the complexities of combining residential, office, and retail space and renovating an aged structure injected a high degree of uncertainty into the project at the outset. Unforeseen design dilemmas could pop up, requiring the firm to assign a dozen or more architects to work out the solution. Construction costs could rise significantly. They wanted to make sure their base pay kept pace.

The developers agreed to pay a fee equal to 4 percent of the construction cost for the basic design of the complex. On top of that would come additional-service fees for any redesign efforts, which would be calculated on an hourly basis. The contract also contained a clause in which both parties agreed to submit any disputes to arbitration.

When the contract was signed in the summer of 1984, the rough estimate for the overall construction cost of the project was around $60 million. That meant Pereira Associates would receive a basic design fee in the neighborhood of $2.4 million, plus any redesign fees.

Randy Verrue wasn't worried about the fee arrangement. He expected to keep the lid on all costs by retaining control of the project budget. And he believed that Tutor-Saliba's dual role as general contractor and part owner would give the firm plenty of incentive to keep costs down.

On the last Friday of July 1984, Scott Johnson was in his Los Angeles office preparing for a meeting in San Francisco on Monday with Randy Verrue and Jay Mancini in Perini's offices in the Alcoa Building. They were to discuss the general concept for the project. Over the past year, Johnson had been immersed in the design of Fox Plaza, a thirty-four-story office tower in a high-profile location that Johnson hoped would signal the new Pereira firm to the Los Angeles market and beyond. By late summer of 1984, that project was at the working-drawing stage and Johnson could turn his full attention to the new project. Bill Pereira still showed up at the firm's offices once a week or so, but as his health deteriorated, his contributions dwindled. Johnson needed some help for a project of Rincon's complexity.

Soon after he had arrived at the Pereira firm, Johnson had begun firing most of the existing staff of design architects. Within two months, he had gotten rid of eighteen architects, some with many years at the firm. He felt that their skills did not match the new directions he and Bill Fain had in mind for the firm. And the empty slots had not been a problem since Fox Plaza was the firm's only big project.

Now, the Rincon commission offered Johnson his first opportunity to hire the type of bright young designers he needed. The week before, in anticipation of the contract, he had interviewed two young architects, Craig Jameson and Edmund Einy. He had told them the firm might win the commission for a major mixed-use project in San Francisco. On Friday, he telephoned both men, told them he had got the job, and offered them positions as junior designers.

"We need to get started right away," Johnson said in the phone calls. "Can you meet me in San Francisco on Monday?"

The plan was for the two newcomers to join Chuck Grein, one of only two designers Johnson had kept on at Pereira, in San Francisco for the initial meeting. Grein, who was respected as a gentle and effective senior architect, would oversee the day-to-day work as project architect.

Einy, a twenty-five-year-old Californian with a master's degree in architecture from the University of California at Los Angeles, had worked at architecture firms since he was sixteen years old. After graduating from UCLA, he had tried working for a couple of larger firms, but was disappointed with the scale of the projects. He wanted to do high-rises, but he wound up designing homes and pieces of mundane buildings. Einy shared Scott Johnson's displeasure over the state of high-rise architecture in Southern California. While he admired much of the residential architecture in the region, he felt that nobody was doing the kind of cutting-edge, major commercial projects he dreamed of designing. So he had left the big firms and gone to work for himself, figuring that if he had to design houses he could at least be his own boss. This new job offered the chance he had been waiting for and, in Johnson, he felt instinctively that he had found a worthy mentor. He dropped everything else and promised to be in San Francisco on Monday morning.

Jameson, also a talented young designer, had a more conventional job at another architecture firm and had to give proper notice. He would not be able to join the small design team in San Francisco for a couple of weeks.

On that Monday morning, as the official design work began, the architects knew that the basic outline of the project had already been defined by the requirements of the Postal Service and the city. They knew there had to be two new buildings on the vacant portion of the site and that the renovated post office had to contain a central core of shops. Carving out the atrium would not have an adverse impact on the historical aspect of the post office because, with the exception of the lobby, the interior of the building was little more than a partitioned warehouse or factory. But there were other limitations that would have at least as great an impact on the eventual form of Rincon Center.

In 1981, the San Francisco Board of Supervisors had declared the Rincon Annex Post Office part of a blighted area that ran from the post office south along the waterfront to an area known as South Beach. Responsibility for restoring the area's economic health was given to the San Francisco Redevelopment Agency, which had been created as part of the urban renewal movement of the 1960s. Using the stick of specialized zoning requirements and the carrot of tax incentives, the agency hoped to channel specific types of development into specific areas within the zone.

The post office was the centerpiece of the blighted area. It was the location closest to the thriving financial district and therefore the most likely spot for the next development. Further, the Postal Service had already indicated it wanted to sell the property. Under its authority, the redevelopment agency set forth the basic requirements that would have to be met by a developer, such as the overall size of the project and some of the uses for the buildings.

In addition, the city planning commission was circulating a draft of its new downtown plan for reining in the building boom that had altered the skyline over the past decade. The draft stressed that new skyscrapers had to be tapered at the top to allow more sunlight to reach the streets. The planners did not want large, bulky buildings that would shade the narrow streets where so much of San Francisco's vitality is found. And the planners wanted the tops of new buildings to be varied so that the skyline did not turn into a giant Lego city of squared-off glass or granite rectangles.

The downtown plan was not yet ready for formal consideration. But the planning commission and the redevelopment agency, in an uneasy alliance of two rival agencies, had made it clear to the Perini development team that the structures at Rincon would have to comply with the spirit of the downtown plan, if not the unformed letter.

Under the redevelopment agency plan, a maximum of 500,000 square feet of new construction could be added at the vacant south end of the site, along Howard Street. Of that amount, 260,000 square feet would have to be housing. The owner would have a choice of setting aside 46,000 square feet of the housing for low- and moderate-income residents or paying the city $5 million, which could be used to offset the market-rate rents. The affordable units had to be spread throughout the new construction, not restricted to the least desirable locations.

The old post office itself would be restored and turned into a museum or commercial center. It was acknowledged that the post office had been constructed in 1940 to allow the addition of two new floors, and they could be built so long as the owner allocated another 12,000 square feet in the new construction for affordable housing.

These limitations formed the parameters for Rincon Center that July day when Johnson, Einy, and Grein sat down with Verrue and Mancini to discuss the initial design concept. The two developers discussed their criteria for the overall development in broad terms. The project needed what Verrue described as "identity and clarity" in terms of separate structures and circulation for each of the elements of the mixed-use project. The residences had to be differentiated clearly from the offices so the people who lived there would have the sense of coming home instead of going to another office, Verrue said. Equally important, the project had to be "commercially viable," which meant completing the project within budget and providing space that could be leased readily to commercial and residential tenants. In the case of Rincon Center, the plan had to be functional and flexible because it was not being built for a specific major tenant, as often happens with a major office project. Instead, the design would have to appeal to yet-unknown tenants, so the floor plans would have to be able to accommodate many different types of businesses.

There were two basic types of office tenants who might find Rincon Center attractive, and they would probably gravitate toward opposite ends of the project. In the old post office, the existing floor plans, or floorplates as they are called, were very large—up to 45,000 square feet per floor. That meant a lot of interior offices, without views. These layouts tend to attract tenants who have a large clerical staff, such as insurance firms or accounting firms. They don't mind if the bulk of their employees have offices with no view and they can take advantage of the larger depths so that large departments can be on one floor.

The new construction, however, with its panorama of San Francisco Bay, should appeal to more upscale businesses, such as lawyers and maybe advertising or consulting firms. They are the operations that demand a high percentage of perimeter offices with views and other amenities.

Verrue felt that the preliminary design done by Peter Bolles had failed to provide a means for creating enough offices with views that could be leased at premium prices at either end of the complex. The old post office was going up two stories, but it still would be dwarfed by the buildings around it. There had to be some way to create space with the kind of views that would bring the higher rents within that structure despite the large floorplates. And Bolles's plan for the two new buildings had allowed one tower to obscure the views from significant portions of the other tower. There had to be a way, Verrue explained to the three architects, to change the configuration of the new structures.

"The developer's job is to give direction to the architect," Verrue said later. "We give the project as much definition as we can and then have the creative geniuses go to work."

One of the design dilemmas, Johnson told Verrue and Mancini, would be dividing the project into the distinct elements that Verrue sought without chopping the entire development into separate parts and losing a sense of continuity essential to making the whole thing work together. Another dilemma concerned the bulk of the new construction. The redevelopment agency's insistence on two buildings, rather than one, had an obvious impact on the size of the new construction. So did the agency's restriction on the height of any new construction at the site to 240 feet. This is pint-size for most skyscrapers these days; Sears Tower, the world's tallest building, soars 1,454 feet above the streets of Chicago; San Francisco's tallest building at the time, the Transamerica pyramid, rises 853 feet. The architectural significance of Rincon Center would not come from its height, but from a variety of other factors that would evolve over the course of the project.

Einy had brought a suitcase along and, after the initial meeting was over, he moved into a hotel. Since Perini's space was limited at the Alcoa Building, Einy set up shop in an office at Chin & Hensolt, the structural engineers on the project. A few days later, he was joined by Jameson, who had cut short his notice in his excitement to get started on the new project. This temporary design studio in San Francisco was necessary in large part because of the unusually high degree of involvement by the staff from the redevelopment agency. Once the preliminary approvals were obtained, the bulk of the design work would be shifted back to Los Angeles.

The first assignment for Einy and Jameson would be creating the models that conveyed Scott Johnson's evolving vision of the design for Rincon Center. A familiar pattern developed within the first week: Johnson, who had returned to Los Angeles, came back with some rough sketches for a new design along the Howard Street end of the project. Einy and Jameson then spent the next few days with X-acto knives, cutting out pieces of museum board and gluing these into the shapes that Johnson had drawn. Museum board comes in many colors, but Johnson invariably uses a shade called Strathmore Alabaster because it neutralizes all other issues, such as color, window pattern, and materials. At this stage, the model's sole purpose is to express the "massing" of the project.

Each week, Johnson would arrive for a discussion with Einy and Jameson. Grein often attended, and every other week or so Jay Mancini stopped by for a progress report.

Several times in this phase, two architects from the San Francisco Redevelopment Agency, Ed Ong and Walter Yanagita, visited the office and critiqued the models. Normally, the architect and developer would come up with what they felt was the strongest design and then present it to the appropriate city officials for modification and approval. But the power accorded the redevelopment agency by the status of the site as a blighted area created what the city officials perceived to be a much stronger role in the creative process.

"Our purpose is to come up with a project that will remove the perception of blight for the entire area," Yanagita explained to Johnson at one of the sessions. "We want to see how the form of the building can be broken up so it will not be massive and will allow as much daylight as possible into the space. Our intent is to provide for the benefit of the people in the city who use the building. These are quasi-public spaces and we have a role to play."

It was a role that Johnson understood, but found difficult to embrace. "I am an esthete," he said late one night over coffee near the end of the project. "That is clearly my bias. But designing a building is not something done in an ivory tower and sent down. Architecture today must be responsive, to government, to the community, to the clients. And it is more interesting if people can have a debate on it. But ultimately someone has to make a decision on it and I like that to be me."

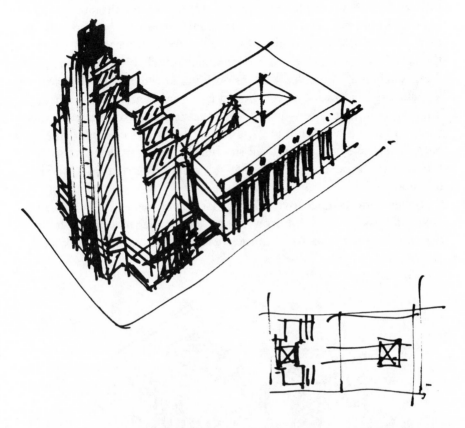

A single building was deemed too bulky to meet city standards.

In his initial sketches for the development, Johnson had come up with a single building designed with enough breaks and articulation that he hoped city officials would feel it met the spirit of the law and would prefer it to the two buildings in the original requirements. The advantages of a single building were many, and chief among them was economics. One building would need only one elevator core, which would obviously be cheaper than two cores. The same was true with the systems that would provide heat, air conditioning, and plumbing to the tenants. While the cost would not be doubled by two buildings, there would be expensive duplication.

But within days of starting the design process, the Pereira archi-

tects agreed that a single building was too bulky for the site, probably would not pass city muster, and would diminish the importance
of the far-smaller post office. So they turned to variations on the
theme of two. One of the early versions, which Einy dubbed "the
Sphinx scheme," involved a larger building at the front of the vacant
lot, closest to Howard Street, linked by squared arches to a smaller
building behind it. The front building was expected to be a hotel; the
back would be condominiums. No one liked the concept, chiefly
because it pushed the second, shorter building too far back on the lot,
too close to the post office. The five-story historic structure would be
overpowered.

Bolles had designed two rectangular structures to be built diagonally across the lot. Johnson wanted more elegance and felt the
diagonal was not responsive to the city street grid. Some of his early

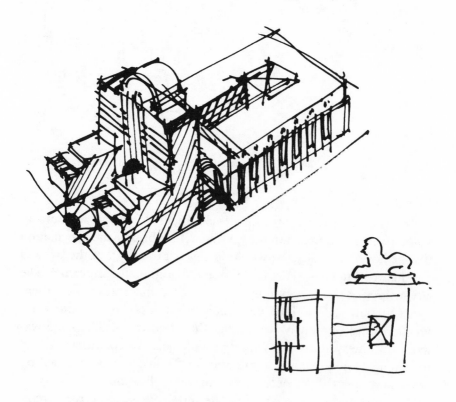

The Sphinx scheme would have overpowered the post office.

designs, however, involved twin Miesian rectangles of glass and steel on opposite sides of the vacant lot, the way the master of Modern had done it at the Illinois Institute of Technology campus in Chicago. Another design called for twin towers with stepped-back tops, one at the front of the lot and the other dead against the old post office. The stepbacks were reminiscent of Republic Bank Center in Houston, which Johnson had worked on while with Philip Johnson. But again, the older building would be smothered. Yet another variation envisioned two similar, curved buildings and a shared lobby. They embraced a skating rink in the open space between the new construction and the post office.

The skating rink was a notion that Jay Mancini had wanted to try after he visited Rockefeller Center, and it was the first of many concepts from other locations that he would try to adapt to Rincon Center. In the case of the skating rink, however, it was an idea that got no further than an early design. Johnson and others convinced the developer that San Francisco was not the place for an outdoor rink.

After about a month of designs and changes and evolution, Johnson produced a sketch of two crescent-shaped buildings that were placed on opposite sides of the lot. Their graceful curves cupped an open courtyard that fronted on Howard Street. The actual models could only hint at the graceful curves, because the museum board could not be bent easily. But the concept was a pleasing one, particularly since it would announce the presence of the project to the public through the large courtyard. The plan also satisfied the shading requirements, since the open space was in front of the buildings.

Mancini, who had informally replaced Verrue as the lead developer's representative on the project, thought over the design and raised objections. He said that he didn't really want the public space to be so public. He would rather find a way to enclose the courtyard so that it clearly belonged more to the tenants in the building than the people on the street.

"We have to market this open space as an amenity for the tenants," Mancini told the architects. "We want them to think of this as their plaza."

The idea of the crescent shapes, however, stuck in Johnson's mind. He began toying with a design that would simply reverse the curves and allow the buildings to cup an inner courtyard, instead of a streetside plaza. He also felt that the two towers should share a single lobby to unify them, since the site was too small for two distinct buildings. Flipping the curves around also would provide the interior offices with views of the courtyard and the skyline and bay beyond; they would not be as popular or as pricey as a bayside view perhaps, but it would be an attractive "amenity," to borrow Mancini's word.

At the same time they had been working on the massing models for the new buildings, the architects had been developing designs for the renovation of the post office. The Bolles plan had envisioned a square, five-story atrium in the center of the post office. A single-story hall would lead out the back of the post office to the new construction. But the Johnson team had a far more dramatic idea in mind.

"Busting out the atrium," Einy called it. The plan that evolved called for enlarging the hallway that would link the atrium to the new courtyard out the back of the post office. The hallway would be widened and the ceiling removed, allowing it to match the five-story height of the atrium. And the atrium skylight would be extended over the resulting allée, providing far more drama to the space. Busting out would mean carving out more of the support beams in the existing building, a potentially expensive proposition, and tearing out the entire rear facade. That final step would require approval from the preservation moguls with the U.S. Department of Interior, who were overseeing the renovation work since the building was on the National Register of Historic Places.

But it seemed worth the effort, since the results would create more drama and expand the number of offices on the upper floors of the post office that would have views of the open interior, a strong leasing point for the developers.

The design that was taking shape over these weeks in the late summer of 1984 was a formal one and reflected two of the forces that had shaped Scott Johnson's vision as an architect. Johnson had developed a strong interest in classical form during the year he spent studying in Italy, and it had been nurtured by frequent trips back to Europe and voracious reading. Growing up and attending college in the Bay Area also had exposed him to San Francisco's architecture. Over the years, the buildings and places in the city that he felt endured were those that had been designed in the 1910s and 1920s by a handful of American architects who had trained at the École Nationale des Beaux-Arts in Paris. Among his favorite Bay Area sites were the Civic Center complex designed by Arthur Brown, Jr., John Galen Howard's schemes for the University of California at Berkeley, the early commercial buildings of Willis Polk and Julia Morgan, and the formal city gardens of Union Square.

So the final design concept for Rincon Center was, at its heart, a Beaux-Arts plan that paid homage to the classical forms in which the style was rooted. Indeed, viewed in its simplest terms, the final design was a crucifix, one of the oldest and sturdiest of architectural foundations. The atrium in the old post office formed one end of the crucifix. The longitudinal axis began with the colonnade and extended through the open courtyard to the new construction. Someone standing in the atrium would have a dramatic and unobstructed view down the length of the project, visually linking the old and new elements yet maintaining their separateness by distance. The bisecting axis would be two entrances on either side of the courtyard where the open space joined the old post office; the midblock entrances would be extended by canopies or banners over the sidewalks to signal the building's presence to people on the street.

Johnson refined this concept and Einy and Jameson churned out more models until they captured the concept that Johnson had in mind. It had taken six weeks, forty-one drawings, and twenty-one sets of models. In the middle of September, with all the alabaster structures lined up like sculptures in the office at Chin & Hensolt, Johnson invited Mancini to come over and see what he thought was an acceptable model. Two towers, their graceful curves only hinted at by the models, sheltered an inner courtyard that connected with the nave that ran out of the atrium in the center of the post office building.

"We held the towers back to the rear side of the lot, so they don't overwhelm the older post office building," Johnson explained to Mancini. "If we hadn't done that, those big towers would seem to lean right over the old building. This way, they each become neighbors. Each is comfortable. Inserting the towers on a curve of forty-five degrees gives us terrific views of the bay and up Nob Hill for the inner apartments. And enlarging the atrium to open it up to the back of the building ties the old building to the new courtyard and buildings."

Mancini liked the concept. There were still plenty of details to work out on positioning, the material and facade design for the

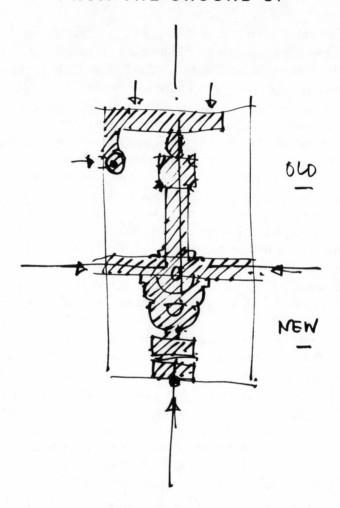

The basic floor plan was a classic crucifix to link the old and new phases.

towers, the number of stories, modifications to the tops of the new buildings, dimensions of the atrium. Myriad details. But this plan struck Mancini as a great beginning.

For Johnson, too, solving the massing problem with a formal design plan and busting out the atrium were just a beginning. Next, he would produce the detailed drawings of the towers and their base, determine the dimensions and impact of the atrium, and refine the master plan for knitting the project into a cohesive whole.

8

A CUSTOM DEAL

If Rincon Center were likened to a serpent, then the atrium would be the head, in which are located the senses, expressions, and brain. The remainder of the project could be muscular, smoothly curved, and boldly coiled as it stretched across the city block and reached into the sky. The head would have to contain its excitement within more precise dimensions. Unless the atrium were a vibrant and exciting attraction, the entire development would be dull. Though it was never a phrase they used, everyone associated with the project recognized that Rincon Center's atrium had to be its sweet spot.

People need reasons for going to a place, and the more reasons there are, the more people will come and the longer they will stay. From Scott Johnson's vantage, the atrium would be this place, the spot where people could interact and do the kinds of things that would draw them to the project. He first envisioned the atrium as a space designed along the lines of the famous Galleria shopping arcade in Milan. There would be a fairly narrow arcade, with stores and restaurants on the first and second floors overlooking the center walkway. He wanted to keep the scale intimate, create a stage where everyone who entered the atrium would be a player. Someone walking into the atrium would be visible to the people sitting at tables along its edges. Eye contact could be made, bits of conversations overheard. The atrium would be a theater.

In a well-designed theater, the distances are close enough for the audience to make eye contact with the actors and see their facial movements from any seat. The maximum distance at which this can occur comfortably is about 90 feet. Early on, Johnson decided that 90 feet would be the maximum distance between the sides of the atrium. From this would flow the basic dimensions of the atrium.

Convincing the owners that the atrium should be carved out of the building to meet these smaller dimensions was difficult and time-consuming. Once the Peter Bolles plan had been scuttled, the developers' attitude was that bigger was better. They wanted a generous square in the heart of the building so that someone could walk in any door and see the front of every store and restaurant.

But Halcyon, the retail consulting firm hired to plan the atrium layout, agreed with Johnson's concept. Their initial design called for a sort of "retail street" going through the older post office building, like an arcade. This fit with Johnson's concept that the atrium should be organized in a way that would draw visitors into and through the retail area with its drama and excitement. With proper design and the right details, people would circulate through the atrium and add to the vibrancy. It was this circulation that would provide the 100 percent visibility sought by the developers.

"The hardest thing for people to understand is that everything an architect does is a custom deal," said Johnson. "It is not like making twelve thousand pairs of shoes. The whole effort is custom. The property is a blank piece of paper. Applying formulas blindly, such as seeing every storefront from every doorway, does not work in good urban architecture. In a world without formulas, it is frequently hard for an owner to make a decision. He needs experience and intuition. And you find people who can make those decisions and people who can't."

For Johnson, the natural process when he is commissioned to do a design is to sit and think about it. He visits the site at different times of the day and night, walks around the neighborhood. As the design begins to take shape in his mind, he isolates the specific problems that must be solved to make the project work. Once the problems are isolated, he begins to examine what he believes are the best examples of the way similar dilemmas were solved in the past. Inevitably he winds up digging through his library in search of previous solutions. The search reflects Johnson's classical roots, his belief that modern architecture should not be cut off from hundreds of years of history.

Rather, architects can look to the past for solutions that are adaptable to today's problems.

Johnson was still examining solutions for the atrium in February of 1985 when he hired a senior designer named Dianna Wong. Wong had attended Radcliffe College and Cambridge University and ended up with a master's degree in architecture from Harvard University. In her first job, with a small firm in Boston run by Joan Goody, she had worked on several smaller mixed-use projects. But she wanted to do bigger projects and she had come to Pereira as a senior designer, despite only three years' experience. At the time, Wong was also the only woman in a senior position at a major Los Angeles architecture firm.

Young architects are often journeymen. A firm will win a big commission and hire several new designers to help out until the job is completed. Then, if there is not enough new work, they are let go. Accompanying this job insecurity is relatively low pay for professionals. In 1985, an architect with less than five years of experience was lucky to earn $28,000 a year. Even experienced architects don't see serious money until they become a partner or principal in a major firm, with salaries averaging $88,000 nationwide.

Wong was hired specifically to work with Johnson on the detailed design of a new performing arts center at a college in the Los Angeles area. The school's board of directors liked the firm's work and was ready to sign the final contract. Unfortunately, the philanthropist who had donated the money to pay for the arts center decided that she wanted an old family friend to design the structure. The job was withdrawn from Pereira Associates and handed over to a rival firm.

Instead of being out of work, however, Wong was moved over to Rincon Center. She was the type of bright young designer Scott Johnson planned to keep. Her first task was working with Johnson on the atrium design. The atrium had to complement the structure that housed it, so Johnson was interested in finding the sort of period details that could be updated and yet still evoke the history of the post office. So he had Wong gather books filled with examples from around the world of architecture from the 1930s and early 1940s. There were volumes on American architecture in the thirties and on British architecture from the same period. A book on architecture in Italy during World War II provided ideas for storefronts. Art Deco books offered examples of strength and simplicity that echoed the design of the Rincon post office itself. A Sears catalogue from 1938 provided furniture with the bold and simple lines of the period. Wong also studied examples of Gilbert Stanley Underwood's other designs, including the famous Ahwahnee Hotel in Yosemite National Park and several buildings along Wilshire Boulevard in Los Angeles.

"It becomes intuitive," said Wong. "You collect a collage of images and you begin to evolve design elements. You distill the elements to what is appropriate. As an architect, you collect visual images in your mind. That is being a literate architect. You don't actually copy, but you examine the essence of a building and extract what is appropriate."

Wong was an integral part of the new wave that Johnson was bringing to Pereira Associates, but the old guard was not yet gone. Bill Pereira still came around the firm in early 1985, as Wong was working on the difficult task of assembling ideas for the atrium and then trying to execute the sketches pouring forth from Scott Johnson. Pereira was aware of the difficulties with the atrium and he occasionally stopped by Wong's drafting table to offer his advice. Less frequently, he would ask Johnson to call a design meeting so he could talk about the work on Rincon Center. But to the young architects being assembled at the firm, Bill Pereira's views seemed dated and they were discounted—courteously but absolutely.

Because Johnson conceived of the atrium as a holder of activity, he and Wong felt that it needed strong vertical walls. Also, because the exterior of the building was so solidly concrete, with few windows, they wanted to sharpen the contrast with an interior that made extensive use of glass. So Johnson designed a glass curtain wall for the atrium, with various colors of glass running in a pattern to carry the eye up the sides of the space. This also would fit into the concept he was formulating for the skin of the twin towers at the other end of the site.

Balconies and small decks would be cut into the upper floors to enhance the interior views for office workers and provide view offices for executives. This use of the interior was expected to be an important selling point. Even with its two new floors, the building would be only five stories high. There would be no commanding views of the bay or the skyscrapers of the financial district. As a replacement, the emerging design emphasized dramatic views of the atrium itself, through glass walls and from balconies.

The design of the upper levels of the atrium was one of the early instances in which Jay Mancini's tight budget imposed serious design restrictions on the architects. The large hole that would be cut in the upper floors of the building was intended to give a feeling of soaring space to the atrium. To emphasize the drama and create an uncluttered look, Johnson had wanted to remove all of the 12-by-12-inch concrete support beams across the span of the atrium. But the developers told him no. They said it would cost too much since new structural walls, beams, and girders would have to be added to keep the building from collapsing into the atrium. So Johnson and Wong came up with a design that left the horizontal beams in place and resulted in a crisscross effect that gave the atrium and long colonnade the flavor of a jungle gym in the minds of some who saw the drawings.

Another key element of the original plan for the atrium involved the Refregier murals. The developers wanted to move them from the old lobby to the new atrium, where they would attract more attention—and more people. An art consultant was hired and, working with Chin & Hensolt, he examined the murals. He found that the works had been painted directly onto the plaster walls. Not only could they not be moved to the atrium, it would take a careful and expensive restoration effort to keep them from being damaged severely in their present locations during the upcoming demolition and construction work in the post office. Out of this restriction came the seed of the notion that new murals could be created in the atrium as a way of visually connecting the old and new portions of the building.

Meetings among the architects, the developers, and the engineers took place every other week, usually in Perini's San Francisco office. At these sessions, progress on various parts of the project was described, decisions were made, and goals were established. By April 1985, enough progress had been made on the rough shape of the atrium for Johnson to have one of his junior architects build a small model out of museum board. On May 5, Johnson and Wong flew to San Francisco to present the model and sketches to Mancini. No one expected this model to be the final representation of the atrium. Countless details remained unresolved and decisions made would be reversed or modified in the coming months. But Johnson and Wong hoped they could secure Mancini's approval for the basic design and move forward from there.

The atrium design unveiled at the May meeting was a combination of the formal and classical and the contemporary. There were elements drawn from nineteenth-century European shopping arcades, such as Milan's Galleria. Yet Johnson's extensive use of glass gave the interior a contemporary flair. There was room for fifteen restaurants and twenty-five shops around the edge of the atrium and down the corridor to the courtyard. The storefronts bordering the atrium were starkly modern, with large plates of glass framed with metal. The skylight ran 200 feet along the building's center and was 68 feet wide, with a wider square of 72 feet on each side above the center of the atrium. The original scheme called for seating in the middle of the atrium and down the corridor, but it had been scrapped because the San Francisco fire code required that those spaces remain open for emergency exiting. As a result, some seating areas were located around the edges of the atrium.

Mancini thought Johnson's plan for a highly patterned granite floor might be too expensive. He also was uncertain about the sharply modern storefronts and the sleek design. He could not decide on the number and sizes of the stores that would line the atrium and the colonnade. And, without the seating in the center of the atrium, the space was blank. It needed something. This dissatisfaction was eventually to spread to many more aspects of the atrium design, and it would be months before agreement was reached. But that day, Mancini was focusing on something for the center of the atrium.

He had spent many days on the road in the previous weeks, visiting mixed-use projects across the United States and in Canada. Though it was perhaps less sophisticated than Johnson's search through the history books, he was collecting his own images for Rincon Center. He had visited Rockefeller Center and admired the symbolism of the Atlas statue. One of the images that made the strongest impression on Mancini was the water fountain at Copley Place, a newer mixed-use project in Boston. He had started to think that Rincon Center needed a water fountain in the center of the atrium. Water would focus attention on the center of the space as well as provide "white noise" to soften the sound of hundreds of simultaneous conversations in the atrium. The background noise would make the decks and balconies more enjoyable for the tenants on the upper stories.

The fountain also could be executed by an artist and its cost

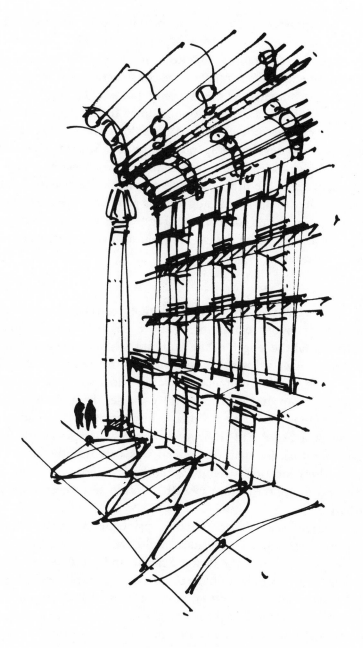

The early atrium design was reminiscent of Milan's Galleria.

deducted from the $600,000 or so that the developers were going to have to spend on art in Rincon Center's public areas. This money was to satisfy the city's requirement that developers of major projects set aside an amount equal to 1 percent of the construction cost for public art. Some developers satisfied the law only grudgingly. But Mancini saw the requirement as a genuine opportunity to add excitement to the project. A cottage industry of art consultants had grown up in recent years to help developers spend this money. At Scott Johnson's suggestion, Mancini hired Tamara Thomas, a Los Angeles art consultant, to help select the proper art and artists for the development. Along with an artist who would address the problem of the fountain, Thomas was asked to find someone who could execute a new series of murals for the atrium, since the existing murals inside the post office could not be moved.

A critical element in the atrium design hinged on removing the rear facade from the post office building to allow the open space and glass skylight to extend the length of the building to the courtyard. Johnson and Wong viewed this as an essential link between the old and new elements in the development. It would allow someone to walk into the atrium from the post office lobby and see through the entire project on one long axis. Beyond this, while the other three sides of the existing post office had rhythm and grace, the rear facade had been a loading dock for mail trucks and was dotted with tiny windows in random locations. Keeping the back facade intact would darken the interior of the atrium as well as divide the project into two distinct halves.

Mancini agreed with the architectural principle, but he expressed deep concern over whether the idea could win approval from the historical experts at the U.S. Postal Service and the National Park Service. The developers had not anticipated any problems with the historical aspects of the renovation, but then they had not anticipated a design that would pull down the rear facade of the older building.

This was a classic clash between money and architecture. Financing for the development depended heavily on the 25 percent tax credits available for historic renovations. It was worth $8 million or so to the developers, based on the cost of renovating the post office. But to qualify for the investment tax credit, the developers would have to come up with a renovation plan that met the approval of the federal authorities. If the Park Service rejected the proposal to remove the rear facade and the developers did it anyway, they would lose the tax credit. That would mean coming up with more of their own money for the project and starting the search for financing all over again. Going against the preservationists on a landmark structure also would bring a heap of trouble, since the architectural integrity of the building was protected by the historic preservation law. However, maintaining the facade to ensure the tax credit and stay out of a court fight with the preservationists would jeopardize what Johnson saw as the architectural integrity of the key element of the development.

Mancini, who cared neither for a fight with the preservationists nor for the loss of the tax credit, argued in favor of keeping the facade and redesigning the rear of the building. Johnson and Wong resisted strongly, contending that this was an issue of singular importance to the vitality of the project. Reluctantly, Mancini agreed that the design could be submitted as drawn in hopes of winning approval. If approval was denied, he warned, the facade would remain and they would just have to design around it.

The preservationists were not the only outsiders who had to approve the design of Rincon Center. The staff of the San Francisco Redevelopment Authority had their own requirements to be met. Since Rincon Center was part of a "blighted" area, the agency's charter gave it power to approve or reject specific development plans for parcels of land within the area. But city politics also were at play here. The agency's power had waned as the number of big urban renewal projects declined. The years when whole neighborhoods were bulldozed in the name of progress were long gone. At the same time, the rival city planning department was becoming more powerful. Many at redevelopment believed they were in danger of being devoured by planning director Dean Macris, acknowledged by many as the most powerful political figure in San Francisco after Mayor Dianne Feinstein. One result of this rivalry was that the redevelopment authority staff jealously guarded the few projects over which they had control—and Rincon Center was the plum.

Virtually from the project's inception, architects from redevelopment had reviewed preliminary models and drawings for Rincon Center. As Scott Johnson worked on the detailing of the new towers and the positioning of the courtyard in early 1985, he constantly had architects from the redevelopment authority looking over his shoulder and raising questions about his work. When he made his presentations to the owners, Ed Ong or Walter Yanagita from redevelopment would often attend and add their comments to the discussion. Johnson grew to resent what he viewed as intrusive micromanagement. Bureaucrats were trying to design his building.

"They are good citizens who may or may not be good architects," said Johnson. "They were trying to help us understand the desire of the redevelopment agency that the finishes had to be light in tone and that the new downtown code requires setbacks, so we just didn't have a massive wall of towers. That was fine. But at a point they became invasive. They were enormously confused about their roles. They never understood the fine line between structuring a dialogue so they get the public amenities they want and actually making specific design decisions. The latter is not their role and they are not particularly good at it."

In a conversation near the end of the project, Walter Yanagita defended the extensive role played by the agency. Yanagita, who had worked as an architect in both Los Angeles and San Francisco before joining the city, said the staff and commissioners who ran the agency were concerned that a Los Angeles architect might not be familiar with the more traditional nature of San Francisco architecture. He said the staff also wanted to ensure that the provisions of the downtown plan, which was moving toward approval as Rincon was being designed, were embodied in the project. That meant restraining height and keeping the new towers as slender as possible.

Two main areas of dispute emerged between Johnson and the redevelopment staff. One involved the exterior material for the two new towers. Johnson favored a facade that was predominantly glass walls framed with aluminum. Even though San Francisco's Hallidie Building had one of the world's first glass facades when it was built in 1917, few structures since then had been erected in the city with curtain walls of glass. The favored material in San Francisco was stone or concrete. The staff was concerned that the glass would look out of place. They worried that it might cheapen the building, give it what Yanagita called "an L.A. look." Their concerns were heightened because Johnson wanted to use glass with two different shades of a light green tint. The architect felt the color would help the building stand out on the skyline, since none of its neighbors used green glass. That was precisely what worried Yanagita and his colleagues.

The second major contested area involved the shape of the towers themselves. Yanagita and his colleagues insisted that the towers be reduced sharply in bulk as they rose. They wanted a series of setbacks at specific intervals as the buildings moved up so that they would cast narrower shadows and impose less massively on the city's skyline. The developers objected, since the setbacks would rob them of rentable space, particularly at the highest and thus most expensive levels. Johnson also opposed them because he was concerned about the impact of the changes on the overall appearance of the towers.

There was one other dispute over the towers, this one involving their tops. Although the towers were designed generally as twins, Johnson felt strongly that each should have a different cap or top. One had been designed with a rounded, vaulted top while the other was triangular. He argued that the towers were going to be homes, not offices, and people would have a greater sense of place and pride if they could differentiate between them and point to their tower, their home. On this issue, Johnson was arguing without Mancini's support. The developer didn't think it mattered at all whether the tops were different or the same. He just wanted to get a design that would pass muster with the San Francisco Redevelopment Agency so he could move ahead with his project.

9

FAST TRACK

Jay Mancini was tired and stretched thin. His marriage was troubled. His wife was a personnel executive at the Bank of America, which was fighting for its survival after a series of eight-figure losses. She spent her days firing hundreds of people—the bank got rid of 10,000 workers in 1985 alone. So she faced her own strains. Mancini had moved out of their condominium and was living at the Bohemian Club, an exclusive men's club best known for annual retreats where statesmen and corporate tycoons run naked in the woods. Meanwhile, Mancini was working twelve-hour stretches trying to cope with an unending string of decisions and dilemmas regarding Rincon Center. Still, it didn't seem to be enough. Now the pace was about to pick up sharply because the decision had been made to put the project on a fast track.

On the afternoon of April 8, 1985, top members of the Rincon team assembled in the offices of Perini Land & Development in the Alcoa Building. Mancini was in charge of the meeting. Scott Johnson had flown up from Los Angeles along with two other architects, Chuck Grein and Charles "Bud" Magee. As the senior project architect, Grein was implementing the main elements of the design. Magee had been named project manager for Pereira Associates, which made him the day-to-day liaison with the construction team. Chin & Hensolt had sent Dennis Oh, an engineer with twenty years of experience who was managing the job for the structural engineers. Ron Tutor, the general contractor, had flown up in his company airplane from Sylmar, his headquarters north of Los Angeles.

At this juncture, the two most important phrases in the lexicon of a project's developers are "on schedule" and "on budget." Mancini had completed the marathon lease negotiations with the U.S. Postal Service and the inch-thick document was undergoing a final review by lawyers for both sides. A set of conceptual architect's drawings had been provided to the Postal Service for its approval on March 22. Once the formality of a design okay was received from the postal authorities and the lease was signed, the clock would start to run for real on the project. Time would be money.

While there are some novel wrinkles in the Rincon Center lease, similar forces are at play in most transactions where the developer is leasing the land from another party. From the perspective of the Postal Service, the lease was set up to accomplish two goals: assure that the agency received a fair rent for the project once it was completed and occupied, and impose a series of financial incentives and potential penalties to ensure that the developer got the project started and finished as fast as possible so that rent would start to flow in.

So the day the ground lease was signed, the developers would pay the Postal Service $450,000 as a demonstration of commitment. It is similar to the earnest money that accompanies an offer on a house. A year after the signing date, the developer was required to post a letter of credit in the amount of $1.55 million. A letter of credit is a guarantee that the specified amount is available and, if demanded under the conditions of the agreement, would be paid to the Postal Service. A letter of credit is generally arranged through a bank and the person or entity obtaining it pays a fee of 1 or 2 percent of its face value. The fee is similar to interest on a loan, although it is less because the money is being held in reserve by the financial institution and is not actually turned over to the entity.

The lease offered Rincon Center Associates yet another incentive to get the work started fast: if construction and renovation had started and construction loans were obtained within a year of signing the lease, the letter of credit would be reduced to $550,000, saving the developers fees on an additional $1 million.

These initial financial obligations are attention getters, designed to make certain the developer doesn't allow the project to languish or, in a soft market, simply sit on the land until the situation improves.

The arrangement with the Postal Service was called a ground lease for the simple reason that it dealt with the ground under the project. The payments to the Postal Service would come from money paid to the developers by tenants who would rent the commercial and residential space in the project. The developers wanted to delay the start of ground lease payments, or at least reduce them for a period, until revenue began to flow from the tenants. Otherwise, it would mean more money out of the pockets of Rincon Center Associates.

The basic rent that would be paid to the Postal Service was set at $3.3 million a year. Payments were delayed until two years after the lease was signed, and only half the $3.3 million would be required for the first year. After that, however, the full rent payment would kick in. The base rent would go up every six years according to a formula based on the Consumer Price Index.

On top of that fixed amount, the Postal Service would receive a percentage of the annual gross revenue paid to the developers by tenants in the renovated post office and the two new floors that were to be added. This so-called percentage rent, which would enable the Postal Service to increase its take as rents rose on its building, did not cover the new construction at the other end of the block.

The lease did, however, require the developers to provide 14,000 square feet of free space in one of the new buildings that would be used as a new postal facility, plus loading docks and free parking for agency vehicles.

Alongside the rent and prepayments, the other primary component of a lease is its length. Standard leases on major commercial projects in which a developer spends millions of dollars renovating existing structures or erecting new ones—or, as in the case of Rincon Center, both—run ninety-nine years. At the end of that period, the buildings and other improvements are turned over to the lessor. Further, the buildings must be free of all loans and other types of liens.

In this case, the Postal Service would become the owner of Rincon Center at the end of the lease, and this included the new buildings on the Howard Street end of the site. In a key issue, however, the developers retained air rights on the new end of the lot, which meant that they could sell the residential units as condominiums and pocket the profits—minus a small share for the Postal Service.

But instead of a ninety-nine-year lease, the Postal Service had insisted on renting the property for only sixty-five years. The time period had been the subject of bitter negotiations and it was the main reason the details had taken so long to work out. But James Wilson, the chief negotiator for the postal agency, had refused to budge on the lease period, which was standard for postal leases at the time.

At first glance, this type of an arrangement appears to defy economic rationality. Rincon Center was going to cost at least $60 million to construct and much more once the development costs were totaled. It would be worth an unknown multiple of that in sixty-five years when the owners turned it over to the Postal Service. But this is where the economics of commercial real estate come into play. An office building, apartment complex, or shopping center provides its owner with income from tenants. If all goes according to plan, the income pays the owner's mortgage or lease and other costs, and provides a profit margin.

If Rincon Center were well planned and an economic success, the developers would receive profits in excess of their original investment and ground-lease payments long before the lease was up. More likely, they would sell the project at a profit well before the lease expired and the new owners would recoup their expenses and make a profit before turning the property back to the Postal Service. This scenario ignores another probability: since the Postal Service is not in the business of managing commercial property, it could be expected to negotiate a new lease when the first one expired.

A lease provides a developer with a key advantage over buying land outright or obtaining a mortgage for it. Instead of coming up with money out of his pocket, the developer's cost of the land is spread out over the length of the lease, reducing his upfront costs and financial risk.

So, crazy as a lease may seem at first glance, the downside is not as great as it appears and there are some advantages. Nonetheless, some developers refuse to build on leased land because they believe it diminishes the resale value of a property. And some large investors, such as certain pension funds, are reluctant to put money into such situations. So the fact that Rincon Center was on leased land added another element of risk.

But as Jay Mancini and the others sat in the conference room that early April afternoon in 1985, the main significance of the lease was that it created pressure to speed up the project. Mancini had discussed the pressures with Randy Verrue, who had in turn gone over them with the brass back in Massachusetts. All had agreed that the project should be speeded up through fast tracking. Indeed, the costs of land and loans, coupled with the desire of many developers and investors to get in and out of projects as quickly as possible, have contributed to the tendency to building skyscrapers on a fast track.

So it came as little surprise to those in the conference room when Mancini announced that they would not be waiting for final city approvals before completing the schematic drawings and getting underway with the partial demolition of the post office interior and construction of the new buildings. They would obtain the overall approvals from the key agencies, and design changes that resulted from unresolved issues would be incorporated into the project as they were settled.

Scott Johnson recognized immediately that this would mean additional work for his designers. They would design the project once and, in all likelihood, have to redesign portions to meet any city demands. When Johnson raised the issue, Mancini agreed that the extra work would be billed as additional services, above the fees set forth in Johnson's base contract.

Fast tracking also meant that the project would get underway without a final budget. Smart developers provide a financial cushion for a fast-track project to cover the invariable extra costs that arise in these situations. But Mancini wanted Rincon Center to stick to a tight, no-frills budget for construction costs. That was why he had been pushing for cheaper materials in parts of the atrium. From Perini L&D's viewpoint, bringing the project in at the lowest possible cost was vital to making it work because of the softening real estate market. When a market weakens, it is usually the buildings in secondary locations, such as South of Market, that suffer the most.

That was the day Mancini also announced the target dates for completing the project. It was an ambitious schedule, calling for completing the renovation of the post office and opening it as phase one by July 1987, slightly more than two years away. Phase two, the new construction, would be finished and ready for occupancy by January 1988. For those dates to work, everything would have to click perfectly.

Mancini also set out the developer's goals for the construction budget for both phases. "This will be a $58 million project," he said. It was a figure he would insist on at some point in almost every meeting for months, long after everyone knew the cost was going to be far greater.

Ron Tutor, who was responsible for determining the budget and seeing that it was met, had come up with an initial estimate of $61.8 million. But Tutor told Mancini not to worry. He said he figured to save $5 million or more by building the new towers out of concrete.

Most people have an image of a skyscraper under construction. They see a huge steel skeleton rising out of a pit. Cranes swing the giant steel H-beams in place. Ironworkers weld the steel girders to the framework, moving higher and higher. The curtain wall, whether of glass, stone, or some other material, is then hung from the framing.

But that is not the only way to build a skyscraper. Tall buildings can also be built with concrete structural elements. Concrete is a mixture of cement, sand, crushed stone, and water. The water and cement fill the void between the sand, and the sand fills the space between the stones and it all hardens, or "sets," to provide a final strength as strong as the strongest stones. Concrete is very good at withstanding the compression resulting from the millions of tons of material. This is called compressive strength.

But there is a second stress on construction material, called tension. Tension is the tendency to pull apart, and it comes from the normal movement of a skyscraper in the wind. It is not visible to the naked eye, but a tall building may move a foot to two off center in high winds and some occupants of very tall skyscrapers can sense this swaying. As a result, structural elements must have elasticity, some ability to stretch without snapping.

Modern steel, with its ability to withstand both compression and tension, enabled American architects and engineers in the twentieth century to erect the tallest buildings in the world. Sears Tower in Chicago is supported by steel columns and beams. Concrete has more compressive strength than steel, but is also much heavier. More important, concrete is brittle and has little tensile strength; pure concrete is too rigid to serve as construction material for a building of any height. The solution to the rigidity is known as reinforced concrete, which was developed in France in the middle 1800s and has been refined dramatically since. In reinforced concrete, bars of steel, called rebar, are embedded in the concrete to absorb the tension and allow the concrete a degree of elasticity. This also is known as ductility.

Reinforced concrete can be found in everything from highways and bridges to stadiums and hotels. It is the most commonly used structural material in the world. But steel remains the material of choice for skyscrapers because it is generally considered to be faster to install and more flexible once the building is finished. For instance, holes can be cut almost anywhere in a steel-framed building to accommodate tenant needs.

Concrete does offer some advantages over steel for skyscrapers, and there are tall concrete buildings, mostly built since the 1960s. In 1985, the world's tallest concrete structure was the seventy-four-story Water Tower Place in Chicago. Because they are stiffer, concrete buildings do not sway as much in wind as their steel counterparts. Occupants are more comfortable because they don't feel the movement as much. Concrete offers natural fireproofing, whereas steel beams must be sprayed with fireproofing material to meet city fire codes. Concrete also provides better soundproofing, which is one reason many hotels and apartment buildings are built with it. And concrete buildings have shallower floor-to-floor heights. In a concrete building, the floor of one story is the ceiling of the one below it. With a steel building, a suspended ceiling must be constructed at the expense of floor-to-floor heights. This would be an important element in the construction of Rincon's new towers.

However, there was another consideration at Rincon Center. San Francisco had been nearly destroyed by the earthquake of 1906. The state of California, because of the prevalence of quakes, had forbidden concrete buildings of more than thirteen stories for most of the century. The restriction was lifted in the 1960s, after heavy lobbying by the concrete industry and advances in concrete technology. But there have been lingering fears among engineers that concrete poses more risks than steel in an earthquake. For instance, heavier buildings are likely to sustain more damage than lighter ones because the force of the quake is drawn to mass. In addition, tall buildings must be flexible enough to sway with an earthquake. They also must behave as one unit, with all the elements tied together. Buildings with more tensile strength are better able to absorb the swaying generated by an earthquake. Concrete buildings weigh more and are less elastic than their steel counterparts, so they attract more force and absorb it less well. To counteract these problems, engineers add more rebar to concrete in earthquake-prone areas in order to increase ductility and allow the structure to sway as a single unit, like a tree bending in the wind. But adding steel rebar means adding money, which tends to take away one of the chief advantages of concrete over steel.

Concrete does have some advantages in earthquake zones. Because it is stiffer than steel, concrete skyscrapers deform less under the swaying movement of an earthquake. Much of the damage from an earthquake occurs when the granite or glass skin of a skyscraper fractures and when structural elements and furniture inside the building start to move in response to swaying. This is less likely to occur in a building that sways less.

Ron Tutor is not prone to long explanations and he offered none for concrete that April day. He assumed the structure would be concrete. After all, he was an owner in addition to being the general contractor. And Tutor was a concrete man, so he also would provide the concrete work for Rincon Center. But the meeting adjourned without a final decision.

By this point, Rincon Center was demanding all of Jay Mancini's time and still it was not enough. Negotiating the lease, working with the architects and the engineers, trying to please the redevelopment agency and predict the demands of the downtown plan—it was all overwhelming him. So he persuaded Verrue to let him hire an assistant.

Bob Mayer was a Citicorp banker who had financed several Perini ventures in the past. Verrue had engaged in some preliminary discussions with him about the big bank's providing the construction loan for Rincon Center. When Mayer heard that they were looking for an assistant on the job, he suggested that Mancini and Verrue take a look at a friend of his, Harry Topping, who was just finishing his MBA at the University of Chicago. Mayer and Topping had worked together as young architects in San Francisco. Two years earlier, Topping had returned to school for his MBA in the hope of starting a career in real estate development.

Topping flew to San Francisco near the end of April for an interview. He is a big, dark-haired, affable Midwesterner who also had an undergraduate degree in architecture and a master's degree in architectural history. He hit it off well with Mancini, who liked the idea of having an expert on architecture to advise him, and Topping accepted the job when it was offered near the end of the trip. He was not to start until after he graduated the following month, but he decided to stick around an extra day to attend a project meeting.

So on April 30, 1985, Harry Topping was sitting in Perini's conference room at the Alcoa Building, where he had once worked for SOM. In the room with him were Mancini, Randy Verrue, Dennis Oh, and Ron Tutor. The topic was the construction material for Rincon Center's new towers. Some of the engineering experts in Perini Corporation's San Francisco construction office favored steel for Rincon. They had worked with it more often and felt it was more predictable. But Tutor was insisting on concrete and, since he was a partner and not just the contractor, and since the project was being led by the firm's development arm, the engineers never challenged Tutor. Nonetheless, Mancini and Verrue had already discussed the issue privately and they raised it now with Tutor at the April 30 meeting.

"This will be a concrete building," Tutor responded emphatically, slamming his hand on the conference table for emphasis. Tutor then ticked off what he considered the compelling advantages of concrete: "It will be cheaper than steel. I'll save you at least $5 million. You can add another floor of residential units in both towers. And it'll go up as fast or faster than steel."

At this early stage of the project, no one in the room had the information to judge whether Tutor's assertions were accurate when it came to cost and speed. Mancini had never been involved in a major high-rise. Dennis Oh had reservations, but he kept them to himself because he assumed that Tutor knew what he was talking about. Only Topping, not yet on the job, pushed the issue. "Gee, don't you think we should consider steel?" he asked.

Tutor gave him a withering look and responded: "Shit no. It will be cheaper in concrete. And it will be quicker, too."

Many developers would have postponed the choice and hired an outside engineering firm to compare the cost and speed of steel with concrete. It would have taken two or three weeks and cost $10,000 or so. But Rincon Center was on a tight budget and a fast track. The project needed to break ground before the end of the year to qualify for the full tax credit for the historic renovation. Missing that deadline would cost a couple of million dollars because the tax credit was being cut back from 25 percent to 20 percent. So they didn't want to wait for a study. They would go with concrete. Besides, nobody really wanted to make Ron Tutor angry.

On top of those reasons, the downtown plan had been approved in late 1984 by the City Planning Commission and seemed likely to pass when it came before the Board of Supervisors for a final vote later in the summer of 1985. The plan set a height limit of 200 feet on new buildings. Rincon's developers had negotiated an extra 40 feet out of the redevelopment agency, since the new plan was not yet law. The ability to squeeze another floor of rentable units into that 240 feet by using concrete instead of steel would mean more rental apartment units. Verrue liked that part of Tutor's argument and it was one of the reasons he approved concrete over steel. It was a choice he would come to regret.

10

THE RIGHT
MESSENGER

The Postal Service and redevelopment agency had granted the developers the right to plan the project. But now those plans would have to be approved for Rincon Center to get underway. The critical agencies were the San Francisco Redevelopment Agency and the City Planning Commission, but the city's Board of Supervisors would also play a key role. Even with a fast-track project such as Rincon, no construction work could begin until these hurdles were cleared.

The effort to win overall approval had begun in November of 1984 when the developers hired San Francisco real estate lawyer Timothy Tosta. He and Mancini had worked together to obtain a critical zoning change for Campeau's small office complex near Candlestick Park the year before and Tosta was a familiar and influential figure in city planning circles.

Tosta still liked to cast himself as an environmentalist, trading on two years he had spent as a lawyer with the California Coastal Commission a decade earlier after graduating from law school at the University of California at Berkeley. He was certainly offbeat as downtown lawyers go, with a beard and shaggy strawberry blond hair. In a corner of his office he kept a keyboard and electric guitar for blowing off steam. But he had come a long way from environmental law. Tosta's specialty was helping developers dodge the obstacles set up by community groups and appease the demands of political inter-

98

ests. He was as much salesman as lawyer, as much master strategist as legal expert. Tosta established new precedents in development law at the same time his lunch tab at Trader Vic's, his favorite downtown restaurant, was running $1,000 a month as he wined and dined planning commissioners, politicians, and others who decided the fate of his clients' multimillion-dollar projects.

"They hire a lawyer, but what they want is for me to get a permit," explained Tosta one day, sitting in his airy downtown office. "We are in the business of cooking up entitlements and making sure they are legally defensible. The law doesn't give you five or seven votes on a board. We don't treat a development as a legal problem. The last thing an official ever asks is, 'What is the law?' A decision has to be defensible politically, not legally. Of course, you want to make sure it is lawful. That is part of it being politically viable."

With Rincon Center, Tosta's first step was to analyze the potential roadblocks. Two primary ones emerged—the threat of Rincon Center's inclusion in the simmering downtown plan, and potential objections from the preservation community to plans for gutting a portion of the interior of the post office. He was less worried about Sue Hestor and the no-growth forces, figuring that the inclusion of affordable housing and the preservation of a landmark building, even if it was only the exterior and the main public lobby, would appease them. Once identified, a strategy had to be developed to overcome the obstacles.

The trick to avoiding the downtown plan was persuading city officials to exempt Rincon Center on some basis or other. Technically, the building was under the jurisdiction of the redevelopment authority since it was within one of the agency's "blighted" areas. But there was concern that the city planning department might try to drag Rincon into the downtown plan "net" out of interagency rivalry. If that happened, it could jeopardize the entire development by destroying its delicate timing.

By the spring of 1985, the downtown plan had been on the drawing boards for nearly two years. It had been passed by the planning commission and was before a committee of the Board of Supervisors, an eleven-member body that functions as a city council for San Francisco. Committee approval was expected by late May, with a vote by the full board soon after.

The central feature of the plan was an annual cap on permits for new office buildings. Three caps were under consideration by the committee, ranging from 950,000 square feet down to 500,000 square feet. Whichever level was approved, the law provided for the planning commission to evaluate all proposals for new buildings and allocate the space each year.

According to the plan, which had been devised by Dean Macris and others in his planning department, at various intervals each year the commercial projects proposed for San Francisco would be put up next to each other and a board of outside jurors would vote on which designs would be built that year. If the plan was approved, developers would face new expenses and great uncertainty. They would have to prepare elaborate presentations, complete with graphics and multiple models, to try to win what had quickly become known derisively as "the beauty contest."

With about half a million square feet of office space, Rincon would eat up a huge portion of a year's total and thus face tough odds in the competition. Tosta had to keep the development out of the beauty contest. He crafted two strategies for winning the critical exemption. One would be a straightforward grandfather clause, stressing that Rincon Center had been under design for months and that it was being crafted to meet the pending downtown plan's requirements. Here, too, Tosta would emphasize that the project offered the city badly needed new affordable housing and retail space south of Market and that it would restore the landmark post office and its murals.

Early on, Tosta persuaded Dean Macris, the planning director, to support the exclusion of Rincon Center. Macris agreed because the building was in a redevelopment zone. With Macris's okay, Tosta had drafted a clause to exempt the project and it had been inserted in the downtown plan approved by the commission. But it was one of many exemptions grafted onto the plan, and the no-growth proponents were gearing up to fight a number of them. The Board of Supervisors committee or the full board would undoubtedly be forced to sacrifice some of the exemptions to muster enough votes to pass the plan.

So the second strategy was to create a broad exemption that would cover Rincon Center without singling it out or even identifying it. Tosta wanted to hedge his bet with another option, but he didn't want to appear too calculating. If both failed, he could always argue that the project was within the jurisdiction of redevelopment and outside the downtown plan's grasp.

San Francisco, like other cities across the country, had seen a dramatic change in its labor force since the end of World War II. Traditional blue-collar manufacturing and distribution jobs were being replaced by office workers. But now, the city was starting to lose a segment of office workers, too—the clerical, technical, and data-entry positions that constitute what is known as the back office. These workers sit at desks in open areas, rather than in offices, and operate computers and process information, rather than interact with outsiders. As a result, back-office workers are most efficiently housed in buildings where there are large expanses of open space on each floor for flexible office planning.

The flood of recent office buildings had been aimed at professionals and executives, those who prized windows along the perimeter of the floors. As a result, the new buildings had small floor plans, averaging about 11,000 square feet. This phenomenon was combining with rising rents to drive back-office operations to the suburbs. Chevron, Pacific Bell Telephone, and Bank of America, three of San Francisco's biggest employers, had all moved back-office operations out of the city in recent months.

Rincon Center would be cast as an antidote to that illness. The forty-five-year-old post office had very large floor plans—around 80,000 square feet. Even carving out the atrium would leave floorplates of 50,000 square feet on the second, third, and new fourth and fifth floors. In addition, the six stories of new office space at the opposite end of the lot would have floorplates ranging from 30,000 to 60,000 square feet. Both buildings would be ideal for back-office operations and that was the point Tosta decided to push as the alternative exemption to the downtown plan. He wanted the decision makers to think about big buildings as a means for taking care of a critical economic need of the city, not just as big buildings.

But he would not suggest to the supervisors that Rincon alone was worthy of this exemption. Indeed, such an exemption would benefit three other clients. So Tosta hired David Dowall, a professor of planning at the University of California at Berkeley, to study the economic benefits of a general exemption to the growth cap for buildings with floor space large enough to accommodate back-office operations. There would be no need to identify the potential beneficiaries. Tosta had commissioned the study several months earlier, spreading its $100,000 price tag among four clients, and it was ready for release as the downtown plan approached a vote in the committee.

A successful defusing of the preservationists obviously hinged on the restoration of the post office, but there was a hitch. While the building's exterior was being saved, its interior was to be gutted—with an important exception, the lobby and its Refregier murals. At community meetings and sessions with historic preservation organizations, Tosta would have Mancini emphasize the salvation and the expensive, painstaking restoration of the murals. It was a hook that was easier to grasp than the whole building.

Devising the messages was the first phase. The second was identifying the officials to whom the messages should be delivered and hiring the proper messenger for each recipient. This can be as simple as personalizing a letter to a public official, but more often involves hiring the appropriate lobbyist or consultant. "What you are trying to do is not blunder," Tosta explained. "You must recognize who has the power and describe the project to each of them with images that evoke a positive response. Part of that is making sure the messengers who carry those images are the proper messengers for the subject."

For example, final approval of the project was pending before the redevelopment agency's seven-member board. Organized labor was a powerful force at the agency, with a majority of its commissioners often coming from the ranks of the city's union leaders. So Tosta recommended that Mancini hire a consultant with strong labor ties to lobby the commissioners. The man he suggested was David Jenkins, an aging and highly respected union leader. Jenkins even claimed to be a character in one of Refregier's twenty-seven murals. "He didn't even have to do that much," said Tosta. "He just had to let them know that he was there and, if they had any questions or saw anything that was awry or amiss, they could let him know."

Another selling point with the redevelopment board was the project's affordable housing, which the agency had required in the first place. Here the issue was persuading the staff and board that their mandate was being met willingly. To work out the specifics of the housing plan and convey that message, Tosta suggested hiring Janet

Roche, who had worked with him and Mancini on the Campeau project.

Roche had spent four years at the redevelopment agency in the 1960s and gone on to a series of jobs as a public housing administrator and consultant, including a brief stint in the administration of President Jimmy Carter. Over the years, she had remained close friends with Wilbur Hamilton, the executive director of the agency. And her uncle was Leroy King, the chairman of the redevelopment commission. As with Jenkins, her role was partly to be a seal of approval for the project.

On May 22, 1985, the city's Planning, Housing and Development Committee held its public hearing on the downtown plan. One of the witnesses was Professor David Dowall, who advocated an exemption for buildings with enough space for back-office operations. To back up his testimony, Dowall provided the supervisors, and the press, with copies of a lengthy study he had done showing that the city had lost 26,000 back-office jobs in recent years. Those in the know were aware that Dowall's study had been funded by Tosta's law firm, but few knew which buildings would benefit from the exemption.

A few days later, Tosta provided the supervisors with language that could be inserted into the downtown plan to embody the back-office exemption for buildings with floorplates in excess of 20,000 square feet. Each letter was tailored for the individual supervisor. For instance, the appeal to Supervisor Carol Ruth Silver stressed that the exemption would protect jobs for women and minorities. Letters to Willie Kennedy and Doris Ward, black supervisors, emphasized the impact on entry-level workers, "many of whom are minorities or single parents."

For Scott Johnson and Jay Mancini and their staffs, much of their time over the next few months would also be devoted to dealing with government—largely, to presenting design details to the redevelopment agency staff. Many of those sessions would also be attended by staff members from the city planning department. Whether the planning department had any authority over the project was open to question. But involving the department in the ongoing design process was seen as a way to avoid provoking a showdown on the issue.

An important joint meeting with both staffs was scheduled for July 18 at the redevelopment agency's office on Ellis Street in San

Francisco. The agenda covered eight items that needed to be resolved in preparation for a presentation to the full boards of both agencies in August. Among them were the color of the glass for the curtain walls on the new towers, whether the tower tops would be different, and the articulation or shape of the towers themselves.

Ten people jammed into a small conference room at ten o'clock that morning. Johnson, Mancini, and Harry Topping were there to represent the project. Among those facing them were Walter Yanagita and other staff members from redevelopment, and Lu Blazej and George Williams from city planning. In a three-hour session, a major issue was resolved by the approval of the general shape and bulk of the towers, which had been designed to taper as they rose, in keeping with the downtown plan. There was a standoff, however, on whether the the tops could be different and on the color of the glass. It was decided that the tops would be decided by the planning commission and the glass would be deferred to the redevelopment agency's board.

On August 20, Johnson and Edmund Einy, his young associate, arrived at San Francisco's ornate City Hall with several museum-board models of the project and a stack of drawings. Jay Mancini was there, too. The planning commission members sat at a large mahogany table on a raised dais in the formal hearing room and the Rincon team sat in the audience as the commission went through the agenda until the project's name was called. Johnson had fifteen minutes to describe the project and he spent several of them on why the tower tops should be different.

"These will be people's homes," he told the commissioners. "Doesn't it make sense to give these homes more identity, more uniqueness? We can't make every unit different, but we can make the two towers different. A tenant can identify his or her own home on the skyline." He got no questions and no response on the subject.

A brief staff report on Rincon Center followed, recommending approval of the project but requiring that the towers have identical tops. Toby Rosenblatt, the wealthy private investor who served as commission president, observed, "The towers look the same to me, so they ought to have the same tops. Done." The commissioners voted unanimously to adopt the staff recommendations. Rincon Center had cleared an important hurdle, although without two different tops.

Johnson and the others then trooped a few blocks to the redevelopment agency offices, where the architect made a similar presentation to the board. The reception was warm and the allocation of affordable housing was singled out for praise. This time, however, glass was the sticking point, though the results, while not particularly pleasing, were less painful. The board decided to approve the project unanimously, with the caveat that the color of the curtain wall and some other issues would be resolved later.

As they left the redevelopment session, Mancini was very pleased. The loss back at planning didn't bother him. He had never understood Johnson's insistence on different tops. He was confident the dispute over the glass would be resolved soon, and he was having his own second thoughts about green anyway. Randy Verrue had told him he wasn't sure he liked the color. He thought it might be too trendy and leave them with a building that would be dated within a few years.

Johnson, angry about the planning commission session, was not in much of a mood to celebrate. It wasn't simply the loss of the two tops. It was that an architectural decision had been made by a political body that appeared to care little about architecture and was not willing to take the time to grapple with its importance. The presumed guardians were, in his view, abdicating their role of dealing with architecture on behalf of the public.

Scott Johnson is extremely charming and articulate. He is the sort of person who flourishes in the limelight, the type of architect who can sell a design to a developer or a planning board by virtue of his intellect and personality as well as his ample architectural skills. And he genuinely values the give-and-take of animated discussions, often observing that architecture benefits from public involvement. It is, after all, the most public of arts. But in the end, Johnson likes to evaluate the points raised in the discussions and make the decision himself. The fate of the two tops robbed him of that chance while at the same time giving no weight to what Johnson considered the architectural arguments.

Some months later, Johnson was having dinner with Hans Hollein, a prominent architect from Vienna, when the discussion turned to architectural criticism by laypeople. "Sometimes I have trouble with a client because I think that when I am presenting a concept, the client doesn't know enough about design and is uncomfortable making a meaningful response," said Hollein. "I say, 'How do you feel about this thing I have done?' They always answer, because of course they feel they must. For me, it would be as if a composer came to me and said, 'Here, look at these twelve scores for all these instruments, do you like this?' I do not read music. If I looked at it, I might say something like, 'Gee, well, I think it's pretty interesting, but it needs more notes over here and maybe there are a few too many at the bottom end over here.' It is the same thing."

But like it or not, the power to make these final decisions rested with the various public bodies overseeing compliance with the city's regulation. And in the summer of 1985, those regulations were about to get much tougher. The downtown plan was approved by the planning committee of the Board of Supervisors and it was wending its way to the full board. The back-office exemption had survived the committee and the *San Francisco Chronicle* had even picked up on the issue in an editorial urging the board to adopt the downtown plan. The law also contained specific language exempting Rincon Center from the new regulations. But there were weeks of back-room negotiations ahead as business interests and no-growth partisans fought over the details of the plan and traded provisions in search of a consensus. Neither measure was assured of survival.

On September 10, 1985, the Board of Supervisors approved San Francisco's new downtown plan. The final language allowed 950,000 square feet of new office space in each of the next three years and required developers to pay for such amenities as open space and child-care facilities. More than 200 historic structures were protected outright and incentives were provided for developers to restore other old buildings. A height limit of 200 feet was imposed for most of the city, and block-shaped buildings, such as the Bank of America headquarters, were out. Tapered buildings, like the Chrysler Building in New York, were in as the city decided it would legislate a more varied skyline. One of the victims in the behind-the-scenes dealing had been the back-office exemption. But Tim Tosta's alternate plan, the grandfathering of Rincon Center, had passed. The project was exempt from the downtown plan.

The week before the board approved the downtown plan, the *San*

Francisco Chronicle's influential architecture critic, Allan Temko, had described Rincon Center as a "dress rehearsal" for the downtown plan in a long piece about the development. The article, however, was far from a rave. Temko, who would later win a Pulitzer Prize for criticism, accused Scott Johnson of "purloining" the sculptured towers from Philip Johnson and Cesar Pelli. Worse, he said the towers would have been more at home on Los Angeles's Wilshire Boulevard than along the Embarcadero.

One aspect of the design that Temko did not have to criticize was the original decision by the developers to leave the existing concrete beams in place in the atrium to save money. In doing his reporting for the article, Temko had discussed the project separately with Johnson and Mancini. He also had been shown the models and drawings. During his session with Mancini, Temko had criticized the beams over the atrium in the drawings and study models.

"Jay, that's a mistake," said Temko. "You'd make the space more vertical by taking them out."

"I think you're right," said Mancini. "We were thinking about removing them. I think we'll just do that."

What Mancini did not say, of course, was that Scott Johnson had wanted to remove the beams in the first place but been thwarted by budget restrictions. Mancini would later deny that, in getting rid of the beams, he was trying to curry favor with Temko, who was very influential in San Francisco and elsewhere even before winning a Pulitzer Prize. He simply said it was a case of having the mistake pointed out to him in time to do something about it.

At the design meeting two weeks after the visit, Mancini announced that he was reversing his earlier decision. The beams should come out to provide more vertical drama. Removing them would weaken the structure, so new walls and beams would have to be built to compensate. Ron Tutor, who had been searching for ways to cut the budget, warned that it would be an expensive addition to the work. Mancini insisted. The atrium would look much better without the jungle gym.

Scott Johnson agreed wholeheartedly with the decision to remove the beams in the atrium, though he was disappointed that it had taken Allan Temko to bring it about. The absence of the beams, however, created a new design dilemma for Johnson. Mancini liked the idea of the space being open and unimpeded to the skylight. But Johnson wanted a ceiling of some sort to contain the eye. "To have no ceiling at all would mean that you would basically be looking up at the sky," he said. "There would be no top to the space. We need a lid to this space, a cap for the energy." So Johnson designed a series of coffered beams across the top of the atrium opening and carried them down the colannade.

11

A DOLLAR BORROWED
IS A DOLLAR EARNED

When a developer gathers his team for the all-important task of deciding what the project at hand will cost, there is never room in the calculations for chaos and innate stupidity. These factors are ignored, not so much because they cannot be priced by the cubic yard or linear foot. Instead, they get buried beneath the thick blanket of optimism that muffles the sounds of reality at the start of any project where substantial amounts of money are to be made.

To say that developers rush out and blindly build is not quite accurate. Their eyes are open. But they often happen to be focused too much on one thing: money. For much of the 1980s, it was difficult not to make money in real estate development. Lenders, unshackled from many federal banking regulations and facing new competition from investment houses, pension funds, and overseas banks, were competing to throw money into commercial real estate. The developers were happy to take the money and build more buildings. "The nature of a developer is to be optimistic and aggressive as long as the banks and insurance companies and pension funds will lend him money," says Jack Sonnenblick, a New York mortgage broker. And they all believe, of course, that their project will be a huge success.

The really nice part about the development game, from a developer's point of view at any rate, is that the gambles can be taken with other people's money. This is perhaps best understood by real estate developers in Texas, who have a saying that applies equally to their counterparts everywhere: a dollar borrowed is a dollar earned. This succinctly reflects the developer's desire to borrow as much money as possible to finance a project, and it reflects the peculiar phenomenon of the 1980s in which builders built to borrow, instead of building to meet market needs.

To be sure, Randy Verrue and the other executives of Perini Land & Development had asked questions about the prospects for Rincon Center before they got into the deal. As corporate developers who answer to a board of directors and ultimately their stockholders, they were more cautious than most of their colleagues, and had a solid record of performance to show for it across the country. But there is a tendency to tilt the answers toward the side of optimism, to ignore certain questions, to be swayed by self-confidence. In this case, Verrue and his colleagues simply discounted many good reasons not to do the project and plunged in. Smart developers do not build blindly, but even the smartest developers often build with blinders.

Given this developer mindset, it's no surprise that Jay Mancini's oft-stated construction estimate of $58 million for Rincon Center, while not moored to much more than wishful thinking, was the benchmark in the early discussions of how much the development was likely to cost. Only later would reality intrude, although it wouldn't be too much later.

The first detailed breakdown of the construction budget for Rincon Center was presented on August 14, 1985, in a meeting at Perini Land & Development's offices in San Francisco. Mancini had been called out of town on personal business, leaving Harry Topping in charge of the meeting. But the show belonged to Ron Tutor, whose office had prepared the budget.

Even Tutor's first detailed budget estimate missed Mancini's target by 10 percent. His calculations for renovating the old post office and building the new phase came to $64,044,377. Tutor emphasized that his figures were only a first pass. They were based on construction documents that were only 20 percent completed. There were plenty of areas, he assured those at the meeting, where costs could be slashed. For instance, his preliminary budget had saved nearly a quarter-million dollars by proposing to substitute plastic for glass in the huge skylight over the atrium.

"Once we get the complete construction documents, I'm sure that we will be within the owner's budget," Tutor said.

Dianna Wong, sitting next to Scott Johnson at the conference table, was highly skeptical as Tutor trotted out his numbers, but she said nothing. She felt that Mancini and Tutor were both under-estimating the complexity of the project and, hence, the cost. Wong and some other young architects at Pereira Associates working on the early design documents had done their own rough figuring. In the drafting room in Los Angeles, the cost of Rincon Center had been pegged at $80 million. Johnson himself figured the cost at $70 million minimum and had already told Mancini so on several occasions.

That day, Tutor provided everyone with a copy of the construction budget for the project. It itemized the major known costs associated with both phases of the project, from $700 for fire extinguishers in the post office to $8,415,611 for concrete for the new building. There was no way to locate the discrepancies by comparing these figures to Mancini's estimate because Mancini's had never been detailed. But the list offered a rundown of the major areas of expense.

Among them was the $2.2 million fee that Tutor-Saliba would collect for overseeing the project as general contractor—3.5 percent of the construction budget. This percentage, which was standard for the industry, would be added to every element of the construc-tion cost.

By this point in the development process, the size of the compo-nents of the project had been determined. The old post office would contain 267,000 square feet of retail and office space, once the two new floors were added. The new building, known as phase two, would have 216,000 square feet of office space in its six-story base, and the two towers would house 320 apartments in 209,000 square feet of space. In addition, there would be room for 500 parking spaces in 162,000 square feet of underground area, most of it on two levels beneath the new towers and the open plaza between the towers and post office. The total rentable space would be about 854,000 square feet. The open plaza, a city-mandated amenity, would bring the total project up to nearly 1 million square feet.

Tutor's breakdown for rehabbing the post office totaled $19,371,289. There were forty-six categories. The largest was $2.7 million for concrete, which would be used primarily for building new walls and strengthening existing walls and columns. The next biggest cost was $2.5 million to demolish the interior and remove the rear facade of the existing building, if that part of the plan got the okay. There was $2 million allocated for the structural steel that would be needed to add the fourth and fifth floors, $1.7 million for the new electrical system, and $1.6 million for new heating and air conditioning. Windows and doors for the retail and office space were estimated at $1.1 million, and plaster and drywall were estimated at $737,500. There were sections for toilet partitions ($15,500), window-washing equipment ($35,000), plumbing ($544,400), painting ($200,000), and elevators ($600,000). The budget set aside $1 million for a category called "general conditions," which included costs that could not be assigned to a specific aspect of the job. They were such overhead items as insurance coverage, rent for cranes that would be used on many parts of the work, and wages for supervisors who oversaw more than one area.

For the new building and its twin towers, Tutor estimated the total cost at $44,673,088 and broke it into fifty-four categories. In addition to $8.4 million for concrete for the major structural elements, there was $4.3 million for the steel rebar to be added to the concrete to improve its ductility. The cost of the glass for the curtain wall, storefronts, and windows was estimated at $3.4 million, and the pre-cast concrete cladding for the exterior of the buildings was expected to cost $3 million. General conditions was pegged at $3.3 million; one reason it was so much higher than on the post office was that cranes would be used more extensively. Heating and air conditioning for the new building was estimated at $2.6 million, and electrical was put at $3 million. Plumbing would cost $2.1 million, and the elevators would run $1.6 million.

Kitchen and laundry equipment for the 320 apartments was expected to cost $350,772; trash compactors and chutes would add $43,000; and there would be $238,200 worth of toilets and sinks. Most of the $373,360 worth of ceramic tile would be in the apartment bathrooms and kitchens. The apartments also would get most of the $635,690 budgeted for wooden doors and millwork and the $210,000 for hardware, such as door knobs and faucets.

The budget also contained three alternatives that would add varying amounts to the final tally. There had been an ongoing discussion between the architects and the developers over the need for balconies on the apartments in the new towers. Johnson and his team favored small balconies as amenities for the units, arguing that San Francisco residents expected access to the outdoors. Mancini couldn't make up his mind. He saw the appeal of balconies and his boss, Randy Verrue, thought they were needed. But he also knew they would add to the costs. So he had instructed Tutor to come up with alternative costs. Adding balconies to 100 apartments would cost $107,000 more; 200 balconies would add $147,000; and 270 balconies, covering every unit that did not already have access to one of the terraces, would cost $231,000. That was a decision that could wait.

There was another category of cost associated with the new building not present in the renovation. Tutor estimated it would cost slightly more than $2.7 million to get the new structure out of the ground—$807,605 to excavate and grade the hole, $660,000 to erect the shoring to keep the hole from falling in while it was being prepared for a foundation and the garage walls, and $1.3 million to buy and drive the hundreds of pilings to support the new building. There was no way Ron Tutor could have known that August day, but this was one of those areas where chaos and stupidity were destined to collide in a way that would make a mockery of his figures.

Later, it would be said by many associated with the project that Ron Tutor did not allow for the necessary quality and complexity of Rincon when he prepared his budget. It would be said that he was accustomed to simpler projects that demanded less expensive materials and fewer architectural flourishes. Scott Johnson, for one, would say that Tutor and Mancini established an unrealistically low construction budget and then tried to squeeze the quality out of the project so its cost fit their figures. He felt that neither man had serious experience in mixed-use projects or with developments with so much public space, where the detail and quality had to be extremely high.

But Tutor had little incentive to underestimate the budget. For one thing, the August 1985 figures were the initial step in establishing a guaranteed maximum price for the project, or GMP. Later, the GMP would be fixed at a specific amount and Tutor, as the general contractor, would sign a contract agreeing to complete the project within the budget. If the costs went over, Tutor would have to prove that his work was not to blame, that there were unavoidable reasons for the overruns. Otherwise the additional money would come out of Tutor-Saliba's pocket.

The construction budget also was necessary to obtain financing for the project. The partnership, which included Tutor, planned to borrow a major portion of the money from a bank, probably New

York's Citibank. The remainder would be raised by selling pieces of the deal to outside investors through a real estate syndication, a procedure similar to selling shares of stock in a company. If the construction ran over budget, the bank would surely balk at increasing the loan and the investors could not be tapped again. So the extra would probably come out of the deep pockets of Perini Corporation. Whichever party footed the bill, the extra costs would delay the time when Tutor and the other owners could begin collecting their payouts since higher costs would extend the point at which the project paid off its debt and began producing a profit. So the financing package depended on a precise construction budget, even though construction expenses would be only one component of the development's total cost.

Since Randy Verrue had taken over as Perini Land & Development's West Coast chief in 1979, most of his major deals had been financed by Citibank. He had developed a solid business relationship and personal friendship with the executive in charge of the account there, Bob Mayer.

A former architect with an MBA from Stanford, Mayer had joined Citibank as a lending officer in the banking company's real estate division in San Francisco the same year Verrue had gone to work for Perini. In a short time, Perini became one of his best customers. Mayer, now a vice-president, and Verrue had discussed the Rincon project earlier in 1985, and it was Mayer who had recommended Harry Topping for his job with Perini. So when Verrue got the first hard figures for the construction cost in August, it was natural for him to take them to Mayer to try to work out a loan agreement.

Financing construction deals is complex and, from a banker's point of view, it can be creative and challenging. It can also be lucrative. Developers are accustomed to paying high interest rates for their money because of the risk involved in real estate ventures. Despite the size and complexity, however, the basics of lending are the same on a $100 million construction loan as on a $100,000 home mortgage.

What counts are the three Cs—character, collateral, and credit. For smart bankers, the most important factor is the character of the

Tutor-Saliba
CORPORATION

CONTRACTORS ENGINEERS

RINCON BUDGET

August 14, 1985

	REHAB ANNEX	NEW BUILDING
General Conditions	1,080,000	3,314,280
Site Grading, Earthwork, Site Demo, Mass Excavation	— 0 —	807,605
Shoring and Lagging	— 0 —	660,000
Existing Bldg. Demolition	2,466,600	— 0 —
Driven Piles	— 0 —	1,250,000
Landscape & Irrigation Allowance	50,000	50,000
Fountain Allowance	— 0 —	50,000
Chain-Link Fence Allowance	2,000	3,000
Site Concrete Paving	— 0 —	148,447
Parking Striping and Bumpers	1,000	2,000
Concrete and Gunite Work	2,665,966	8,415,611
Reinforcing Steel and Post-Tensioning	655,200	4,380,040
Arch. Pre-cast—GFRC	558,000	3,008,100
Concrete Block & Masonry Veneer	44,800	177,000
Struct. Steel & Misc. Metal	2,000,000	856,800
Metal Deck & Insul. Concrete	151,000	— 0 —
Expansion Joint Covers	— 0 —	248,000
Metal Roof	— 0 —	22,400
Rough Carpentry	29,400	46,000
Millwork & Wood Doors	100,000	635,690
Bituminous Waterproofing	— 0 —	304,700
Building Insulation	88,000	42,000
Built-Up Roofing, Fluid Applied Roofing, Elast. Expan. Joints	190,000	190,000
Sheet Metal and Louvers	35,000	35,000
Metal Framed Skylights	480,000	217,500
Joint Sealers	17,000	33,000
H.M. Doors and Frames	48,000	144,000

Overhead Coiling Doors	35,500	35,500
Aluminum Windows, Entrances, Storefronts, Revolving Doors, Glass and Glazing	1,125,000	3,375,000
Finish Hardware	70,000	210,000
Sheet Vinyl	— 0 —	29,208
Lath, Plaster, Drywall, Spray-On Fireproofing, Metal Framing	737,500	2,212,500
Ceramic Tile	70,000	373,360
Acoustic Ceiling	30,000	37,266
Terrazzo Floor and Base	120,800	— 0 —
Granite Work	338,780	338,780
Marble Countertops	8,000	8,320
Painting	200,000	300,000
Toilet Partitions	15,500	15,500
Toilet Accessories (Office)	52,200	— 0 —
Toilet Accessories (Residential)	— 0 —	238,200
Building Directories	8,000	8,000
Fire Extinguishers	700	700
Recessed Entry Mats	8,000	8,000
Accelerographs	7,000	13,000
Window Washing Equipment	35,000	35,000
Parking Equipment	10,000	15,000
Loading Dock Equipment	8,000	12,000
Gate Operators	5,000	5,000
Trash Chutes and Compactors	— 0 —	43,000
Kitchen and Laundry Equipment	— 0 —	350,772
Elevators	600,000	1,630,000
Plumbing	544,400	2,108,000
HVAC	1,599,000	2,600,000
Sprinkler System	425,875	779,125
Electrical	1,750,000	3,090,000
Energy Management & Security	250,000	250,000
Fee 3.5% of Cost	665,068	1,510,684
TOTAL EACH BUILDING	$19,371,289	$44,673,088
TOTAL BOTH BUILDINGS		$64,044,377

Alternate #1		
As Described on Page #5 of Structural Report by Chin and Hensolt and dated July 8, 1985	ADD	$276,000.00
Alternate #2B		
Added 100 Balconies	ADD	$107,000.00
Alternate #2C		
Added 200 Balconies	ADD	$147,000.00
Alternate #2D		
Added 270 Balconies	ADD	$231,000.00

borrower. The second most important is the collateral, or the quality of the project, whether it is a single-family home or a major mixed-use project. The third factor, credit, relates to the financial health and background of the borrower.

In Bob Mayer's view, Randy Verrue and Perini L&D were strong on character and credit. He admired Verrue as an honest, straight-talking developer in a world filled with too many hucksters. He also had worked with Tom Steele, the company president back in Massachusetts, and Citibank had helped finance transactions around the country for the parent company, Perini Corporation. As for credit, the parent company was the nation's fourth-largest construction company. It had a strong balance sheet, with revenues topping $800 million a year, a net worth of $82 million, and substantial assets spread across the country. More than enough to absorb any unexpected costs.

The rub came in the collateral. Mayer had the same doubts about the project that once had steered Verrue away from it. He thought the location was questionable, the uncertainty of a major renovation was troubling, and the San Francisco rental market was weakening. Office rents in San Francisco had risen to record rates in the early 1980s, as much as $35 a square foot. The result was predictable: there had been a rush to put up new buildings and, as those new buildings came on the market in 1985, the oversupply was beginning to depress rents.

Mayer also was nagged by the critical role that the investment tax credits were to play in arranging the syndicated financing. For instance, if construction did not get started by the end of 1985 so it could take full advantage of the credits, the syndication would be jeopardized. Too, Mayer did not like the use of concrete as the main construction material. He had spent long enough as an architect to suspect that concrete was not right for the project. He felt that it would be too slow and possibly too costly. But Verrue had assured him that Tutor had promised to bring the building in on time and under budget. And Perini's track record was indeed reassuring to Mayer. The company had never gone seriously over budget on any project Citibank had financed. Mayer figured they knew what they were doing when it came to choosing the building material and estimating the construction costs. That was their bread and butter.

Mayer spent several days in August going over the numbers and discussing his concerns with his bosses, including Citibank's senior West Coast lending executive, John Pipia. The potential troubles were real enough, they decided. But Perini Corporation had the kind of deep pockets and dependable record that balanced well against those worries. And there was another factor at play here, working in favor of funding the project. It was Citibank's burning ambition to grab a bigger share of construction lending in California.

The nation's most affluent state—with an economy that would rank it sixth among the nations of the world in terms of gross product—had long been dominated by a single financial institution, the Bank of America. Founded in 1904 by A. P. Giannini, the son of Italian immigrants, Bank of America had grown into a globe-straddling giant. For more than thirty years, it was the world's largest bank and California's strongest. But by the mid-1980s, the situation had changed dramatically. Beset by mismanagement and bloated overhead costs, Bank of America was battling to survive by firing thousands of workers and restricting such activities as major commercial lending. Its iron grip on California had loosened.

Plenty of shrewd banks in the state were angling to profit from Bank of America's troubles. The best of them, Wells Fargo, was a specialist in construction lending. New York–based Citibank, which had replaced Bank of America as the nation's largest financial institution in 1982, was restricted by banking regulations from opening branches in California to serve consumers. But there were no such restrictions when it came to lending to developers, so the new giant was eager to cut a bigger piece of that pie for itself.

Near the end of that August, Bob Mayer sat in Randy Verrue's office in the Alcoa Building. He had come to deliver the verdict on whether Citibank would go for the deal. "There are plenty of unknowns in this deal, Randy," Mayer explained. "But we know you and we know Perini and we know that you'll both perform. You've got a great track record. We'll find a way to make this deal work. But it's going to take a sizable hunk of equity."

To Verrue, this was not an unexpected kicker. Equity is similar to the down payment a buyer makes on a house. It constitutes the cash and value that the investor puts into the project. In commercial banking circles, it's sometimes known as "pay attention money." The riskier the project, the more equity a lender demands in order to feel comfortable with the loan. With a project such as Rincon Center, Citibank wanted to make sure that Perini and its partners were paying plenty of attention.

In determining how much Citibank would be willing to lend on the project, Mayer had evaluated the two major financial risks: would the project be completed within or near the budget and would the space be leased within the expected time at the anticipated rents? Mayer expected that there would be some cost overruns on the project. There almost always were. Because of Perini's experience as a construction company, however, he expected no major glitches. The question of the rents was more problematic. Rents were headed down, but no one knew quite where the bottom was. Perini's loan request, called a pro forma, had been conservative: it forecast a net rental rate of $19 per square foot, after management expenses and other costs were deducted. Mayer multiplied this figure by the available commercial square footage of the development, factored in the revenue from the retail space and apartments, considered the time it would take to get the space fully leased, and came up with a loan package that he thought the project could support. Citibank would make two primary loans on the project for a total of $115 million.

The largest of the loans was $79 million for construction and interest. Unlike homeowners, who borrow only the amount they need to buy a house, developers routinely borrow enough additional to pay the interest on their construction loan. This enables them to finance the project until money flows in from a sale or from rental revenues. It is also necessary because developers cannot write off interest on a construction loan as a tax deduction, but instead must count it as a capital expense.

In this case, the construction loan was to be paid off in three and a half years, although there was an option to extend the payoff date for another five years after that. Citibank would earn $792,500 as a commitment fee on the loan. The interest rate would float with the cost of funds to Citibank under the rate that international banks charged each other, called the London Interbank Offered Rate, or LIBOR. The interest rate was projected to average 11.2 percent and interest payments were expected to total $16.1 million over three and a half years.

Under the terms of the construction loan, the developers would be required to contribute a total of $37.5 million in equity. But, according to the developers' plans, only one-third of it would be their money. That third, $12.5 million, would come in the form of a letter of credit issued by Perini Land & Development to Citibank. It was to be Perini's promise to contribute that amount of cash to the project, and it represented the company's entire planned exposure on the deal. Perini planned to raise the other required $25 million by selling interests in the project to outside investors through a capital-raising process known as a real estate syndication. The terms required that this $25 million be placed in an account at Citibank until the construction loan was paid off.

Once the construction was completed, the developers were required to pay off the construction loan by securing permanent financing, known as a "take-out" loan because it takes out the original lender. Mayer likes to call take-out loans "no brainers." A lender can look at the finished project, examine the rents that are coming in or are projected, and determine the long-term risk. Take-outs used to be for thirty years, but in recent years the duration has shortened and the standard length runs eight to fifteen years. Insurance companies often provide money for take-out loans because there is little risk involved and the rate of return can be seen clearly by the rent flows.

Construction loans are trickier, and hence riskier, because they involve an unfinished project and a lot of educated guesswork. The lender, usually a bank, is betting that the developer will finish the project on schedule and within budget, and then be able to lease the space at the expected rents and therefore pay off the loan. If the developer goes under before the project is completed, the bank can find itself facing a loss on the loan or inheriting a half-finished development, which it must then try to resell to recoup its investment. If the project suffers huge cost overruns, someone will have to come up with enough money to complete it. If the market will not support the rents projected when the project was conceived two or three years earlier, the cash flow won't be there to make the payments. (While the savings and loan scandal was a couple years away from reaching its full pitch, thrifts in Texas and a few other places had already begun to feel the squeeze of writing off massive commercial loans that had gone bad and trying to find a way to recoup the losses by selling half-empty office buildings in weakening markets. It was a real estate massacre that shows how badly lenders can be hurt on construction loans.)

To cut down on the risks associated with construction loans, lenders routinely set up procedures to fund the loan through installments pegged to construction progress. At least that way the bank should not wind up paying 100 percent of the money for a project that is only 50 percent finished. As with most construction loans, Citibank and the Rincon partners agreed to hold monthly meetings to review progress and pay the next installment on the loan. These are called "draw meetings" because they allow the developer to draw on his loan balance once he has demonstrated a level of progress on the work.

As another protection for the bank, the contract stipulated that the developers could spend no more than $25 million of the loan before they raised an equal amount in equity. Perini guaranteed this cash infusion into the project, and they planned to raise the money through the syndication to outside investors. The syndication still left Bob Mayer a little uneasy because it depended so heavily on the tax credits. But billions of dollars were being raised each year through these types of offerings, so his concerns never rose to the level of a deal breaker.

The second major component of the loan agreement called for Citibank to issue a $36 million letter of credit on behalf of the developers. The letter of credit was to guarantee the repayment of $36 million worth of tax-exempt bonds. The San Francisco Redevelopment Agency had agreed to issue the bonds on behalf of the developers to raise money for the two new towers because of the affordable housing units in the project. At the time, San Francisco had a residential vacancy rate of about 1 percent, which was very low. The construction of new apartments for the working and middle classes had come almost to a stop, largely because all the new units were upscale condominiums. The cheap financing available through the tax-exempt bonds was one of the only ways that apartment construction could be profitable for a private developer. The money raised through the bonds could be used only to pay for building the residential portion of the project under the agreement with the re-development agency.

Citicorp, the parent of Citibank, had pioneered these types of transactions, and they were taking place in major cities across the country in 1985. To some, the process amounted to little more than a taxpayer subsidy for private developers. City governments or agen-cies with bonding authority would back bonds that would be sold to investors by developers to raise funds for a specific project. The developers would pay the regular interest to the investors until the bonds matured and were paid off. However, the interest rates were far lower than if the developers had borrowed the money from a bank because the interest payments were tax-exempt for the investor.

The idea behind these deals was to allow a city government to assist developers on projects that would benefit the public but might not qualify for financing without the extra push of tax-exempt bonds. These projects were supposed to help rebuild disintegrating neighborhoods or create jobs in poor areas. This occurred in many cases, including Rincon Center to some extent. But there was another side to these deals. Developers with the right connections at City Hall could obtain cheap financing for their projects, often regardless of need or value to the public. Further, the subsidized financing helped launch some developments that would not have made eco-nomic sense under normal conditions. So there were instances in which the tax-exempts favored certain developers.

To gain a credit rating that would make the bonds attractive to investors and assure the redevelopment agency of not getting stuck with the payments if Rincon went bankrupt, Citibank would issue the letter of credit agreeing to pay off the investments at their matu-rity in twelve years if the developer was unable to do so. This was basically an insurance policy, and to obtain it the developers would pay Citibank a hefty "premium" in the form of a one-time commitment fee and annual fees. The deal called for the bank to receive a commitment fee of $742,488, and yearly fees of 1.87 percent over the twelve years that would total about $8 million. It would be a nice profit for Citibank so long as the bank never had to make good on the letter and pay off the bonds.

Working out the details of the construction loan and the letter of credit would require about three months. Along with the financial aspects, there had to be changes in the lease with the Postal Service that would allow the developers to obtain separate take-out loans for the first and second phases of the project. But Mayer felt confident that the transaction could be done before the end of the year to preserve the tax credits critical to the second phase of the financing, syndicating the deal to investors.

As devised, the construction loan and the tax-exempt bonds would raise a total of $115 million for Rincon Center, far more than the $64 million in construction costs forecast by Ron Tutor earlier in August. In addition, the executives at Perini Land & Development expected to raise another $38.6 million through the syndication. That would bring the total money available for the project to almost $154 million.

So what happens to all the extra money? Following the trail of those dollars provides a revealing look at the complexity of financing and constructing a major real estate development—and at the staggering potential profits associated with such a project. Most of the following figures come from a prospectus drawn up a few months after Citibank's preliminary agreement to finance the project. While the figures ultimately changed for the Rincon project, they offer a road map to the pot of gold developers envision when they embark on a project of this scale.

According to the prospectus, the construction cost was to be $60.9 million of the nearly $154 million. The estimate was $13.5 million for tenant improvements, a category that is separate from the basic construction costs and usually represents an "allowance" to outfit the interior needs of a tenant. The category covers such things as interior walls and doors in commercial space, carpet or other flooring in commercial and retail space, and the counters and special mechanical features for restaurants and similar areas. Payments to the architects, engineers, and consultants were budgeted at $4.2 million. Commissions to agents who would lease the commercial and residential space in the development were estimated at $2.6 million, and legal and recording fees connected with the project were expected to total $1.3 million. The various fees and interest payments to Citibank and the tax-exempt bondholders exceeded $27 million.

The prospectus specified that $39.1 million would be paid to the developers, the general partners, and their affiliates. Not all of this is profit. At least, not right away. Rather, the figures illustrate the scope of the overhead for the project and the ways in which the developers compensate themselves for their outlays. Perini would be required to deposit $25 million of this money in an account at Citibank. The principal would serve as the remainder of the company's equity on the project and the interest from the account would be used to offset the interest on the construction loan. A fee of $3.2 million was to be paid to the firm hired to arrange the syndication's sale to individual investors. Another $2.4 million would pay the commitment fee once permanent financing was arranged through a take-out loan.

Other chunks were smaller, but they benefited the owners more directly and demonstrate the ingenious variety of ways that developers take money out of projects on the front end.

The partners were to divide $272,523 to reimburse them for their original out-of-pocket costs. About $650,000 was to be paid to the developer as a fee for supervising the rental of the commercial and residential space. A $1.55 million chunk was designated for Perini Land & Development as a management fee for administering the project. Perini Corporation was to receive $853,706 as the anticipated profit on its share of the construction costs in the joint venture with Tutor-Saliba. About $3 million was to be paid in commissions to the brokers who were actually to sell the syndication shares to individual investors. Additional amounts would pay for office overhead, insurance, and some salaries that were not covered by the management fee.

The prospectus allocated a development fee of $22.6 million for Perini Land & Development as the general partner and developer of the project. But the company would have to wait to receive this money until construction was completed and a take-out loan was arranged. At that time, the plan called for borrowing enough money to pay off the entire $79 million construction loan from Citibank, thus freeing up the $12.5 million letter of credit and the $25 million cash on deposit. The $25 million would then go to the developers as their fee and the first payout to the investors.

It was a deal loaded with profit potential, so long as events unfolded pretty close to the lines that had been mapped out by the developers, the banker, and the general contractor. But, as Bob Mayer had worried during the loan negotiations, this was not a done deal. The financial structure depended on the successful syndication of the project to a few hundred wealthy outside investors. That, in turn, depended on convincing the guardians of the post office's history to permit the developers to tear off the rear facade, a strictly utilitarian part of the structure that had been used solely for truck loading and delivery. It also hinged on events that were unforeseen and would prove to be totally out of the control of the developers.

12

MAKING THE DEAL

Perini Land & Development started seeking outside capital for Rincon Center in the spring of 1985. They had once considered selling a chunk of the project to one of the likely institutional investors—a major pension fund or a life insurance company. But they soon found that institutional investors were not particularly interested in buying into a project with a big residential component. They were more accustomed to straight office-building transactions, and they had learned the advantages of maintaining a distance from new ideas, such as mixed-use projects. New ideas usually cost money. In addition, pension funds are not taxed on their earnings so the tax-shelter aspects of the deal had no appeal to these big investors.

The list of early potential investors also included the Japanese, who were eagerly snapping up major office buildings across the country in 1985. But the Japanese are very risk-averse, preferring to acquire completed structures with tenants in place in the unfamiliar U.S. market. They weren't interested in getting in so early. Like the pension funds, the Japanese had little use for the tax-sheltering aspects of the construction project since they paid their taxes in yen, not dollars.

So, early that summer, Perini sent out packages of documents and brochures describing the deal to about twenty investment firms that specialized in assembling real estate transactions for wealthy individual investors. These firms had proliferated through the 1980s as hundreds of private real-estate partnerships were assembled to invest billions of dollars in new projects offering huge tax breaks. The federal government had created the shelters in the 1970s by allowing developers and builders to pass on to investors the tax deductions generated by investments in new construction. The investment firms served as the middlemen in these deals, finding projects to syndicate and then organizing the sales through brokers to a roster of rich people with income to shelter. The syndicators were well paid for their trouble; as a rule of thumb, their fees often consumed 10 percent of the total take and sales commissions could add nearly as much.

Some of these partnerships were driven solely by the tax benefits and invested in highly speculative developments—nursing homes in Florida, resort hotels in Arizona, shopping centers in Texas, shoddy apartments in Southern California. Others were well-conceived investments that would turn out to be profitable for all concerned. Rincon Center seemed to fall into the latter category, with its high-profile San Francisco location and the track record of its developer. So the chance to syndicate it attracted a lot of interest from the middlemen.

"It was the kind of project that gets everybody to stand up and pay attention," recalled Bruce Kiernan, a syndicator at the Boston Financial Group, a major investment firm. "It was in downtown San Francisco, mixed use, Perini Corporation. What more could you want to catch an investor's eye?"

Securities and Exchange Commission regulations and state securities laws covering real estate syndications restricted offerings to people in upper-income brackets, so-called accredited investors. They had to have a net worth of at least $1 million or an annual income of at least $200,000. The reasoning of the regulators was that these were sophisticated investors who were smart enough to evaluate the deals themselves, since the SEC did not review the offerings and their state counterparts barely glanced at them. In reality, the investors in these deals were usually wealthy doctors, lawyers, dentists, athletes, and show business personalities—people with substantial annual income to shelter from taxes but without the time or expertise to handle their own investments. Whether they were sophisticated investors was in the eye of the beholder.

The package that Perini sent to the syndicators initially indicated that the corporation wanted to raise $50 million from private investors. As the responses began coming into the company's headquarters in Framingham, Massachusetts, no one thought the project would generate that much investment money. The potential returns did not seem to support that kind of outside investment. Even in their eagerness for the business and their expectation that the deal would sell well, the syndicators had a legal responsibility to make certain that the tax benefits and potential return on investment for the buyers matched the money that Perini was trying to raise.

They had some of the same doubts about Rincon Center that had been expressed earlier by others. While it was in downtown San Francisco, the exact site was not top drawer, and the city's rental market was softening. In a weakening economy, investors often retreat to premium locations. The complexity of a renovation added uncertainties to the ultimate cost of construction. There were also concerns about the size of the floorplates in the commercial areas. What Tim Tosta had sold to the city as a major advantage for Rincon Center in keeping back-office workers in San Francisco was not a plus to the experts evaluating the projected revenue flow from the project. Back-office operations do not pay front-office rent.

Facing up to the fact that the deal would not work at $50 million, Perini began negotiations with a few firms to put together a transaction that would raise less money. After several weeks of exchanging offers and counteroffers, Perini decided to go with Boston Financial Group, a financial consulting and syndication firm that had worked extensively with developers and investors since its founding fifteen years earlier.

Additional negotiations between Perini and Boston Financial, principally over the amount that would be raised, resulted in a preliminary twenty-page agreement. It called for Boston Financial to assemble a syndication that would raise $38.6 million for investment in Rincon Center. Perini wanted the deal to be done by late spring of 1986 so the money could start flowing in by early 1987.

Boston Financial had added a couple of kickers as hedges against some of the risks of the project: Perini Land & Development agreed to cover all cost overruns on the project out of its pocket and to lend up to $5 million to the project for five years to cover possible operating losses. The Perini loans would be repaid out of operating income from the project, but only after the investors had received a cumulative return of 8 percent of their money. Also, Perini was required to guarantee that it would secure permanent financing for the development, a take-out loan, by the end of 1989 at an interest rate no higher than 11.2 percent. If the permanent loan rate exceeded 11.2 percent, Perini would pay the extra. This was a risk, however, for which Perini was compensated. The developers were allocated $9.3 million out of the syndication proceeds to pay for interest above 11.2 percent. If they secured a permanent loan at less than that amount, they could pocket the $9.3 million.

This $9.3 million was augmented in the syndication agreement with $16 million earmarked to pay the interest on the construction loan from Citibank. Since the $79 million construction loan included enough money to really pay the interest, the $16 million would be combined with the $9.3 million to form Perini's cash deposit to fulfill its equity requirement with the bank. In this neat way, the outside investors would be putting up all the cash Perini planned to invest in the deal. And once the construction was completed, the money would go to the developers as profit, if all went as planned.

The syndication agreement also contained an escape clause for the outside investors that would increase the pressure on Perini to finish the project on time. If the development was not completed by January 31, 1989, the investors could vote to force the developer to return their capital contribution. Despite its Draconian nature, the clause raised few concerns at Perini. Their construction schedule offered plenty of cushion. The renovation of the post office was to be finished by July 1987, and the new building would be done by January 1988. Also, to soften any concerns, Perini would be paid $947,000 upfront for the risk of facing the disaster clause.

Of course, this was in addition to the other upfront payments that had been arranged to benefit the developers, such as the $1.55 million management fee and $650,000 leasing fee. And, as a partner with Tutor-Saliba in the construction work, the parent company was expected to receive $853,706 in profits. Another affiliate, Perini Investment Properties, was contracted to manage the entire project once it was up and running.

All of this, however, was not without risk. Plenty of glitches were possible in this prosperous scenario. For instance, the $9.3 million earmarked for Perini in exchange for guaranteeing the interest rate on the permanent mortgage could be devoured if interest rates soared.

As important, the cost of any overruns on the construction budget would come out of Perini's pocket and force the company to commit its own money to the project.

In the following six weeks, Boston Financial developed the specific terms and language for the offering, as well as its marketing strategy. The syndication would be divided into 400 investment units at $96,600 each. The payments were to be staggered over five years, with each installment tied to certain performance conditions that had to be fulfilled by the developers. Among the conditions were finalizing the construction loan with Citibank, completing various stages of the project, and leasing specific amounts of the commercial and residential space. In much the same way that Citibank sought to protect its exposure through the monthly draw meetings, the outside investors wanted to make sure work was progressing before kicking in their shares of the money.

For the investors, the returns were divided into two distinct components. The short-term benefit was the ability to shelter income from other sources through huge deductions available through investment tax credits, paper losses in the early years that could be passed through to the investors, and depreciation write-offs. An investor paying in $96,600 for one unit would receive total tax deductions of $179,894 over twelve years. For a taxpayer in the 50 percent bracket, the highest level at the time, this was a direct tax savings of $89,947. The tax credit for historic rehabilitation offered investors a bonus. Unlike deductions, which reduce taxable income, the tax credits could be subtracted at 100 percent of their value from an individual's taxable income. Tax credits would total $18,898 per investor between 1986 and 1990, when they ran out. So the tax benefits of the investment alone surpassed the actual cash outlay.

There were other types of investments that may have offered more muscular deductions, such as oil-and-gas partnerships. But this one had something else going for it. The tax-shelter aspects were augmented by the potential long-term benefits, which would be based on a share of any operating profits or profits resulting from the sale of the project. Calculating long-term benefits is trickier than analyzing the tax aspects of the investment since the eventual profit will depend on revenue and the sales price of the project. No one expected the developers to hold on to the project longer than necessary to satisfy their obligations to the city agencies and maximize their profits.

Assuming reasonable appreciation, Boston Financial projected a selling price of $219 million for the entire project on January 1, 2000. At that price, the outside investors would each realize a total after-tax gain of $284,688—a return of 295 percent on their money, not even counting the huge savings from the tax shelter. Even using a fire-sale price of $115 million—equal to the expected mortgage on the project in the year 2000—Boston Financial expected each outside investor to receive $120,024 in benefits after taxes, a gain of 124 percent.

So, as syndicator Bruce Kiernan explained it, the deal offered the tax benefits to get investors through the early years when the project was not going to be making any money. Then, about the time the tax benefits were used up, the long-term earnings would kick in as the development started to turn a profit.

For its expertise in assembling such an attractive and clever investment package, Boston Financial was to receive a $3.2 million syndication fee and a $4 million consulting fee once the shares were sold. Out of that $7.2 million, the company anticipated overhead costs of $3.4 million, bringing its compensation to a handsome $3.8 million. As the syndicators, Boston Financial also would be entitled to 1 percent of the profits from the eventual sale of the property. The major expense for Boston Financial would be an estimated $2.9 million in selling commissions to the brokers who would actually place the units with investors.

While it had been independent for a number of years, Boston Financial retained strong ties to the New York–based investment house of Paine Webber, which had created it in 1969, and planned to use its brokers to sell the Rincon Center package. For each unit sold, a broker would receive a commission of $7,245.

The total take for Boston Financial and its selling agents on the Rincon deal would amount to nearly 20 percent of the $38.6 million investment. Taking such a substantial amount off the top in fees and commissions was one reason that some sophisticated investors viewed real estate syndications as gimmicks that were most profitable for the syndication firms and brokers themselves; the people putting the packages together were assured of their money upfront, while the investors had to depend on real estate markets and tax laws over the long haul. Yet, when coupled with the tax benefits, the potential long-term return on the Rincon deal would carry a considerable appeal in the marketplace and hordes of rich people were finding the allure of such packages impossible to resist.

Beyond the obvious financial aspects, the marketing strategy developed by Bruce Kiernan and his boss on the deal, Jim Hughes, was designed to stress the location and nature of the project. They conceived a dog-and-pony show for potential investors that would highlight the neighborhood as the next area of rapid development in San Francisco. The presence of residential units, a liability to institutional investors, would be turned into an advantage by pointing out that a mixed-use project did not depend on any single market for its income. If residential rents were down, commercial might be up. If commercial revenue was lagging, maybe the stores and restaurants would be generating lots of revenue. The drama of the architecture and the renovation of the historic post office also were identified as selling points.

By the end of 1985, Boston Financial was preparing a videotape that brokers could show clients. The tape featured Scott Johnson discussing the architecture of Rincon Center. It pointed out that the same firm had designed the Transamerica pyramid, one of the best-known buildings in America. Randy Verrue was on the tape, lauding the financial strength of Perini Corporation and the overall virtues of the development, and Peter Fallon of Boston Financial outlined positive investment trends in San Francisco.

The syndication seemed to be on track, and plans were made to host a lavish pre-sale party in San Francisco in late March or early April for the brokers who would sell the investments. By that time, demolition would be well underway at the post office and the excavation should be started for the new building. The party would be a way to excite the brokers. The printed prospectus and other offering material would be ready by then, and sales could start by the middle of April. The timing seemed perfect—hit the rich doctors and lawyers just as they are in their annual tax-induced shock.

Most of the millions in tax benefits being offered as bait to the outside investors would be generated by the expenses and depreciation allowances associated with the new building. But about $7.5 million of the benefits were linked to the historic tax credits associated with the renovation of the old post office. If those credits were lost, the potential return on the deal for investors would drop sharply and new terms would have be drawn up that would reduce the total outside investment.

So as the year drew to a close and the developers were rushing to break ground and secure the full tax benefits, the outstanding matter of whether the rear facade of the post office could be removed had become critical. Jay Mancini had remained adamant that the facade would not be stripped off if it meant losing the historic tax credit. Scott Johnson and Dianna Wong continued to insist that the success or failure of the atrium hung in the balance.

Architects in the local office of the United States Department of Interior, which administers the historic renovation code, were equally intractable. Not only were they insisting that the facade remain. They wanted some partitions that had been installed on the second and third floors of the post office after the building was completed to remain in place to assure what they saw as the interior integrity. Mancini and his assistant, Harry Topping, both felt the partitions cut into the floor-plates in such a way that rents for those floors would have been reduced sharply.

One night in early December, Mancini and Topping were eating dinner at Vanessi's, an Italian restaurant not far from the Rincon site. The subject was what to do about the historic tax credit. As they talked, it became clear that the issue would have to be appealed to the Department of Interior in Washington, D.C. With millions of dollars in financing hanging in the balance, most developers would either have solved this problem much earlier in the process or hired a team of high-powered lawyers to argue the appeal. But Rincon was a fast-track project, and a woefully understaffed one at that. Mancini and Topping knew that one of them would have to fly to Washington and make the presentation. They talked at length about who would be best suited and, finally, Mancini looked across the table at Topping and said: "Harry, you go. If you win the appeal, fine. If you don't, don't bother to come back."

Topping was stunned by the ultimatum, which had been delivered with a straight face. He didn't know whether Mancini was joking. And he was so frightened that his boss was serious that he decided not to ask.

Harry Topping was a good choice for the assignment, if you did not have a team of well-connected lawyers to grease the way. Along with his undergraduate degree in architecture and his MBA, he had a master's degree in architectural history. He felt it would give him additional standing as he argued that the unattractive rear facade, with its loading docks and oddly placed windows, had to go. The following morning, Topping telephoned Washington and arranged an emergency meeting for the next day with John Connolly, the crusty architectural historian who served as chief of the appeals office at Interior and final arbiter on matters of preservation. That night Topping was on the red-eye to Washington, D.C., with architectural drawings rolled into a long tube and an uncertain sense that his six-month-old career was on the line.

He checked into the Willard Hotel a few blocks from the Department of Interior offices, showered, and spent the next few hours putting the finishing touches on his presentation. At two P.M., he was ushered into a conference room at Interior where he faced Connolly and five or six young preservationists. For the next ninety minutes, Topping argued that economic prospects of the project hinged on removing the rear facade and taking out the interior partitions. He stressed that the rear facade was an ugly duckling, and the three sides of the post office with architectural and historic significance were being maintained scrupulously. The department's own regulations, Topping pointed out, said contemporary designs for alterations should not be discouraged when the changes do not destroy significant architectural material. There were few questions and, when he finished, Topping was told to go wait in the nearby cafeteria. "We'll let you know in an hour or two," said one of Connolly's young aides, who escorted Topping to the cafeteria.

Shortly before five P.M., Topping was summoned back to the conference room to hear the verdict. He found no hint of the decision in the blank faces as he walked toward a chair. When Topping was seated, Connolly said the panel had considered his arguments and examined the reports of the San Francisco office. They had decided, said Connolly, that the rear facade and the partitions could go. They added little to the historic significance of the building, the official explained, and should not be allowed to stand in the way of the overall project.

Topping was jubilant. He immediately telephoned Mancini and

reported the news. It didn't occur to him then to ask whether he really would have lost his job if the decision had gone against them. Flying home to San Francisco that night, he decided never to ask Jay Mancini if his job had been on the line. He just didn't want to know whether his future could disappear so abruptly. Not with all the other difficult decisions still ahead.

13

DECISION AND INDECISION

The approval to remove the rear facade was a major win for the developers, but it was only one of the complicated battles fought in the war to get the development underway officially before the end of 1985, so the full benefits of the tax breaks could be ensured. Since the start of the project in the summer of 1984, it had been marred by the inability to make final decisions on a number of key issues. Some of this was inevitable on a project as complex as Rincon Center. In other cases, the responsibility rested with Jay Mancini, whose ability to make a choice at times seemed in direct and inverse proportion to the significance and urgency of the matter at hand. A proliferation of consultants often served only to compound the problem. Blame also could be apportioned to the architectural team, which had trouble providing workable design documents in a timely fashion. And certainly the unusual intrusion of the staff of the San Francisco Redevelopment Agency into the planning and design of Rincon Center was a factor. Wherever the responsibility lay, the fact was that key choices were not made in a timely fashion and the resulting delays would reverberate throughout the project for months and months to come.

One of these oft-delayed decisions was the shape of the atrium in the old building. A critical question about the renovation of the post office was whether the foundation and underground pilings could withstand the weight of the two new floors. If calculations showed that they could not, the developers would face the costly alternative of spending millions of dollars to upgrade the foundation and pilings on which it rested or cancelling the new floors and losing the additional revenue and a substantial portion of the tax credits. Two factors would determine the answer to the question: the quality of the pilings and soil surrounding them, and how much the weight would be increased. This last part of the equation, the weight, could not be determined until the shape of the atrium itself was finalized. But the first portion of the question could be answered well in advance.

In 1850, the year California became a state, the post office site was under ten feet of water as part of Yerba Buena Cove. Hundreds of ships were abandoned there as their crews ran off to seek their fortunes in the gold fields. Through the 1870s, portions of the cove were filled in and wharfs were laid out in a pattern roughly the same as the streets that now exist. After the 1906 earthquake, the rubble of flattened buildings and houses was pushed into the cove, creating a larger land area. Still, even when the post office was completed in 1940, the land was unstable and bedrock was 100 feet or more below the surface.

When bedrock is out of reach, a system of pilings and a foundation must be constructed. Since ancient Rome, tree trunks have been stripped of bark and driven into the ground to support buildings. In the case of the original Rincon Annex Post Office, 3,800 wooden pilings were driven down to depths of sixty to seventy feet. The pilings were made of Douglas fir and they were about fourteen inches in diameter at the top, tapering to a base diameter of eight to ten inches. These are called bearing piles, and they were intended to transmit the load of the post office to firm soil. Depending on their exact location, the pilings traveled through twenty to thirty feet of rubble fill and an equal layer of the soft, compressible clay known as bay mud to reach a stable layer of dense sand.

The original planning documents showed that the pilings were grouped in clusters of 100 to 200, with each cluster capped by a slab of reinforced concrete. These slabs served to link the pilings into a single unit, which could support the weight of a huge vertical column. Atop the slabs, a foot of concrete was poured to form the basement floor of the post office.

In the summer of 1985, a geotechnical engineer named Michael Praszker had been hired to conduct a series of tests aimed at determining whether the pilings and soil would sustain the new weight.

Praszker, the principal in a firm called Lee & Praszker, had spent forty years examining soil conditions in the San Francisco area. The firm had performed tests for the underground tunnels of the Bay Area Rapid Transit (BART) system, and evaluated the stability of the landfill where San Francisco International Airport was built. Praszker liked to refer to himself as "a Bay man," and he didn't venture into strange territory to ply his specialized trade.

Praszker's critical evaluations for Rincon started out in a damp, dark, four-foot space between the ground and the underside of the elevated basement floor, which rested on top of the pilings and piling slabs. The first task was to cut a trench alongside several separate groups of pilings so that they could be inspected visually. Since the work was conducted below the water table, a subcontractor continuously pumped the seepage out of the trench to allow the men to work. In addition to the sight inspection, chunks were sliced out of twenty-six piles and replaced with concrete to bind the wood together again. The chunks were sent off for laboratory tests to determine if there was dry rot or other deterioration. Praszker found precisely what he had expected: once the mud was washed away, the chunks of wood looked like new, and the tests found no sign of any sort of deterioration. The water in the mud, which had entombed the piles for more than four decades, had preserved them perfectly.

Next, Praszker's engineers conducted three types of tests to discover and chart the strength of the piles and the stability of the soil.

The first test was for compression. The top of a piling was sliced away where it met the concrete slab and a fourteen-inch-high jack, powered by compressed air, was inserted into the space. The jack could be calibrated to exert downward pressure against the piling equal to various amounts of weight. The result would be a stress curve that measured the ability of the piling to withstand the downward push of the building's weight. The tests were run on forty to fifty piles and only two snapped under the strain.

The second test involved evaluating the capacity of the piles to withstand tension. When a material is pulled or stretched, it is said to be in tension. Very elastic materials demonstrate tension readily, like a rubber band that is stretched to twice its length. Tension occurs in a building when one side sinks slightly or the building sways fractionally in a wind. This creates a pull on the foundation on the opposite side. Proper pilings have enough tensile strength to withstand the pulling without snapping, yet they will not stretch so far as to allow the structure to topple. To determine how much tensile strength remained in the pilings, the jack was reversed to pull up on the wood. The result was another series of charts measuring this type of strength.

When these two tests were finished, the gaps between the pile tops and the slab were filled with concrete so no strength would be lost. The jack was moved into yet another position for the final series of tests. This time, the device was placed horizontally between the tops of two pilings and the pressure was increased gradually to try to drive the pilings apart. This was a measure of the ability of the pilings to withstand the lateral forces that push a building sideways. It also gauged how well the soil had settled around the pilings, since the pressure was transmitted down the length of the column.

These tests were conducted over several weeks, and evaluating the results was not a matter of saying simply that the pilings were good or not good. The lab tests showed that they had not deteriorated, and the visual inspections showed that they looked like new. The three strength tests resulted in charts that demonstrated the pilings were capable of withstanding significant additional weight.

The next phase of the question was how much weight could be added, and that answer would come from the structural engineers at Chin & Hensolt. It was their job to calculate the gross weight of the building with the two new floors. Even if the pilings could withstand a lot of additional weight, it was inadvisable to push them to the maximum because it could change the settling patterns of the soil and disrupt the stability created over the past forty-five years. The idea was to keep the building weight as close to the original as possible while adding the two floors.

One part of the solution was to make the new floors as light as possible. The top of the three-story building would serve as the floor for the new fourth level. Rather than concrete, the walls for the fourth floor and the entire framing and floor for the fifth floor would be constructed out of steel to lighten the weight. The other part of the solution was to make way for the new weight by taking out some of the old weight by cutting away floors for the atrium. But the shape of the atrium had not been decided, so the engineers didn't know how much the demolition crew would be chopping out. Since the old floors weighed 110 pounds per square foot, the amount was of great consequence.

"The real way we are going to accomplish the two new floors is to unload the whole structure by carving out the atrium," P. Q. Chin explained to Jay Mancini in urging him to settle the question of the atrium's shape. "The soil doesn't know what the hell you're doing. We unload the center of the building, recalculate its weight with the new floors. We can do it fast with a computer. But the computer can't work until we know what to feed into it."

Removing much of the old, heavy flooring was vital to being able to add the two new floors. But it was not without costs in other areas. The concrete-slab floors contributed to the strength and rigidity of the building. Eliminating them would weaken the structure and require new reinforcement. This aspect of the planning had been complicated by Jay Mancini's decision to remove the beams across the atrium, which would weaken the center of the structure even more than envisioned originally.

A building must withstand three basic load forces. The most obvious is the weight of the structure itself, weight made up of beams, floors, arches, and walls. This is called dead load. The building also must support the live load, which means people, furniture, equipment, and stored items. These two forces are primarily downward-acting, and they are supported by the walls and vertical columns that transfer the load to the foundation. A third type, dynamic load, results from the natural movement of a building in response to wind pressure or, in a more extreme case, an earthquake. To withstand this lateral movement, the structure must be stable enough to move without collapsing yet elastic enough to give a little. Part of this elasticity comes from the material itself: steel or reinforced concrete. But engineers also must use horizontal beams and girders to knit the vertical columns and walls into a cohesive whole that withstands dynamic load.

The weight factor was complicated by another problem. San Francisco's building code required that structures erected in 1985 withstand much higher loads than those that had been built in 1940, when the post office was completed. Because the planned renovation was so extensive, the building would have to be brought up to the current code by strengthening existing walls and columns. The finish would be stripped from the interior side of the eight-inch-thick concrete exterior walls and they would receive another four to six inches of concrete. It would be sprayed on through a pressurized system called "shot-crete," and the new concrete would be tied into the old walls using steel rebar. The existing columns were hollow and had been used to help ventilate the post office. Many of them would receive steel cladding from floor to ceiling to bring their strength up to code. In addition, new freestanding steel columns would be installed around the perimeter of the atrium to support the dead and live loads. Steel girders would span back from the new columns and tie into the existing concrete columns. The steel would be encased in concrete to blend with the building, and the effect would be of contemporary "flying buttresses."

These plans allowed for removing large sections of floor for the atrium; exactly how much would be cut away depended on the atrium's final shape. But the calculations by the structural engineers had counted on leaving the cross beams in place to maintain the knit effect. Now removing them would demand additional strengthening of the building against lateral movement. Otherwise, it would collapse in response to normal wind, never mind what might happen in an earthquake.

In part, accommodating the new plan meant more of the same. More walls would be strengthened, and more columns would receive steel cladding. But the engineers from Chin & Hensolt wanted to build fourteen new concrete walls to make up for the weakness in the core of the building caused by removing the beams, and that was going to cost more. The proposed walls were called shear walls. Shear is a destructive force that results from lateral movement; as its name suggests, it is the tendency for material to split (or shear) apart.

After Allan Temko's visit in September and Jay Mancini's decision to remove the cross beams, Chin & Hensolt had written a letter to Mancini pointing out the need for new walls. At a meeting in Pereira Associates offices in Los Angeles on September 27, an engineer from the firm again stressed the necessity of new walls. But Harry Topping, who was filling in for Mancini, said the developers were concerned about the costs. He urged the engineers to come up with a redesign that would minimize the number of new walls.

A few days later, Dennis Oh, the project manager for Chin & Hensolt, met with Topping and Mancini in the post office building.

He wanted to find some way to make them understand that this was not an area in which costs could be cut. Oh had spent nearly twenty-five years as a structural engineer in San Francisco. During that time, he had seen standards for protecting against earthquakes improve, seemingly with each new tremor. There was no way that he would approve a renovation for Rincon Center that applied less than 100 percent of the latest knowledge.

Standing in the open room that constituted most of the first floor of the building that day, he gestured toward the ceiling and said: "You're going to have a skylight up there. You want it falling down in an earthquake?"

Dennis Oh had made his point. At a meeting on October 18, the general contractor reported that the new shear walls would add $276,000 to the cost of strengthening the post office, and the expenditure was okayed without further objection.

Still undecided, however, was the shape of the atrium. This delay was having troubling consequences for the entire construction schedule because the city refused to issue a demolition permit until it saw the final design drawings for the renovation. City officials didn't want to okay tearing out the inside of the structure until they knew what was going to replace it and whether it would be structurally sound. The staff of the redevelopment agency also was balking at providing the approvals necessary to secure the construction loan and officially start construction. But, while the staff wanted to see the final design of the atrium, their concerns focused on the color of glass that would be used in the curtain wall for the new towers.

Fast-tracking meant that work would progress without some city okays. But the demolition permit and the final loan approval were hurdles that had to be cleared before any work could start, fast track or not. Mancini still was not satisfied with Scott Johnson's design for the atrium. He thought using three different colors of glass and draping the five-story space in a glass curtain wall was too brash. Also, the storefronts were too modern, with aluminum where Mancini preferred wood, which he believed a more subdued and richer material.

Objections also were still on the table concerning the layout of shops and restaurants proposed by Halcyon, the consulting firm hired by Mancini. Halcyon envisioned bringing the storefronts right out to the edge of the atrium, which encroached too much on the potential open space to suit the developers. Harry Topping had taken to referring to the plan as "the bowling alley." He and Mancini even disagreed with Halcyon's proposed mix of shops and restaurants. They were beginning to feel that the development needed more restaurants to help attract people and provide the exciting atrium they sought, and the Halcyon plan was heavy on shops and light on restaurants.

Johnson and Dianna Wong had been revising the atrium in response to the developers' concerns. From their point of view, the process was being slowed terribly by Mancini's inability to decide what sort of atrium he found acceptable.

At a meeting in October, Johnson presented new sketches that called for lighter colors in the curtain wall and less obtrusive metal cross members. The space also had been opened up by the elimination of the concrete beams. Tom Sargent and Sandra Lipkovitz from Halcyon attended the meeting and they defended their retail plan, contending that the depth gained by bringing the stores to the edge of the atrium would provide more leasable space. They also liked Johnson's highly contemporary atrium design.

But Topping, who attended the meeting without Mancini and was assuming more of the responsibility for the atrium, was unconvinced by either the design changes or the defense of the retail layout. He saw the atrium as the linchpin of the development and he wasn't happy with the direction in which it was going. By the time of the October meeting, he was thinking seriously about bringing in a new retail consultant for a fresh perspective.

There is nothing unusual about a $150 million project employing a lot of consultants. In the case of Rincon Center, Jay Mancini was coming to rely heavily on them because he liked to hear a variety of opinions before making up his mind. He had even gone so far as to hire architects to review Johnson's design work. In response, Johnson felt that Mancini surrounded himself with consultants because he didn't trust his own judgment or, unfortunately, that of his architect on many matters. But the architect was most disturbed by what he saw as a breach of the profession's informal guidelines.

"Dealing with many consultants on a job is not an irritant in itself," Johnson later explained. "On most complex jobs, there are scores of them and it is common to work with them. In fact, it is impossible without them. What was at issue here, and remains a very current topic, is that I had never worked with an architectural office which agreed to work on an overlapping scope of work for which another architect was already retained. It was my background, both at Skidmore, Owings & Merrill and at Johnson and Burgee, that we would never touch a piece of work unless another architect was let go and we would contact him to verify that he was no longer working on the project. Then, if we were interested, we would study what they had been studying. This principle is based on what most everyone in the business knows to be true: while one professional may be better or worse than another, architecture is still an interpretive and somewhat subjective practice. This was basically a self-monitoring code within the profession."

For the first time in his experience, Johnson had a client who would hire multiple consultants on all fronts. None of these consultants irritated him as much as Kenneth Tardy.

Tardy was a San Francisco architect in his fifties who had been brought in to plan the interior office space of the two buildings. But from the start, Mancini had pressed Tardy into the role of professional second-guesser on almost every aspect of the design. If Mancini wasn't sure he liked an aspect of Johnson's design, he would have Tardy do a sketch of his own and then compare them. He did it for lobbies, for the atrium walls, for the layout of the courtyard between the old and new buildings.

Tardy didn't object to this kibitzing, largely because he viewed the much younger Johnson as faddish. He liked to refer to him as "the architect from 'Miami Vice.' " In Tardy's mind, their differences were clear: he was traditional, realistic, and San Francisco; Johnson was flashy, artsy, and Los Angeles.

Ken Tardy is an inside man, and that has molded his view of the proper role of the architect. He specializes in laying out floor plans that create the most rentable space for the owner, positioning toilets so they are the proper distance from the elevators, determining the number and location of elevators. These sound like mundane jobs, but they are integral to ending up with space that is functional and rentable. He believes these tasks are often ignored by architects with loftier ambitions than making sure the toilet doesn't end up too close to the reception area.

"You see, I know what I do for a living," said Tardy. "Architects don't know what they do for a living because they are trained to create art and they are really being hired to make money for the owner. I fight the architects because I want to have the inside of the building work for the owner. You can have your massing. You can have your cute arch. That's fine. But don't screw up everything from the windows inward so the owner can't lease his spaces."

Mancini offered a more tactful description of the roles he assigned Johnson and Tardy: "Scott really is a great artist and his medium is buildings. But he is less conscious of how it will work on the inside. A developer wants great art, but it has to work. Ken was more pragmatic; not a great artist. At what he does, Ken is as good as Scott. Now, you can get a consultant to tell you anything. You have to decide who is the guy to believe. You have to tear down their arguments and pick the best. An awful lot of that goes into the formative stages of the design process. The developer must be rigorous. The devil does lie in the details, and the developer's job extends from the macro to the micro choices."

As Tardy looked at the project that fall, he believed that Scott Johnson was well on the way to screwing up the inside of the building. For one thing, the toilets *had* been designed too close to the reception areas. It would create disruptive traffic flow around the reception area. He insisted that they be moved. But far more important to Tardy, Johnson had designed the windows in the new six-story office tower and those overlooking the atrium in the post office on a section that was five feet wide, the standard in the marketplace. In recent years, however, Tardy had become convinced that four-foot-six modules allowed tenants more flexibility in dividing space along the perimeter of a floor, the premium location.

An interior wall can only be built on a line with the window module. So if the module is five feet wide, the widths can be five, ten, or fifteen feet. With a four-foot-six module, the widths will be on multiples of four and a half feet. The difference between a ten-foot-wide office and a nine-foot-wide one is only 10 percent, and Tardy maintained that there's very little noticeable difference to the occupant. That 10 percent, however, can mean more perimeter offices across an entire floor and more flexibility in dividing the interior space.

When Tardy proposed the four-foot-six module at a meeting in

October of 1985 and offered his reasoning, Johnson did a slow, characteristically invisible burn. He was well aware of the desirability of perimeter offices; he had come up with a unique design for Fox Plaza in Los Angeles to optimize the number of such spaces. But he felt that Rincon Center was a totally different building, which would appeal to a different type of tenant with far less need for perimeter offices. Further, the narrower window modules would force him to redesign the entire pattern of the curtain wall on the two towers after they had already been approved by Mancini. Responding to Johnson's objections, Tardy said, "I'll bet you dinner that we could go to five buildings and you won't be able to tell me what the window module is from the street." It was a challenge that Johnson could ignore easily, for he had no desire to eat dinner with Ken Tardy. As for the window width, Mancini said he would take it under advisement. A month later, he decided to go with the four-foot-six modules and told Johnson to redesign the curtain wall pattern to reflect the narrower windows. The decision added more weeks to the design time.

Johnson already had redesigned several sections of the project more than once, and that time would be billed as additional services. The duplicate designs requested of Tardy's office for some portions of the project meant duplicate costs, and Tardy's bill was mounting steadily. So the architectural fees on the project were climbing fast and appeared certain to outstrip the budget. Other costs were rising, too, and some involved far larger numbers than the architectural fees.

The ground lease required the developers to provide 14,000 square feet of free space to the post office on the first floor of the new building for a new consumer facility. The terms required a loading dock for postal trucks, and the plans called for placing it at street level on the Spear Street side of the building. For months, the staff at the San Francisco Redevelopment Agency had been complaining that the location would be unsightly and cause traffic problems on the narrow street.

The only alternative was moving the docks to the first basement level of the two-level underground parking structure. Mancini did not like the solution for several reasons. The most obvious was that parking stalls would be lost, which meant revenue would be lost. The height from the floor to the ceiling would have to be raised from ten feet to fourteen feet to make room for the big trucks. That meant the plaza between the buildings would have to be raised to accommo-

Rincon Center, under construction in the lower left corner, assuming its place on the San Francisco skyline.

Pioneers Receiving Mail *is one of the murals by Anton
Refregier that were saved in the historic lobby.*

Patrons line up on one of the building's last days as a post office.

Aerial view of the site when it was still operating as a post office. BILL WASSON

Carving the atrium and installing new columns and girders for the renovation.

Work nears completion on the renovation, but the new portion is just rising out of the ground.

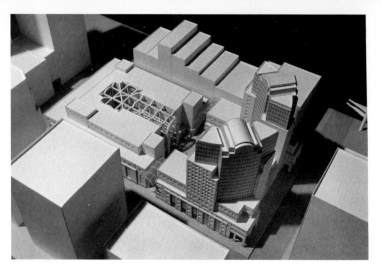

An early study model shows residential towers with two types of tops, and the atrium before the crossbeams were removed.

The architect's detailed sketch with pre-cast concrete panels for the facades of the new towers.

The presentation model for Rincon Center at a scale of ⅛-inch to 1 foot.

An atrium view, with the rain column on and the pool surrounded by the offending plants. STEVE WHITTAKER 1990

Interior of the residential lobby, one of the last arenas of design dispute.

Apartment interior with a low beam crossing at a diagonal.

Outdoor plaza and Joan Brown obelisk viewed from the renovated portion looking toward the new building.

The completed project viewed from the south end of the block facing northeast.

The partners: Scott Johnson (left) and Bill Fain.

date the increased height, since it would be even more expensive to dig deeper. The floor of the upper parking level also would have to be strengthened with additional rebar to withstand the weight of the trucks. Moving the docks would cost $1.2 million.

Despite the extra cost, Mancini decided to go ahead and tell the city officials that he would move the loading docks. But he would point out to the redevelopment staff that the change came at great expense. What he would not say was that he had in fact come to agree that the docks would work better away from the street. He would keep silent on that point because he hoped to build up some reserves for the other battles that were still pending.

Both the architect and the developers were chafing over the extensive and, in their minds, intrusive involvement of the redevelopment agency staff. One of the most significant and stubborn debates was over the color and density of the glass for the curtain wall. The developers wanted gray glass and the redevelopment officials wanted light green glass. They were very alarmed that the gray would be a dark and dull blot on the city's skyline. And anyway, there were no gray-glass buildings in San Francisco, a fact that caused the bureaucrats untold consternation. The decision had been made that the only way to resolve the debate was to set up a display of the actual types of glass proposed for the curtain wall. Then maybe the staff could be persuaded that the color and density of the gray were acceptable and the project could move forward.

This was important because the redevelopment staff refused to sign the design-development documents until they had approved the color of the curtain wall. Without redevelopment's signature on the documents, Citibank could not sign off on the construction loan and allow the work to begin. And work had to start by the end of the year to assure the full tax credits for the development.

With his back to the wall over the deadline, Mancini didn't think he could win a fight over the color. The redevelopment staff was too adamant in its opposition to gray. Mancini wanted to buy some time to go around the staff and persuade the redevelopment commission that this decision was too important to leave to underlings. So Mancini, who fancied himself something of a strategist as a result of his military background and history degree, envisioned this scenario: he would give in grudgingly on moving the loading docks and, in exchange, would ask the staff to do him the favor of signing the design documents without a decision on the glass color. He would then promise to stage the glass demonstration as soon as possible after the first of the year.

Mancini put his plan into effect at a meeting on November 23. He told Walter Yanagita and Frank Cannizzaro from redevelopment that he had agreed to move the loading docks at great expense to the owners. Redesigning the new portion to accommodate the move also had added to the pressures on the development team, he said. Couldn't the staff see its way clear to okay the design documents without deciding on the glass? After several minutes of consideration, Cannizzaro agreed. He said the glass and some other unresolved design issues, such as the atrium, could be worked out later.

By the middle of December, Jay Mancini could sit quietly in his office, hands folded in front of him, and reflect on several victories. Harry Topping had won the okay for removing the rear facade. The demolition permit had just been approved and work would start officially the following week. The design okay from redevelopment had cleared the way for the construction loan from Citibank, and the syndication plans seemed to be progressing nicely.

Not that plenty of pressures didn't remain. Mancini was still not happy with the atrium, though he had not decided what would be a better design than the galleria-type of layout proposed by Johnson. And the price of moving the loading docks had been a high one, but it was only one reason the budget was being pushed further out of whack.

14

AN ORCHESTRAL
PERFORMANCE

On a Tuesday morning in the middle of January 1986 at about ten o'clock, Jay Mancini got the word on the budget problems. Ron Tutor and his staff had spent the first days of the new year revising the construction costs on the basis of the design documents approved by the redevelopment staff. The numbers were going up.

As Mancini sat at a conference table in Pereira's Los Angeles office, Harry Topping to his side and Scott Johnson and Dianna Wong across from him, he listened to Tutor explain the principal areas that had driven up the estimate. The decision to add balconies to 270 apartments cost $231,000. New shear walls required by the elimination of the atrium beams added $276,000. Moving the loading docks upped the costs $1.2 million. A decision by the developers to increase revenues by adding parking spaces beneath the old post office had meant lowering the basement floor to provide enough headroom at a cost of $1.8 million. These and other changes had pushed the estimated cost of construction to $65,079,336.

"I can still do it for less," said Tutor. "I think we can bring this in at $63 million."

Tutor said he did not believe he would need all the money budgeted for concrete, and he had identified other areas where costs could be cut to offset some of the increases. He wanted Mancini to consider shaving expenses in areas the contractor deemed nonessential. He proposed eliminating the on-again, off-again balconies, and economizing in areas that wouldn't show. For instance, thousands of dollars could be saved by building basement walls with wooden studs and drywall, instead of concrete block as planned. Money could be saved by reducing the quality of the interior finishes, too, such as reducing the amount of expensive granite used on the floors and wainscoting.

Mancini knew that Randy Verrue dearly loved the elegance of Citicorp Center, its forty-one stories wrapped in a skin of glass and creamy white pre-cast concrete, with sleek rounded corners. Large surfaces of the new building and its towers were to be covered with pre-cast concrete panels, and Verrue had often said he would like to replicate the color of Citicorp Center. Standard nonpremium concrete has gray cement in it, so its color is gray and often less uniform, panel to panel. To achieve the white that Verrue wanted, white cement would have to be added to the concrete mix at a cost of $200,000 or more. Tutor proposed a major saving by not only eliminating the white but by replacing the pre-cast concrete with less expensive, thin, concretelike panels (called GFRC—gypsum fiber reinforced concrete) on the exterior cladding. He did not put a figure on the switch, but it probably would cut half a million or more.

Mancini agreed to consider the proposed changes, including eliminating the balconies and substituting GFRC for pre-cast concrete. He instructed Johnson, who said little in response to Tutor's comments, to change the basement partitions, minimize the use of granite in the lobbies, and reduce the amount that would be spent on the floor finishes in the atrium and courtyard.

As he left the meeting shortly after noon to catch a plane for the short flight back to San Francisco, Jay Mancini thought it was a hell of a way to start the new year. If he'd known what was going on inside the offices of Pereira Associates, he might have been even more concerned.

William Pereira had died on November 13, 1985. Before his death, he had insisted that the seven partners add Scott Johnson and Bill Fain to their ranks. Without the new blood, Pereira was worried that his firm might not survive. The proposal met considerable resistance from several of the partners. But Pereira had pointed out that Johnson and Fain were bringing in the firm's commissions. Without them, the business seemed doomed.

Indeed, Fain had recently won a commission to plan part of a massive new city being built by the Japanese on the Hawaiian island of Oahu, and construction was underway on Johnson's Fox Plaza in Century City. The gleaming granite and glass monolith would sit on a knoll in full view of the city's movers and shakers. It seemed sure to catapult Johnson into the limelight in Los Angeles and bring in new commissions.

The other partners put their futures ahead of their pride and dispatched Roy Schmidt, the firm's president, to make the offers in the fall of 1985. To Schmidt's surprise, neither Johnson nor Fain jumped at the chance. The two young architects were in somewhat different circumstances at the firm then. Johnson had been promised a partnership as part of his agreement to move to Los Angeles from New York. He had not taken the firm up on the promise yet because, as he delicately phrased it, he was uncomfortable with the current composition of the partnership. Fain had arrived as a senior planner, but without a partnership commitment. Bill Pereira, however, had pushed the other partners to bring both Johnson and Fain into their ranks. Aware of Pereira's push on their behalf and their own value to the firm, Johnson and Fain had joined forces and responded together to Schmidt's partnership proposition. They drew up a list of conditions for accepting partnership and presented them to Schmidt. Only half facetiously, they had dubbed the list the "ten commandments."

Some of the demands were straightforward and businesslike. An annual business plan should be instituted. No partner could act on behalf of the corporation without notifying the others. Offices in Irvine and the Mideast nation of Qatar—a testament to more prosperous days and to what the young Turks viewed as the firm's uneven quality of work—would be closed and all design and planning done in the central office. Preparations would begin to move out of the huge space on Wilshire Boulevard into more affordable quarters that also would reflect the smaller size of the operation. The marketing department would be eliminated for a direct savings of $200,000 a year, and regular staff evaluations would be started.

Most dramatically for the other partners, all benefits for the firm's principals would be cut in half immediately and remain there until business improved. Revenues of architectural firms are often cyclical. Staff designers and planners are hired and fired as big projects come and go. But the financial difficulties at Pereira Associates ran deeper, and so did the cuts that Johnson and Fain wanted.

Some of the other "commandments" were designed to concentrate in their hands what they deemed their fair share of the power. Johnson was already director of design, but Fain would be elevated to director of planning with complete control over the department. They would review all prospective project budgets before contracts were signed to ensure that the jobs had been budgeted with sufficient manpower (some architectural firms underassign a job to increase profits, but it occurs at the expense of good design), and all contacts with prospective clients would be handled through them.

"To be fair to the firm, I have been in enough big organizations to tell you that the things happening here happen in a lot of older organizations," Fain recalled later. "In order to head out in the future, a lot of things had to be swept away. We were not going to attack any individuals. But we felt very strongly that the people who do the work need to be the people who represent the firm."

Not unexpectedly, some of the partners were indignant. Two would resign in a matter of weeks. But in the end, those remaining accepted the new rules. The only choice seemed to be to watch Johnson and Fain walk out the door, probably taking the future of the firm with them.

Even this budget cutting was not enough. Other reductions were implemented in the following weeks in an effort to keep the firm afloat. In a decision that would have repercussions later, the partners agreed to reduce the firm's errors-and-omissions insurance—the equivalent of malpractice insurance—to $2 million, down from $5 million. The reduction was made even though the contract with Rincon Center Associates required that protection be maintained at $5 million.

Roy Schmidt would later recall that he telephoned Jay Mancini about that time to discuss payments that were overdue from the developers. During the conversation, he mentioned that Pereira Associates was considering reducing its E&O insurance. Mancini said it sounded okay, but he would check with his lawyers and get back to Schmidt. According to Schmidt, there was no return call on the issue and the company went ahead with the reduction. Still, despite the cost cutting, as the new year rolled in, Pereira Associates seemed to be sliding toward insolvency.

In early 1986, the focus of Scott Johnson's frustrations on Rincon was the atrium. Jay Mancini and Harry Topping were dissatisfied with his design and with Halcyon's plans for the retail layout. But the developers were unable to articulate their objections or come up with an alternative from which the architect and the retail consultants could work.

In his plan, Johnson had tried to remain close to his original vision of the atrium as a space akin dimensionally to Milan's nineteenth-century Galleria, whose name has been invoked in countless retail spaces in the United States. The great Italian original, which he had visited many times, represented much of what Johnson sought for the atrium. It is a vibrant crossroads, an extension of the surrounding streets, and a magnet that draws life from the streets. It is covered with a tunnel-vaulted skylight, but it is airy, open, and lined with stores and cafés.

Johnson had conceived Rincon's atrium as a similar promenade. Since his version would be cut off from the streets by the building itself, Johnson wanted to evoke the sense of its surroundings by giving the interior a strong visual tie to the new towers. He also wanted to establish a powerful visual counterpoint to the exterior of the post office, which had few windows in its great concrete expanse. The result was a plan for contemporary storefronts of metal and glass overlooking the long walkway from two levels. Above them, glass walls would dramatize the vertical space and pick up the pattern and colors of the curtain wall on the towers. Livelier than the exterior curtain wall, the atrium would use three colors of glass panels. There would be lightly tinted gray vision glass and two shades of bluish spandrel glass, which would be opaque. He planned to stitch them together with a bold grid of aluminum mullions.

Halcyon had laid out a series of deep stores that fronted on the edge of the atrium and essentially turned it into a five-story retail street. There were plans for a few sit-down restaurants and lots of retail stores, such as clothing boutiques and convenience shops. The atrium would narrow to a more traditional promenade, also lined with additional stores, which would lead out the rear of the old building into the open courtyard. Halcyon planned a series of kiosks in the open plaza between the old and new buildings as a way of continuing the retail flow of the development.

The design envisioned the atrium as sort of a wide galleria leading into a narrower throat that would channel traffic out the rear of the building and into the courtyard. Mancini and Topping had focused their criticisms on the narrowness of the atrium itself, and the depth of the stores that resulted from that narrowness. Halcyon had tried to respond to the criticisms by pulling the atrium storefronts back from the edges, creating more of an open court in the center of the post office. But they could not satisfy the developers, at least in part because Mancini and Topping had expressed their dissatisfaction in vague terms. The developers knew they were unhappy with the atrium, but they did not know why. The answer was a familiar one: get another opinion.

"At some level, Halcyon just did not gain our confidence," said Mancini. "I asked a lot of questions trying to figure this problem out and, in that interplay, I did not feel that I was getting back an understanding of how to solve the problem. We needed a fresh view."

Halcyon was out, and the replacement was Bob Carey, the president of Urban Centre Developments, a prosperous retail consulting firm across the bay in Oakland. He had recently finished plans aimed at enlivening the retail space at Rockefeller Center, a credential that Mancini found particularly impressive.

Carey had started out as a retailer, working as an executive assistant to Cyril Magnin, grandson of the founder of the prestigious I. Magnin chain of fashion stores. An imaginative retailer in his own right, Cyril Magnin had created a small empire of Joseph Magnin stores that catered to fashion-conscious women on the West Coast. After Magnin was bought out by a conglomerate, Carey wound up working as the retail consultant for the first of four buildings that would become Embarcadero Center.

The office space in the first building at Embarcadero was almost entirely leased when he was hired in 1973, but the retail space on the first three floors was nearly vacant. Carey developed a master plan for that building and wound up as the retail consultant for the entire development and the adjoining Hyatt Hotel. From that base, Carey created his own company and capitalized on his success at Embarcadero and his background as a retailer to develop a lucrative business, with projects around the world.

Early in the development of Rincon Center, Randy Verrue had approached Carey about serving as the retail consultant for the project. When he got a look at Carey's fees, Verrue had decided not to hire him. Halcyon got the job instead. Then, when concerns were first raised about Halcyon's retail plan, Verrue had approached Carey again and asked if he would take on the job of leasing the retail space. Carey took a look at the Halcyon plan for an arcade through the development and said he was not interested.

Jay Mancini telephoned Carey in January of 1986 and invited him to lunch. There, the developer asked him what was wrong with Halcyon's plan.

"Jay, do you know the definition of an arcade?" asked Carey. "I'll tell you. An arcade is a connector between two vibrant streets. It is a 'through,' not a 'to.' This is a 'to' place, and so an arcade will not work, by definition."

Carey grabbed a napkin and sketched out his idea for how the retail space should be formed at Rincon Center. He drew pictures of two large public spaces, one in the atrium and the other in the courtyard. "These must be two museum-quality public spaces," he said. "You've got to make people want to come to the development."

Carey wanted to pull the storefronts way back from the edge of the atrium and create a space more in keeping with the traditional definition of an atrium courtyard. He did not want Johnson's sense of intimacy, but an open area where shoppers and diners would congregate. Mancini took the napkin and the ideas to Verrue and got the okay to hire Bob Carey to rework the retail layout. A few days later, Mancini, Topping, and Carey went to Los Angeles to present the concept to the architect. What they were carrying was more than a new retail plan, however; it was the seed for a major redesign of the atrium itself.

Unlike Mancini, Scott Johnson was not particularly impressed with Carey or his background. As he listened to his presentation, laced with stories of his earlier successes and his flawed definition of an arcade, Johnson began to view Carey as someone whose only concern was a theoretically correct plan for the retail space alone. He was not interested in the other functions that a successful mixed-use project must perform, and Johnson was deeply concerned that his proposals would damage the overall development. "Carey was a problem because he felt that he had a valid opinion on everything in life, and I didn't care much for that," Johnson said.

In his discussion that day, Carey criticized the Halcyon plan for creating stores with too much depth. He said retailers do not want long, narrow spaces; they want a location that offers lots of windows along the front to attract customers. Aligning the stores around a larger open space in the atrium, a space he kept referring to as "museum quality," would create shallower depths and more frontage to attract potential tenants, he said.

Mancini had long objected to the modern look of the atrium. His vision of the entire project had always been more subdued than that of his architect. He felt Johnson's design was too cold. He had bought a book with pictures of the great shopping arcades of Europe and found that they all had plenty of stone. He liked the richness of stone. And he saw in Bob Carey's suggestions a way to remake the entire atrium.

"San Franciscans have a European bias," Mancini said to Topping one day after the trip to Los Angeles. "The metal and glass might go well in San Diego, but it would be a bust in San Francisco."

The importance of the atrium to the success of the project was never underestimated in anyone's mind. That undoubtedly was one of the reasons that the wrangling over its design extended for months. Even Randy Verrue made certain he had his say about some elements of the atrium. He wanted a stone floor and he wanted balconies on all of the upper floors to provide tenants with the chance to enjoy the space. Not only would it make the building more attractive to tenants, but the balconies themselves could be counted as additional square footage in calculating rents.

In part, the final shape of the atrium at Rincon Center was the result of a market study. About the time of the Carey-initiated debate, a market study done for the developers concluded that the surrounding four-block area had a severe shortage of retail space. The survey used a rule of thumb that said twenty square feet of office space would support one square foot of retail space. In the neighborhood around Rincon, the survey found the ratio was 54 to 1. The reason for this skewed ratio was the economics of real estate development: with office rents rising, the surest money for developers in San Francisco in recent years had been building office buildings. Office leases were also a safer bet than retail rentals, since shops and restaurants tended to fold with more frequency. Assuming the pattern continued, the market study predicted that the shortage of retail space would increase sharply over the next fifteen years.

The lease with the Postal Service and the agreement with the redevelopment agency dictated that Rincon Center not be all offices. Both governmental agencies had sought a mix of uses for the space as part of the effort to revitalize the neighborhood. The Postal Service had gone so far as to impose restrictions in the lease that prohibited the developers from leasing a large enough single space in the old post office to attract the sort of anchor tenant that draws shoppers to a location, something such as a Saks Fifth Avenue or Nordstrom's. So, if the project was to take best advantage of the demand for retail space pointed out in the study, an alternative anchor or anchorlike concept had to be developed. Halcyon's fairly even mix between shops and restaurants certainly did not offer anything like an anchor. But the market study offered a suggestion: it proposed devoting a heavy proportion of the retail space at Rincon to restaurants and drinking establishments.

Various studies have shown over the years that office workers spend two out of every three retail dollars on food and drink. According to the Rincon study's calculations, the 20,000 workers already in the area were each spending an average of $1,530 a year on food and drink, a total of more than $30 million. That level of spending would support 130,000 square feet of restaurant space. But the market area at the time had only 40,000 square feet of restaurant space, and devoting half of Rincon's retail space to restaurants would add only another 40,000. So, even once Rincon was operating, there would still be a shortage of restaurant space and that should translate into high demand at Rincon. In addition, since the competing restaurants were spread out, the study predicted that Rincon could capture a market share in excess of its size by concentrating a large number of restaurants under one roof. Anyone who has ever gone to lunch with a group of colleagues can see the advantages of several types of fast-food restaurants under a single roof.

The use of food as an anchor fit neatly into Bob Carey's planning. He had explained to the developers that he felt their project was too small to compete head-on with the Embarcadero's 260,000 square feet of retail space. But Rincon's developers could create something that the much larger development lacked—a core of restaurants, a "critical mass of restaurants."

The idea made sense to Mancini and it had the reassuring advantage, to him, of matching the findings of his market study. So it was decided that food would become the anchor attraction for the atrium. And Topping and Carey reworked the retail floor plan to create a bustling food court, with lots of small ethnic restaurants where customers would buy their lunch over the counter and eat at tables in common dining areas.

This type of food service does not need as much space as sit-down restaurants because diners can share common eating areas, so Topping and Carey devised a new marketing plan and Johnson responded with a new floor plan. The new plan pulled the storefronts back from the edge of the atrium, tucking them under new, larger second-floor balconies. The retail space on the second floor was replaced by more offices. Since commercial space rents for less than retail, it would reduce the revenue flow a bit. But the results would concentrate activity on the ground floor. The plan would also avoid the higher failure rate associated with second-floor stores. Further, Johnson developed the concept of using raised seating areas in the common area to provide some definition to the space. But he balked when Topping and Carey wanted to replace his metal storefronts with wooden ones.

Scott Johnson disdains the use of the word *compromise* in describing the circumstances he faced in designing the atrium. "To most people, in an artistic way, compromise is de facto a negative term," he says. "I think, for complex projects in cities today, the design process has to accommodate participation."

His job, as he perceives it, is to listen to the client (and, in other instances, to the public agencies) and try to allow his architecture to grow out of their needs while still retaining the qualities he believes are essential to good design and function. So when Carey's new ideas for the atrium were adopted by Mancini and Topping, Johnson had figured that he had to listen carefully and make use of them.

The most difficult change for him to make was eliminating the glass curtain wall, which he thought brought zest and excitement to the atrium. Mancini had said he would like stone for the walls to evoke the feeling he'd had looking at the pictures from Europe. But as they discussed the costs it became clear that the budget had no room for material that expensive. So Johnson came up with the idea of substituting panels of gypsum board, which would be heavily rusticated and painted to give an illusion of depth and richness.

Johnson also was willing to recess the storefronts around the atrium and create the raised seating areas, which would provide an edge to the space. But he would insist on keeping the promenade along the wide hallway between the atrium and the rear of the post office, where it opened onto the courtyard. That would still provide the strong sense of longitudinal axis that Johnson felt was essential to tying the old building to the new one.

Throughout March and early April, he and Dianna Wong worked long hours revising the design and searching for elegant ways to illustrate the changes. On April 16, Mancini and Topping, accompanied by Bob Carey, returned to Pereira's office in Los Angeles to review the new concept. What they saw were four raised seating platforms, storefronts recessed beneath overhanging second-floor balconies that were supported by granite-clad pillars. The atrium itself was a much larger, airier open space extending up five stories to the giant skylight. The stores on the second floor had been replaced by offices. The walls were sketched to reflect the solid gypsum board, and glass had been restricted to large windows tinted light gray on the upper floors, with clear glass for the storefronts. All of the upper floors had recessed balconies. The coffers that defined the space by providing a symbolic lid were still in place.

The floor plan called for smaller spaces on the ground floor to accommodate a dozen small restaurants as well as a couple of larger areas for fancier dining accommodations. Around the edge of the atrium, beneath the second-floor balconies, space had been allotted for a series of murals to echo the Refregiers in the old lobby. Johnson suggested that an illuminated water fountain or figurative work of art could be placed in the center of the enlarged atrium.

Mancini and Topping both reacted positively to the changes. Mancini said he thought the design reflected the "Art Deco" feel of the historic lobby and the exterior of the building. He loved the walls. They would fit in the budget and, with the paint and rustication, someone would have to examine them awfully closely to see that they were not real sandstone. He liked the idea of a fountain, explaining that the white noise would help muffle conversations in the atrium. The background noise would also allow office workers to use the balconies for conferences and small meetings. Mancini, who had

Walls and seating were pulled back to create a more open atrium.

favored a fountain from the start, particularly admired the one in Boston's Copley Place, and he wanted to fly Johnson out there to see how it had been done.

For Johnson, the Rincon atrium perfectly fitted his definition of what a contemporary architect does. The world no longer was a place where an architect could design a building in the solitude of his studio and impose it on the public or the owner. Public forces, embodied in the redevelopment agency and the downtown plan, were shaping Rincon Center. And the debate over the atrium was a clear illustration of the role of the owner, though Johnson certainly wished for a more decisive owner. But the process reflected his belief in the direction architecture was headed.

"The execution of architecture at the highest level, the most serious level, is no longer a solo performance," said Johnson. "It is truly choreographic. It is an orchestral performance. I see the process more in terms of a moving target, of identifying influences that will impact on the design. One of them may be Jay Mancini. One may be Randy Verrue. One will be the city of San Francisco. A very important one will be me. Another will be the talents and limitations of my staff."

In a sense, this is also an old-fashioned definition of architecture and it reflects Johnson's grounding in classical interpretations. The word *architect* is derived from ancient Greek. As the archbishop was the top bishop, so was the *architekton* the chief *tekton*, meaning he was the chief carpenter. There can be little doubt the carpenter took his instructions from the building's owner. The idea that the architect was designing to please himself or his muse would certainly have seemed misguided to the Greek-trained Roman architect Marcus Vitruvius Pollio, who wrote the first known architectural treatise. He dedicated it to the emperor Augustus, on whom he relied for patronage.

So then, the practice of designing a building to respond to the broad demands of its owners need not seem extraordinary. The trick in the case of a project as complicated as Rincon, a project with as many influences as Rincon, was finding a way of doing so that retained, or even enhanced, the elegance and usefulness of Scott Johnson's original conception.

"You have to let information come as it comes, and it takes months really for it to happen," said Johnson. "Of course, that doesn't mean that you don't start with the Big Bang theory. You want to start with a big idea or a series of ideas and see which one works, which one gets seventy-five or eighty-five percent of it right. And you may spend the next two years getting the other twenty percent or so to work."

The atrium had changed substantially from the original concept of Johnson, Dianna Wong, and the other designers who had worked on that part of the project. And it would change more before it was completed. The four raised seating areas would be refined by the addition of wide edges so that people could sit along them, a variation on the steps of Italian piazzas. The platforms would be gracefully rounded and the shape would echo the second-floor balconies. Balconies and small decks would be recessed into the upper floors to enhance the interior views for office workers and play up the atrium. Johnson also had persuaded Mancini that Ron Tutor's idea of using plastic for the atrium skylight was a very bad solution. He pointed out that even high-quality, thick plastic would have a tendency to warp slightly through the constant exposure to the elements. While the warp might not be visible, it would break the seal and result in leaks that would be quite visible, and quite expensive to repair. (This can, of course, also be a problem with glass when the frames themselves warp.)

Final decisions on many of the other matters were months away, and there would be plenty of discordant notes in between. Even at the design meeting in Los Angeles that April 16, Carey objected to what he perceived to be a lack of space for signs for the storefronts. Too, he said he wanted to have new entrances created by cutting into the lobby walls so that the space would be opened up for shoppers.

But Mancini and Topping were satisfied that they finally had the basic plan for the atrium. They instructed Johnson to create the additional drawings to show Chin & Hensolt where the demolition crew would cut the floors. P. Q. Chin would be happy, too, because the opening for the atrium was larger than had been planned. The old post office was going to lose more weight.

Near the end of the meeting that day, Harry Topping raised another issue briefly. He almost forgot to bring it up at all. Most of the design attention had focused on two places, the atrium and the exterior of the new towers. Topping had been reviewing the floor plans for the new apartments, and he thought some of the layouts looked cramped. Also, beams seemed to be cutting across some of the ceilings in odd places. He wondered whether these apartments would rent for the premium prices that Perini hoped to get for them. He wondered whether it might be a good idea to have a housing consultant take a more serious look at the floor plans before the process moved much further.

Scott Johnson had just solved a major design problem. He had little interest in launching another battle. Johnson was principally a designer and much of his work went on in the imagination. Yet he believed firmly that the architect's vision was not the end but the start of his job. Equally important to the proper performance of his job was orchestrating the execution of the design ideas. Since his experience in laying out high-density, multifamily housing was limited, he had assigned the primary supervision of the floor plans to Chuck Grein, a senior architect at the firm who had experience with multifamily housing. Johnson, however, had constantly reviewed every step of the design work.

Johnson felt that the results, which had been approved by Jay Mancini months earlier, met the standards set forth by the developers. Perhaps the problems that Topping was now raising actually lay in those standards.

When the apartment floor plans were approved by Mancini in late 1985, the budget was already under assault. The developer had responded by trying to cut costs by reducing the size of the apartments. Building codes specify minimum room sizes for apartments, and Johnson told Mancini that the smallest legal standards for rooms were those of the federal Department of Housing and Urban Development. Johnson had cautioned Mancini that the sizes were probably too small to bring top rents on the market. But the developer said he felt the project would provide other amenities to compensate for the size.

As he sat and listened to Topping's assessment, it occurred to Johnson that perhaps Mancini had not had the time to really assess whether the small apartments would be rentable at premium prices. But making any changes at this point would be very expensive and very disruptive.

15

FROM INEVITABLE
TO IMPOSSIBLE

Later, it would seem to a few that they had been dancing on a grave. But at the time, no one knew a calamity was waiting on the next page of the calendar. Only bright hopes seemed called for on the first Thursday of April in 1986 as fifty or so brokers from Paine Webber arrived in San Francisco, wives and girlfriends in tow, for two days of partying and presentations on the attractions of Rincon Center. It was a grand kickoff for the coming syndication.

All of the brokers were men, and most of them had experience selling units of syndications put together by Boston Financial Group. This party was as much a thank-you for work done as an incentive for work to be done. Boston Financial was picking up the tab, which included round-trip airfare for two and a room at the Westin St. Francis Hotel on Union Square. Plus, in accordance with the tradition of these affairs, each person was given $50 cash as walking-around money.

On Thursday night, the brokers, suspenders and yellow ties predominating, were feted at a catered dinner at a private mansion rented for the occasion. They listened as Jim Hughes, the lead principal on the deal at Boston Financial, outlined the financial aspects of the syndication, and as Randy Verrue from Perini L&D described the project itself. It also was opening night for the videotape of Rincon highlights, which had been prepared by Boston Financial and featured Scott Johnson and others discussing the architectural and financial aspects of the development.

But the centerpiece of the trip came on Friday. Demolition was in high gear at the post office building. Dust was everywhere and the noise level was high, especially for people accustomed to the rustle of paper and the blips of a Quotron machine. Workmen with sledgehammers were knocking down interior partitions and others were erecting the temporary shoring to stabilize the structure. Portions of the second and third floors had been removed in the center of the building. On the other end of the lot, the old post office docks and some storage sheds had been been removed, and bulldozers had recently begun the preliminary excavation for the thirty-foot hole that would be the starting point of the new building.

Donning the obligatory hard hats, the brokers were led in groups of ten or so through the post office building, picking their way among the workmen and piles of debris. Pieces of twisted steel rebar stuck out of walls and the floor where sections of concrete had been smashed away. Standing in the center of what would be the atrium, they could look up three stories through a narrow hole that would ultimately be extended through the new stories, widened and shaped into the atrium. Canvas tarps were nailed over the doorways to the lobby to protect the murals that lined the walls there. The guides for the day were Jay Mancini and Harry Topping, who provided a running technical commentary and shared their visions of how the grime would be transformed to glitz.

After the tour, the brokers were taken to the roof of a nearby parking garage. From there they could see the sparkling bay and the graceful span of the bridge to Oakland and imagine the same view from the offices and apartments of Rincon Center.

"Everybody got to dream a lot," said Boston Financial's Bruce Kiernan, one of the trip organizers.

Chances are the dreams that day were not so much blue, as in bay view, but green, as in money. The brokers would collect a commission of more than seven grand for each of the units they sold to investors at $96,600 a piece. Multiplied by 400 units and divided among the fifty or so brokers there that day, that amounted to serious money.

The thick prospectus outlining the financial terms was not available yet, but each broker was given a twelve-page summary of the offering. The first page of the summary listed five highlights of the deal. These emphasized the location of the development, the experience of Perini Land & Development, the projected tax benefits, the favorable construction financing, and the investor protections provided by the developer, including the promise to cover all costs through 1989. According to the summary, construction was scheduled for completion on the post office by July 1987, and on the new building by January 1988. The document also provided instructions for customers to wire the first installment, $7,300, to the First National Bank of Boston after they received the official offering documents.

The brokers were confident there would be little trouble selling the Rincon deal. The project sounded like a winner. The numbers worked from a tax standpoint. And the syndication market was hot. Sales of tax shelters had risen to phenomenal levels by 1986. Hundreds of private sales made coming up with exact figures impossible, but tax-shelter sales were believed to have jumped from under $2 billion in 1976 to nearly $25 billion in 1985.

While the variations on these shelters were many, the basic structure was to bundle together several different tax incentives, such as credits for rehabilitating buildings, interest deductions, rapid depreciation write-offs, and low capital-gains rates. In 1986, investors were putting their money in horse-breeding farms, oil and gas wells, coal mines, movies, and research-and-development projects. A group of dentists in California put up thousands of dollars each to finance a three-year project designed to determine whether a jojoba bean plant is female and therefore capable of producing more beans. The scheme drew a scathing denunciation from California Congressman Fortney "Pete" Stark, who said, "We shouldn't be giving tax breaks to anything that takes three years to figure out its sex."

But the most popular shelters were real estate partnerships. Under these schemes, investors made relatively small individual contributions to a project through a syndication, and the developer borrowed the rest of the money. The partnership would turn the interest deductions and the accelerated depreciation write-offs into huge paper losses, which were divided among the investors and written off on their individual tax returns. These were known generically as "passive" losses because the taxpayers did not play an active role in the business. When the building was finally sold, the income would be taxed at what was then a low 20 percent capital-gains rate. It was all legal, and it was virtually unbeatable.

These tax schemes had altered the economics of commercial real estate. As with Rincon Center, they made it possible for developers to build new buildings even when demand was soft. They also had drastically altered the income-tax patterns of the country and cost the treasury billions of dollars. A 1985 study prepared by the Treasury Department for Texas Congressman J. J. Pickle found that in 1983 alone, 30,000 taxpayers with earnings of more than $250,000 paid less than 5 percent of their income in taxes. Three thousand of those taxpayers were millionaires. And all of them were the targets of tax syndicators.

There was a similar pattern among big businesses. Over the previous three decades, U.S. corporations were paying an ever-decreasing share of the nation's tax bill. From just over 25 percent in the 1950s, the corporate contribution to government revenues had declined to a little over 6 percent in 1983. Some of the most profitable corporations in America had found ways to pay little or no corporate taxes.

Confidence in the tax system had been undermined by the antics of corporations and individuals alike. But at least the corporations could argue that they were providing jobs in exchange for the benefits. Rich people had few such defenses and their tax-shelter scams seemed to be the larger irritant to the average taxpayer. People saw themselves subsidizing the rich life-styles of wealthy Americans with well-paid accountants and clever tax lawyers who exploited the loopholes. And their sentiments were showing up in public-opinion polls and congressional mailbags. Little wonder that rumblings about tax reform in Congress were loudest when it came to tax shelters for the wealthy.

"The people who Congress saw as being the biggest pigs at the trough, from the political point of view, were the high-income individuals who were paying low shares of their income as taxes," acknowledged Kiernan, the syndicator.

Tax reform was on the front pages of the nation's newspapers almost daily during the first months of 1986, as congressional leaders struggled to devise a system that would redress what many viewed as the wrongs of the rich. The House of Representatives had passed a tax-reform package shortly before Christmas. But the Senate had yet to come up with its legislation, and the $300-an-hour lobbyists representing businesses and special interests were sure that the conservative upper body would not approve any radical changes.

It was expected that the powerful real estate lobby would flex enough political muscle to stave off any serious damage to rules governing tax shelters, which had become so important to its members. Indeed, when House Democrats had floated a trial balloon suggesting a prohibition on the use of passive losses to offset other taxable income, the idea was shot down quickly by the industry and the proposal not included in the House legislation.

In Boston that spring, Jim Hughes and Bruce Kiernan were keeping a close eye on the newspapers and having regular conversations with lawyers and lobbyists in Washington to get a behind-the-scenes reading. Nothing that they heard really alarmed the executives at Boston Financial. The conventional wisdom still prevailed: the Senate Finance Committee, which had willingly created many of the tax breaks in the first place, would keep reforms bottled up. Concerns were even less serious when it came to the pending Rincon offering, since changes in the tax law always provided a period for grandfathering in deals in the works. However, since their livelihoods depended in large measure on the tax laws, Hughes and Kiernan could not afford to ignore the debate.

Not far outside Boston, at the corporate headquarters of Perini Corporation in Framingham, tax reform was even less troubling to the executives. In the middle of March, John Schwarz, Perini Land & Development's chief financial officer, seemed to sum up the attitude when he told Tom Steele, the firm's chief executive officer: "It looks like tax reform is dead. The members of Congress are too busy squabbling among themselves."

All of this changed over the weekend of April 26–27. Staff members from the major tax-writing committees in Congress—Senate Finance, House Ways and Means, and Joint Committee on Taxation—gathered in a cramped room on the House side of the Capitol. Their job was to reach a series of compromises that would overcome the factionalism and bickering, the influence of special interests, and the self-interest of the various congressmen. Their job was to assemble the pieces of a plan that would lead to the biggest tax reform in decades.

A key element of this plan was an assault on tax shelters that would prohibit using passive losses to offset taxable income from any other sources. For instance, the plastic surgeon in Beverly Hills would no longer be able to shelter income from his practice through an interest in a horse-breeding farm in Kentucky or an office building in Albuquerque.

The concept was virtually the same as the House version, which had been torpedoed by the real estate lobby earlier. But this time there was a crucial difference. The elimination of passive-loss provisions would be linked to a reduction in the maximum income-tax rate to somewhere around 25 percent. The centerpiece of tax-reform efforts had been simplifying the tax-rate structure by reducing the number of brackets and bringing down the maximum rate, then 50 percent.

Those supporting the reduction, such as Senator Bob Packwood, the Oregon Republican who was chairman of the Senate Finance Committee, wanted a maximum rate somewhere in the twenties. But that would be a great windfall for the rich. So, to make the reduction palatable to the Democrats in Congress and to the public, there had to be a means for offsetting the tax benefits for the wealthy. Eliminating tax shelters, a prominent symbol of inequity, had the political advantage of appearing to hurt wealthy people exclusively and blunting the size of the tax break they would receive through the rate reduction.

Shortly after midnight on May 7, the Senate Finance Committee voted 20 to 0 to approve a proposal for legislation that would eliminate the passive-loss provisions for wealthy individuals and reduce the maximum income-tax rate to 27 percent. The actual legislation had not been drawn up and it would have to be approved by the full Senate, a conference committee of members from both the House and Senate, and signed by the president. But the proposal broke the logjam over tax reform. The curtain was about to fall on the magic show of tax shelters.

The timing could hardly have been worse for Rincon Center. By early May, the syndication was nearly sold out. Investors had indeed found the package attractive, and more than 300 of the 400 units had been purchased since the offering hit the streets two weeks earlier. However, the syndication would not be finalized until all of the units were sold. Even then, the investors had the right to vote on whether to cancel the transaction and get their money back. Tax reform was going to throw everything off course, though even then no one knew just how far awry things would go.

Tom Steele at Perini L&D and Jim Hughes at Boston Financial agreed that the best course was to move ahead with the final sales and closing of the offering as quickly as possible. The tax lawyers would come up with new language to insert into the offering to protect the investors in the event the law changed and made the investment less attractive. Unconsidered was the possibility it would become completely unattractive.

Two main hopes were keeping the deal alive, along with the sort of wishful thinking bred when millions of dollars hang in the balance. First, changes in U.S. tax laws had never been retroactive. If they could get the deal done in time, it would be grandfathered in under the old rules and the passive-loss provisions would be retained. The deal could be adjusted to reflect changes in the tax rate that would reduce the benefits to the investors. Steele had innumerable conversations with auditors, lawyers, and tax specialists during late April and May. The experts were unanimous in assuring him that the law would not be retroactive. Second, even if the worst occurred and the new rules were applied to existing deals as the Senate Finance proposal suggested, Steele was told that it was likely that Congress would approve no more than a slight reduction in the tax rate and some restrictions on shelters. Again, adjustments could be made to keep the deal alive.

The most likely scenario in the minds of those connected with Rincon was that the loss provisions would be grandfathered in but the deal would have to be restructured to reflect a reduction in the income-tax rate. This meant investors would have to be offered a stronger financial return to make up the difference in lost tax benefits. This money would come out of the pockets of the developer, but there still seemed to be plenty of room to maneuver.

A memo drafted by tax lawyers for Boston Financial and dated May 30 explained how it could work if the maximum tax rate was cut to 27 percent in the Senate proposal. The capital required from each investor would be reduced to $92,549 from $96,600. At the same time, each investor's share of the eventual proceeds from operating income and the anticipated sale of the development would be increased by $37,456, to be effected by reducing the amount due the developers. This meant less money upfront for Perini and more payouts down the road. But there was enough cushion for the deal still to work for the developers.

Other developers across the country took the prospects of substantial tax reform more seriously. Or they at least decided some insurance was warranted. Dozens of developers persuaded friendly congressmen on the tax-writing committees to stick language into the final law that would specifically exempt their current projects from the changes. This was an arcane, but far from secret, practice and Tom Steele discussed taking that route with other executives at Perini and at Boston Financial. But they decided it was unnecessary. They were certain the project would be grandfathered in.

The final version of the Tax Reform Act of 1986 was approved by the House on September 25 and by the Senate two days later, in a rare Saturday session. President Reagan signed the bill on the South Lawn of the White House on October 22, marking the single most sweeping change in the history of the nation's income tax. In his speech at the signing ceremony, Reagan mentioned a *Washington Post* headline that he felt summed up the months of work in which tax reform had gone from a long shot to a sure shot: "The Impossible Became the Inevitable."

The top tax bracket would be lowered in phases to 28 percent. To balance the decrease, tax breaks for the rich were swept away with the signing, including the passive-loss provision for tax shelters. This unprecedented overhaul of the tax code also took the unprecedented step of making the law retroactive to January 1, 1986. Astonishingly, there would be no grace period for the billions of dollars in tax-driven deals in the works, no grandfathering. In fact, the new restrictions would cover tax benefits from 1986 forward on deals that had been set up years before. The spigot was turned off tightly and immediately.

There were cries of protest from all sorts of special-interest groups and criticisms that Congress had hurt more than just wealthy individuals. Some of the squawks were justified. For example, the new law slashed the tax credit for the rehabilitation of old and historic buildings. Now, only $7,000 a year in tax credits would be available to individuals, and severe restrictions were imposed on the availability of the credits to people with gross incomes of $200,000 a year or more.

The historic tax credit had been enacted by Congress to encourage the revitalization of the nation's older commercial areas and historic residential neighborhoods. And, despite the inevitable abuses that seem to accompany any tax regulation, it was working. The number of historic buildings rehabilitated under the law had been rising steadily since the late 1970s. In 1985, the figure hit a record high as more than 3,100 historic buildings were renovated using the tax credits. Not all of these projects were megadeals like Rincon. Indeed, in fighting to save the tax credit in the spring of 1986, the National Trust for Historic Preservation had argued passionately that most of the buildings using the tax credit were in small towns. But the scaffolding propping up the tax-reform package had been so fragile that removing any single piece might have brought the entire structure down. So the historic tax credit went the way of other tax shelters.

"Congress decided to eradicate a problem with a massive nuclear attack which killed not only the enemy but the wildlife and good things as well," Gerald Portney, a tax specialist with the accounting firm KPMG Peat Marwick, would later say.

For Rincon Center, a variation of the *Washington Post* headline might have been in order. The financing deal that seemed inevitable now looked impossible.

Bruce Kiernan was stunned. "Frankly, we couldn't believe that what was passed was coming," he lamented after the measure was signed. "It really was unprecedented. We expected some alternatives, rates cut and benefits reduced. But there would still be a way to make this a good investment. By stripping out all of the tax benefits, that option was not open to us."

Boston Financial Group had invested more than $750,000 in the syndication, paying for such expenses as tax and legal advice, evaluations by accountants, printing costs, and the party in San Francisco. So they wanted desperately to salvage some sort of transaction. Indeed, the entire syndication industry was on the verge of collapse. Stunned investors were demanding their money back on earlier deals or refusing to pay future installments. Syndication firms everywhere were scrambling to save sinking deals and come up with strategies to confront the new tax environment. Most were destined to fail.

Perini L&D also had plenty of incentive for finding a way to raise money from outside investors. Their alternatives were limited and each was potentially costly. They could bring in a new partner to provide fresh money. They could come up with the additional money themselves. They could try to sell the entire project to another developer at that point. Or they could persuade Citibank to lend them the additional money. This last was an unlikely prospect: Perini had not yet put any real cash of its own into the project, so the bank would probably not be willing to put up more of theirs. It was also the most appealing to Perini.

"We probably could not have sold the project to someone else because we had guaranteed the post office that we would be the ones to finish it," Randy Verrue later recalled. "Getting more money out of our own pockets would have meant other projects could not be funded. A financial partner would want their money at the least amount of risk. It seemed better to complete it yourself and sell it yourself. And, of course, try to get Citibank to up the loan amount."

First, however, there was another stab at offering the deal to investors on a strictly economic basis. The problem with that was that the project was expected to operate at a deficit for a number of years, partly because of the soft market but largely because all large commercial projects do so. That meant returns on the investment would not be generated for years, and that made the deal much more speculative. It soon became clear to everyone that the idea would not sell.

To bring in outside investors, there would have to be some sort of tax hook. So the financiers at Boston Financial decided to restructure the offering around the surviving historic tax credits. But they could only be used by individuals with incomes under $200,000 a year as a result of tax reform. The original syndication had been directed at people with incomes of $250,000 or more. It would not have been regulated by the Securities and Exchange Commission, since it was offered to wealthy investors who were believed by the SEC to be sophisticated enough to protect themselves from a scam. This new offering, however, would have to be registered with the federal agency and examined by the regulators for fairness since it was going to investors who earned less and were therefore considered less able to protect themselves. The new offering would be called a registered placement, and the process was costlier than an unregistered syndication because underwriters and lawyers would have to attest to the

SEC that it was a sound investment. But that was only one of the problems with it.

The numbers for the placement proposal illustrate how drastically the tax legislation had altered the economics of Rincon Center, and how dramatically the landscape of financing had changed for real estate developers across the country. This time around, the plan called for raising $39.6 million from outside investors. But the units would be reduced to $5,000 each, with a minimum investment of four units, or $20,000. The projected tax credits were confined to the first three years of the deal and amounted to $4,155 in 1987, $276 in 1988, and $249 in 1989. The total tax benefit was a paltry $4,680.

Since this was clearly not to be a tax-driven transaction, the developer had to promise the investors a quicker return on their money. Cash distributions were guaranteed to investors by the developer at a rate of 7 percent in 1987, minus the value of the tax credit. These payments would begin even if the post office renovation was not finished; if there was no revenue, the payments would have to come out of Perini's pocket. The distribution rate was set at 8 percent in 1988 and 1989, also minus the tax credit. In following years, the projected cash distributions were expected to increase from 8.1 percent to 17.2 percent by 1999. Under the projected benefits, investors could expect to receive cash distributions totaling $19,105 each between 1987 and 1999, a far cry from the six-figure tax deductions and hefty tax credits available under the old law.

For Perini, the economics of the offering also changed in a dramatic way. Since the project was not expected to generate a profit until at least 1993, the cash distributions were going to rely heavily on loans to the partnership from the developer, particularly in the early years. As part of the new offering, Perini agreed to loan the development itself more than $22 million to cover projected operating deficits and shortfalls in the cash distributions. Plus, the developer had to pledge 95 percent of the proceeds from the eventual sale to the investors compared with 89 percent under the previous deal.

The economics of the new deal left Tom Steele uneasy, and the uncertainty was echoed by the board of directors of Perini Corporation. The company would be on the hook for substantial cash payments for years. The deal would be a hard sell.

The collapse of the original syndication had brought with it new pressures for Randy Verrue in San Francisco. Bob Mayer at Citibank had questioned him repeatedly about where Perini planned to come up with its $25 million cash equity. The project had not reached the $25 million limit on what could be drawn down on the loan before the company put in its equal amount. But Mayer wanted to be certain that something was underway, particularly since he had been hearing ominous reports about the excavation for the new building.

16

THE $6 MILLION HOLE

Beginnings are auspicious moments. Cultures throughout history have begun the practical work of construction by consulting providence or enacting an appropriate ritual. Elaborate ceremonies were observed from the earliest days of Roman civilization and long before that among the dynasties of China. To this day, Hindus honor the start of a building by having a holy man dig a hole at the corner of the foundation and place in it objects of religious and spiritual significance, such as water from the Ganges, grains, and spices. This ceremony is used not only for homes but for office and apartment buildings, too.

There was no ritual or appeal to spirits to mark the start of the excavation for the new building at Rincon Center. Just a bulldozer grinding off the first layer of earth. Our society has become too pragmatic for such practices. It is too bad. They could have used all the help they could get in digging the hole for Rincon Center.

The foundation excavation would dig about thirty feet into the ground, the equivalent of three stories. The reason for going down was to build the foundation on more stable soil, although the stability of the soil at this location was poor at any reasonable depth. The excavation also automatically reduces the distance that the pilings supporting the foundation must be driven. Once the excavation was completed, test borings could be made to determine the precise stability of the underlying soil in the locations selected for the hundreds of pilings that would support the new foundation.

Digging a hole that covers half a city block is expensive. The excavation itself was expected to cost about $800,000. The shoring to support the sides of the hole was budgeted at $660,000, and buying and driving the pilings was pegged at $1.2 million.

The asphalt that covered the site when it was a parking lot for postal employees and trucks had been removed in March 1986 as part of the early demolition work on the project. In the following weeks, a wooden fence was erected around the site to keep the inevitable gawkers at bay and some preliminary surface excavation work had begun. During the early stage, archeologists had worked alongside the excavation crew and their finds, while not amounting to a major discovery, brought to life a chapter in San Francisco history.

An opium tin and ceramic pipe bowl were recovered from a location along the Steuart Street side of the site, where one of the city's more than 2,000 Chinese laundries had stood in the 1880s. Garment fragments, a clothes iron, and two cakes of soap were also recovered from the location. Elsewhere, the diggers found a decorative hair comb stamped with the date 1851, a Hohner harmonica of brass and wood, a child's writing slate, pieces of a porcelain doll, and dozens of ceramic pots, pitchers, and dishes. Unlike the better-known and much more rowdy Barbary Coast area of San Francisco's waterfront days, Yerba Buena Cove had been a bit more family oriented.

The early excavation also turned up the remains of a major wharf near the old post office building on the Steuart Street side of the site. The wooden pilings extended forty feet or so into the ground, marking the time when the site was under water and part of the cove. After a brief consultation with the general contractor's job foreman, the decision was made to extract the pilings by wrapping chains around the top and pulling them out with the bulldozers. To the amazement of the workers, 300 pilings were laid out along the edge of the old building and out into the vacant portion of the site. The pilings, which were about twelve inches square, were yanked out over a period of several days and the holes left unfilled.

Withdrawing a handful of pilings from their century-old homes in the ground this way could have been done without endangering the stability of the soil. But proper procedure in the extraction of so many required that some sort of grout be pumped into the holes so the stability of the soil would not be disturbed. Otherwise, the soil moves in to fill the vacuum created by pulling so many plugs and the result is instability. It would be weeks, however, before the effects were noticed. By then, the soil was causing plenty of other problems.

By May of 1986, the bulldozers and backhoes were beginning to excavate the main hole. Dump trucks roared out of the deepening pit, hauling away tons of the rubble-filled dirt and soft bay mud. As the hole deepened, sixteen workers from the Bridge, Wharf and Dock Builders Union welded steel beams and braces in place to support a wooden wall. The combined structure of the walls and the temporary steel supports is called shoring.

The obvious function of shoring is to keep the sides of the pit from caving in. Equally important, however, is maintaining the stability of the ground surrounding the excavation. If one side of the Rincon pit caved in, it could pull down the street and possibly destabilize the ground under neighboring buildings. A massive, unseen network of utility cables and sewer and water lines runs beneath the streets of every major city. Disturbing the soil around them could cause breaks that would disrupt entire city blocks.

The structural engineering and shoring design for the excavation was subcontracted to a San Francisco firm, Shapiro Okino Hom and Associates. Once the hole was dug and the shoring in place, the number and placement of the new pilings would be done by Lee & Praszker, the firm that had evaluated the pilings supporting the old post office and had examined soil conditions for dozens of buildings along the San Francisco waterfront over the past four decades. Its engineers were intimately familiar with the risks associated with excavations involving layers of rubble-filled soil and bay mud. While he believed it was outside his contract, Michael Praszker had offered the developers some advice based on his experience.

A hole three stories deep and half a block in size is excavated in sections. Usually the bulldozers and trucks work from the center out. As they get to what will be the edges, they are followed by the workers who install the shoring to keep the sides from moving in or, in the worst cases, collapsing. Praszker said the sides of the hole should be excavated in a staggered pattern, digging out a space in one spot, then skipping a space of equal width before digging out again. These spaces are known as "windows." The widths of the windows should be no more than forty feet, he said, and there should be at least as much distance between the windows. Shoring should be built to stabilize the window before further digging was done next to it. He also said that the earth berms that would remain in place as additional, passive support for the lower section of the pit while the shoring was being built should not be cut at too sharp an angle. The lower the angle, the more support the berm would provide. This all was a slower method than simply digging away huge chunks and leaving steep berms, but it would minimize the risk of soil movement.

On July 17, Michael Majchrzak, an engineer with Lee & Praszker, visited the excavation site to get ready to drive the first piles. As the excavation had been planned, a portion of the hole would be stabilized so that the initial piles could be driven before the remainder of the hole was completed, to save time. But what he saw disturbed him. The digging was proceeding in a manner that he felt was potentially dangerous. The bulldozers and huge mechanical shovels were carving out broad expanses on the wall, much larger than forty feet. The earth berms appeared too steep to provide the necessary stability. Both instances of what Majchrzak viewed as potential problems, the larger windows and the steeper berms, were the result of an effort to proceed as fast as possible on the excavation.

Majchrzak returned to the office and wrote a memo to Steve Sabo, the foreman on the construction project for Tutor-Saliba. He cautioned Sabo that similar methods at a nearby site with almost the same soil conditions had resulted in soil movement that caused long delays. "In our opinion if the current excavation procedures continue at the site the results will be similar," warned Majchrzak. He also asked for a meeting at the site to explain the potential problems.

A few days later, Sabo met with Richard Rodgers, the senior engineer on the project for Lee & Praszker. Rodgers described his company's concerns to Sabo and urged him to change the techniques. As they inspected the edges of the excavation along both Spear and Steuart streets, Rodgers pointed out the small fissures that indicated soil movement and warned that they would grow unless the proper steps were taken. Sabo seemed to agree with Rodgers and promised to take up the issue with John Costello, the developer's construction manager for the project.

Every developer should have an on-staff construction manager with extensive experience in the field work of the business. Usually the manager will have spent years as a foreman with a big general contracting firm, so he will be familiar with every aspect of what it takes to make a construction job go smoothly and efficiently. If a job falls behind schedule somewhere, or part of the budget is out of whack, the construction manager's job is to raise holy hell until the problem gets fixed. The concept is the same as a barking dog.

John Costello had been hired a few weeks earlier as the barking dog on Rincon Center. He had supervised public-works construction projects for the state of Oregon, but this complex project was his first job managing a major development in the private sector. Along with helping Jay Mancini and Harry Topping cope with the burgeoning scope of the project, Costello was supposed to keep a sharp eye on the construction costs and report directly to Randy Verrue. While there still was no final budget figure, the estimates were climbing and Perini L&D was concerned enough to offer Costello an unusual incentive. At the end of the project, he would be paid a bonus based on a percentage of the amount he could demonstrate had been saved by his direct actions.

Perhaps because he was new to the job, perhaps because he was pressured by the delays that had set back the construction schedule before he even arrived, Costello wanted the excavation to proceed as fast as possible. So the news that Steve Sabo brought him was highly unwelcome. Nonetheless, Costello met with Rodgers.

"I don't like your method of excavation and I'll tell you more," Rodgers said to Costello. "We are not experts in excavation. You are not experts in excavation. You never worked with mud. Your assistants never worked with mud. I know shit-all about digging and you do, too. You better get yourself an engineer who knows something about it."

Costello agreed to consult with the engineers from Shapiro Okino Hom, who had designed the shoring to support the walls and existing streets, and he discussed the issue with Jay Mancini. They saw no need to stop the excavation, but they did agree to some modifications in hopes of resolving the difficulties. The degree of incline would be reduced on the new earthen berms in an attempt to stabilize the lower part of the hole's sides. Dirt would be hauled back to the site to add to some of the berms that had been dug already. And the shoring would be redesigned and strengthened through the addition of more support beams and braces. Meanwhile, however, Costello wanted to go ahead with plans to drive the first piles in sections of the holes that were ready.

Larry Barr, a foreman on one of the two eight-man welding crews on the job, had spent twenty-five years erecting shoring and performing other structural work. He had seen the minor soil movements at Rincon and recognized the potential for a big problem. "The ground around there is pretty fluid," he said. "If it moves an inch, then you are in trouble because it kinda turns to jelly and everything is on the move and escalates. You have got to redo everything in the shoring and stiffen it up and make adjustments. We doubled up on a lot of beams and put in extra struts."

Even after the modifications, Richard Rodgers told Costello that he was not certain the method would succeed. He cautioned the construction manager again that his firm was not a qualified excavation contractor, but had only agreed to review the techniques to avoid foreseeable problems.

The modifications did not work. Between the latter part of July and the middle of August, the soil movement continued along the Spear and Steuart sides of the excavation. The actual movement could not been seen on a daily basis, but within a period of less than three weeks, the weakening walls had pushed the wooden sheeting in about five inches from the edges of the pits. The hole was slowly collapsing. The soil movement had created small fissures along the edges of the excavation that were spreading back toward Spear and Steuart streets. Among the areas where the soil movement was most severe was the edge nearest the spot where the 300 timber pilings from the old wharf had been removed.

In the middle of August, Michael Praszker went to the site to examine the movement himself. The excavation was continuing on expanses wider than forty feet and workers were now erecting shoring twenty-five feet below the surface. Praszker was alarmed. He feared that huge sheets of earthen wall could come tumbling down, and he immediately summoned Jay Mancini.

"Jay, I'm afraid this is going to collapse on men," he said. "I order you to bring that soil back."

Praszker realized that he was overstepping his expertise and his authority, and perhaps inviting trouble down the road. "Jay, you know what I am doing. This is not my domain. I am not a structural engineer. I am a soil engineer. My wife is going to throw me out for going on a limb this way."

"Mike, old friend, we are all one family," Praszker later remembered Mancini saying that day. "Nobody sues anybody."

Up until this point, Mancini had devoted most of his attention to the continuing decisions on the design of the development. He, too, had been reluctant to call a major halt to the excavation and investigate the need for a total redesign of the shoring. He had, for the most part, relied on Costello. But Praszker's alarm infected him. He held an emergency meeting with Costello, Sabo, and Dennis Oh, from Chin & Hensolt. The decision was made that lives should not be risked. Men were pulled from the hole. Dirt was hauled back in to reinforce the walls along the east and west perimeters of the site, where the movement was worst. While the excavation was halted, the shoring was reinforced once again. This process stopped progress on the excavation for several days, but it seemed to work. There was no discernible movement for more than a month and a half.

By the end of September, the excavation was nearing its completion. In the rush to make up for the time already lost, wider sections were being dug out again. On September 29, Dennis Oh wrote a memo to Costello and Sabo urging them to narrow the opening, as Lee & Praszker had recommended. A few days later, the walls moved again, buckling shoring near the top of the hole and sending jagged cracks through the sidewalks on both Steuart and Spear streets. A handful of new pilings had been driven in a small portion of the excavation. When the sides of the hole moved, the movement rotated the soil at the bottom of the excavation, too, bending the pilings and essentially making them useless. They would have to be replaced. Some medium-size water lines beneath the streets cracked. There was a fear that major sewer and natural-gas lines would rupture. The concrete piling that held up one of the cast-iron sewer lines beneath Howard Street had to be replaced to prevent the line from shifting and breaking. The hole was evacuated again, and this time the delay would last longer and be very expensive.

Further excavation was delayed until the shoring could be modified once more and additional tests could be run on the soil conditions. Because of the new fears over soil stability, the entire foundation structure for the new building had to be redesigned to incorporate stronger elements and more concrete than originally planned. Work on the new portion of the project came to a virtual halt that lasted for weeks. Costs were mounting.

Eventually, the developers would break out what they said were the additional costs resulting from the problem-plagued excavation. Pulling out the old timbers without backfilling the holes had forced a redesign of the foundation in that specific area to incorporate additional pilings and beams to tie them together. The cost was estimated at $400,000. The failure of the shoring system itself, with the resulting additional work on design, reinforcing the shoring, and redoing the excavation, cost $2 million. The developers said the biggest item, however, was the overall delay in the project schedule, which translated into increased carrying costs on the loans and pushed out the management and administrative costs. The price tag for those delays was set at $3 million.

If the figures seem stiff, consider the potential losses associated with delays. At that point in the project, the projected rent for Rincon Center was slightly more than $17.5 million in its first year of full occupancy. Dividing that figure by 365 days translates to nearly $48,000 a day in lost rental income for delays that pushed back the project's completion. The figure does not include the carrying costs of the construction loan, the payments to holders of the tax-exempt bonds, and lease payments to the Postal Service. Interest on the $79 million construction loan, for instance, was nearly $15,000 a day, whether the project was open and generating income or not. In a letter to one of the shoring designers months after this financial disaster, Jay Mancini predicted that the failure of the shoring and related problems would add $6 million or more to the final cost of the project.

Other target dates had already been missed and more would be missed before the development was finished. The final design approval from the redevelopment agency was late, delayed by continuing squabbles over design details. The debate over the design of the atrium had dragged on for months. Ron Tutor's final cost estimate to establish the guaranteed maximum price was still not in when the shoring failed. But those were more amorphous problems. With the hole, the developers could point to a specific event that had caused specific delays. Here, it was easy to see the cause, and harder to assess the blame.

"The whole thing was unnecessary," said Michael Praszker much later. "They bungled it because they wouldn't do anything without having three decisions. There is one thing that Jay Mancini didn't do right. There was no coordinator. So instead of stopping and saying, 'Let's get our heads together,' they would start pointing fingers."

Even the most sophisticated design techniques and the most efficient construction schedules cannot always avoid a misstep. Considering the thousands of calculations and decisions necessary in erecting a major real estate development, structural failures that result in major property losses or deaths are extremely rare. However, the number of minor failures is large enough that insurance companies report that about one engineering or architectural firm out of three is involved in a claim for financial damages every year.

Soon after the final problems developed in early October, Praszker began to hear rumors that the developers were likely to sue someone over the extra costs and delays. Among the complaints he heard was that not enough test boring had been done to determine the viscosity of the soil, which resulted in a weaker shoring design than required. In forty years, Michael Praszker and his firm had never faced a lawsuit, so he was gravely concerned. On October 9, he wrote a letter to Jay Mancini in which he sought to memorialize the various concerns that he and his engineers had expressed over the summer about the excavation techniques. He outlined his dissatisfaction with the large windows and reminded Mancini that visible soil movement had been reported on several occasions. He also complained about the steepness of the slopes leading up to the walls.

Praszker was not sure whether he would be sued. He still was obligated under his contract to supervise the installation of the pilings for the foundation once the excavation was completed. Perhaps if that went well, he could avoid being blamed in court for an expensive mistake that he felt he had done his best to avoid.

Some tests had been performed on the soil in small areas of the excavation for driving the first piles, which had been replaced after they were ruined by the soil movement. Once a stable hole was available, the remaining test borings were performed to determine precisely what type of soil lay beneath the excavation. Uniformity underground is rare, and layers of soil and rock typically flow in an undulating pattern. But with Rincon, there was a complication.

Beneath the project lay a geologic structure that can be best visualized as a valley, a V-shaped gorge dropping down about 300 feet to the floor carved by a river millions of years ago. The development itself sits on one of the valley's slopes. This does not create immediate peril. The block is not going to slide down into a prehistoric gorge. Just across Mission Street from the post office building was One Market Plaza, which was built in 1976 over a deeper part of the gorge. That building rests on 200-foot-long piles, the deepest ever driven in California. For Rincon Center, Praszker and his colleagues felt they would not have to go that deep. But they would need to sink long pilings of differing lengths to accommodate the underground contours of the site.

The uppermost soil, which contained a heavy component of bricks, rocks, wood, and other debris from decades of fill, had been stripped away by the excavation. So had the top portion of the next layer, which was the soft compressible clay called bay mud. The remaining bay mud ranged in thickness from 50 to 70 feet. Beneath that was a layer of dense sand, gravel, and residual soils that was up to 30 feet thick. The depth at which bedrock was found varied from 90 to 155 feet, with the seismic mapping and test borings showing that the deepest submersion of the bedrock was nearest the old post office.

The next step involved driving more than twenty test piles into the ground at various locations around the site. By applying pressure to each pile and measuring the response of the earth surrounding it, Praszker's engineers determined the exact load that each pile would be able to carry. With the working drawings of the building as an overlay, they then determined the number, depth, and precise pattern of the pilings that would be required to support the new structure. Most would obviously be placed beneath the two towers, since they would contain most of the weight.

The calculations called for driving 1,182 pilings into the ground in clusters across the site. The figure was less than a third the number of pilings supporting the old post office building, which was only three stories high when it was built. But the new pilings would be capable of supporting far more weight because they were to be made of prestressed, reinforced concrete. They would come in two thicknesses—12 inches square and 14 inches square. The depth of the piles would vary from 67 feet to 113 feet, 6 inches. The longest piles would go closest to the post office building. Even the longest, however, would not reach bedrock. Instead, they would be imbedded in the dense sand layers above it. Each location would be predrilled to a depth of 30 feet in order to facilitate the descent of the pile.

The actual driving of the piles was done by single-action and double-action diesel-powered hammers. The hammers, suspended above the piles from cranes, drive in the concrete lengths by repeated blows.

Since the thickness of the mud varied and the contouring sloped gently down, the sand layer was not uniformly horizontal beneath the locations of many of the piles. This slope created a hazard that the pile would slip sideways when it made contact with the dense sand, much as a nail can bend when struck a glancing blow by an amateur carpenter. A crooked pile, like a bent nail, does not function properly. In order to avoid the slips, H-shaped steel beams were imbedded in the end of each pile. The beams, called stingers, extended out ten feet from the end of the pile and bit into the sloping layer of sand to stop sideways movement.

Once driven, the pilings stood in parallel rows along the outer edge, where the walls would be, and clustered in bunches across the floor of the excavation. They were only the first element of the foundation. The next was tying the 1,182 concrete pilings together in a unit that would support the weight of the structure and withstand lateral movement as well.

The first step in this process was pouring two-foot-thick concrete slabs, called caps, on top of each cluster of pilings. The caps covered twenty or forty pilings each and were as large as twenty foot square. Once poured, the caps were linked with a series of poured-in-place concrete beams on the floor of the hole, the level known as grade. Wooden forms were built for the beams and cages of steel reinforcing bar were constructed inside the forms. The concrete was then poured into the forms and allowed to harden until it formed a link between two caps. Much like the structural elements of a building itself, these beams were designed to knit the slabs and pilings into a cohesive unit.

This was essential because the area is earthquake-prone. No building can withstand the force of a major earthquake without some movement. When the earth moves, a building must follow. Tying the pilings together meant that the building would move as a single unit in an earthquake, rather than having one portion going off in one direction and another section in another direction. This was particularly important with Rincon Center because the structure would stand on mud. Scientists have long understood that soft soils, such as mud or landfill, shimmy far more than bedrock in an earthquake. So buildings erected on such sites are a special risk.

The final step in preparation of the foundation was pumping in a vast layer of concrete (called a mat) on top of the caps and beams. Since the building would be built out of concrete, and therefore would be extremely heavy, the mat would be two and a half feet thick and extensively reinforced with a network of steel rebar to ensure that the building moved as a single unit in a quake. The mat would double as the floor of the lower of the two underground parking levels.

The foundation work was completed late in 1986, about four months behind schedule because of the excavation woes. Finally, the new phase of Rincon Center was ready to start its climb out of the ground. This part of the job, driving the piles and tying them together, had gone smoothly. Michael Praszker still did not know whether he would be sued, but he hoped his performance had lessened the chance.

The millions of dollars in extra costs associated with the excavation riveted Jay Mancini's attention to the budget. He began to harp at Harry Topping about the extra money being spent on design consultants, the delays caused by the problems with the redevelopment agency, and a host of nickel-and-dime issues. The working environment for Mancini and Topping was miserable even without the added tension. They were working twelve hours a day, six days a week, trying to keep up with the countless decisions that had to be made. In the summer of 1986, the two men and their secretary had moved from the Alcoa Building to a makeshift office in the historic lobby of the post office building. It amounted to nothing more than three desks and a couple of telephones pushed up against the wall at one end of the lobby.

"The philosophy of this company is that the project team should be on-site," Mancini had told Topping. "You are on top of things that way. Problems and issues jump out at you. You begin to get an intuitive sense of how things are going. The building becomes like a living object. You form a symbiotic relationship with the building."

Later Topping would wonder how things had got so screwed up if they had a symbiotic relationship with the building. But at the time, the move had seemed logical. A move that had seemed logical in summer had turned most uncomfortable by early winter. San Francisco does not get the sort of bitter winter temperatures that afflict the Chicago area, where Topping grew up. But the cold along the bay is damp and penetrating, particularly in an unheated building with thick concrete walls. To add to the discomfort, dust and noise were everywhere because of the construction underway in the rest of the building.

Topping started wearing long underwear to work and a sweater beneath his suit coat. He took the sweater off only when he went to lunch, so he would look like a real businessman. He bought a small space heater and placed it next to his desk. Mancini, however, was a good Marine; he led by example. He eschewed long underwear and a heater.

On a day when the damp cold was particularly unbearable, Topping drew his heater so close to him that the upholstery on his chair caught fire. He quickly put out the fire, but the chair had been damaged badly. Mancini was out of the office when the accident occurred, which was a good thing because his frayed temper might have ignited, too. Fearing that even hearing about the silly accident would send up his boss, Topping tucked the chair away in another part of the building and found another to use. He telephoned a repair shop, had the damaged chair picked up, and planned to pay for the repairs himself. But before he could get the chair fixed, Mancini discovered the scheme and confronted Topping.

"Knock that off," Mancini said sternly. "That's a battle casualty. We'll pay for the chair."

17

THE TOOTHBRUSH
AND THE CAM

Much as the new towers of phase two were designed to blend harmoniously with the existing post office building, the developers wanted a series of murals in the atrium of the old building that echoed the historic paintings in its lobby. By July, they had decided that these new murals would be executed by Richard Haas, a prominent New York painter whose art had an architectural flavor. His extravagantly huge murals had been painted on the blank walls of buildings across the country, providing a dose of fantasy and humor to otherwise dull spaces. The *New York Times* would eventually describe him as "the greatest architectural muralist of our time."

One of his murals, a trompe l'oeil version of a building facade on the side of a building in Chicago, had caught the eye of Harry Topping when he was getting his MBA at the University of Chicago. So when Tamara Thomas, the Los Angeles art consultant hired to help select the artists for the public spaces at the development, suggested Haas as one of the artists for Rincon, Topping jumped at the chance.

Near the end of July, Haas had flown to Los Angeles to discuss the murals with Johnson, Mancini, and Topping. He then returned to his studio in New York to work on preliminary sketches for the series of murals in the atrium that would complement the paintings in the historic lobby. They would be far smaller than his signature outdoor works, but the hope was that they would convey some of the same excitement.

About the same time Haas was hired to paint the new murals, restoration had begun on Anton Refregier's works in the historic lobby. Since their completion in 1948, the scenes depicting the history of California had become caked with grime. The residue was being painstakingly removed under the supervision of Thomas Portue, a San Francisco art conservator. He had first seen the murals while working his way through college for a mail-delivery service, a job that meant he made frequent trips to the Rincon Annex post office.

Refregier had painted the murals on a gesso base that was applied directly to the plaster walls of the post office lobby. A water-soluble cleaner, the easiest method for cleaning the paintings, would have dissolved them instead. So Portue resorted to a simpler but more time-consuming process. He used a soft plastic eraser to rub off the dirt and occasionally resorted to an electric drafting eraser for difficult areas. Once the murals were cleaned, the original paint was touched up and repaired where it had flaked away or been damaged. A clear coat of synthetic resin varnish was applied to imitate the original sheen and protect the murals in the future.

There was a second type of restoration required to save the murals. The walls on which most of the murals had been painted were thin, plaster-coated partitions, rather than the heavy concrete of the exterior walls. Over the years, new window openings had been cut into these partitions beneath some of the murals. As a result, the walls themselves were weakened. The vibrations of the demolition and new construction caused concern that the supports might deteriorate further, allowing the plaster to crumble and destroying some of the murals. To solve the problem, Chin & Hensolt developed a new steel frame that was attached to the original metal studs in the partition. The new design was stiff enough to protect the integrity of the murals.

With work on both the new and old murals progressing, attention had turned to what Mancini was now calling "the water event" for the atrium. Mancini had a high regard for Harry Topping's artistic sensibilities; that had been one of the reasons he had hired him in the first place. So he turned over the preliminary work on the water event to Topping.

A few months earlier, Jay Mancini, Scott Johnson, and Dianna Wong had flown to Boston to visit Copley Place, the 1.5 million-square-foot mixed-use downtown development. The middle of the atrium at Rincon Center was still a blank, and Mancini was leaning toward putting some sort of fountain there. He wanted the architect's opinion of the Copley Place fountain. He wondered if something similar could be designed for Rincon Center. Johnson had suggested a fountain as one of the options for the atrium. But lately the architect had enlarged his thinking about what might go in the space. He had been trying to envision some sort of water-based element that would tie the entire project together, linking the atrium in the old building with the courtyard facing the new structure. He had not formulated a concept of what sort of device or art would accomplish that ambitious task, but the Copley fountain had seemed like just another fountain to him.

Since the trip, Johnson still had not come up with a concrete idea for what sort of artwork would fill the space in the middle of the atrium. But he had managed to convince Mancini that something more than a fountain should be considered. The assignment for coming up with an alternative had been handed over to Topping.

In addition to the list of painters, Tamara Thomas had provided the developers with the names of fifteen or so artists who specialized in the sort of major public works that the developers had in mind for the atrium, including some who were expert fountain designers. Scanning the list and examining photographs of their previous works, Scott Johnson was intrigued by a San Francisco artist named Doug Hollis and he pointed out his work to Topping.

There is a type of artist the public rarely encounters in a gallery, museum, or other traditional exhibition space. The work of this subspecies is called variously environmental sculpture, earthworks, or public art. Doug Hollis prefers the last label and describes himself as a "public artist." His works are site-specific, meaning they are designed with a specific location in mind. And they often involve the use of sound as well as visual elements. He first began to acquire a reputation in San Francisco during the 1970s with constructions called wind harps. One in Berkeley, called Wind Organ, consists of thirty-six tuned metal organ pipes permanently installed on a slope behind an academic building. As the wind passes over them, the pipes emit an eerie melody.

But the attention of Johnson and Topping had been drawn to some of his other works that involved water, such as a wind-activated, walker-responsive, floating sound structure on a lake in Delaware and a series of terraces surrounding a tidal cloak on the coast of Washington. Nothing resembled a water fountain, but the men saw a uniqueness and excitement that they wanted for the atrium.

After being contacted by Topping, Hollis flew down to Los Angeles, where he met with Johnson, Mancini, and Topping at the architect's offices. He was shown some study models of the project and a series of drawings. The architects had designed a series of gazebolike kiosks in the interior courtyard that were intended to extend the flavor of the atrium into the outdoors. Hollis nearly laughed aloud at the kiosks. To him, they symbolized an architect's attempt to create a "meaningful object," and reaffirmed his long-held view of the profession. "They think they are artists, too," said Hollis. "I tell them, 'Just be a good architect.' "

It is an interesting and narrow view. Hollis had spent twenty years expanding the boundaries of art into new dimensions, many of them intruding on areas traditionally viewed as architecture. Yet he maintained this restrictive and dismissive attitude toward architects.

There is art in a well-designed building. That is part of what distinguishes architecture from engineering or carpentry. And it is one of the criteria that differentiate good architecture from bad architecture. Unlike Hollis's "public works," which simply exist in space, a building must contain space and simultaneously respond to and define the larger area around it. You may admire a Henry Moore sculpture. You can even glide your hand across its pleasing surface. Hollis's wind chimes create a beautiful sound. But you do not have to live in them or work in them. As the architect-author Witold Rybczynski has said, "Making space is social art." And that makes the task of the good architect the most difficult of all arts.

But Doug Hollis was not thinking along those lines that day. Instead, he listened as Johnson, Mancini, and Topping said they needed something that would unify the ground-level experience of the entire project. They wanted something with water, something dramatic. Mancini kept using a phrase that struck Hollis as silly. He kept calling it a "water event." He said he would pay Hollis $2,000 to come up with a concept and a few sketches. If he and Topping liked the concept, they would proceed to development. Hollis, who had never before worked with a real estate developer, took Mancini and Topping quite literally when they said they wanted to unify the exterior and interior.

Over the next two months, Hollis developed a unifying concept and, instead of a few sketches, produced more than a dozen detailed drawings. As Scott Johnson had drawn on historical antecedents for elements of his design, so too did Hollis transform an ancient structure, the water sluice, into a piece of ultramodern art. It conveyed elements of a Roman aqueduct and a gold mine's water slurry.

He was scheduled to unveil the drawings at a fairly formal presentation in Johnson's Los Angeles office. The architect would be there, along with Topping, Mancini, and some leasing consultants from Cushman & Wakefield, a real estate firm. But when Hollis woke up the morning of the presentation, he had food poisoning and had to cancel the meeting. He would always feel that missing the formal presentation had damaged the chances that his grand design would be approved. In fact, food poisoning or not, it didn't have a prayer.

A few days later, Hollis made an informal presentation to Topping, Mancini, and the leasing consultants in San Francisco. He posted his drawings along the walls of a conference room at Perini's offices. They showed a funnel-shaped water tower nearly two stories high in the courtyard, close to the arch leading into the new building. A glass trough came out of the tower and, supported by stainless-steel arches, crossed the plaza, pierced the new facade of the post office, and ended above a pool in the center of the atrium. Other drawings showed water coursing through the trough and cascading in a double vortex into the pool. Sunlight filtered through the falling water and fell in a pattern across the atrium floor. Hollis told Mancini and Topping that the water would create a pleasing, mild roar that would echo through the courtyard and the post office.

For several minutes, as they walked around the room examining the drawings, there was silence. Topping scratched his head and did not say anything. Mancini and the consultants did not say anything. Finally, Topping said, "Well, Doug, this is interesting. We'll have to think about this. I'll get back to you pretty soon." Topping and Mancini had been dumbfounded by the scope of the concept. They could not imagine constructing this huge device in the heart of their

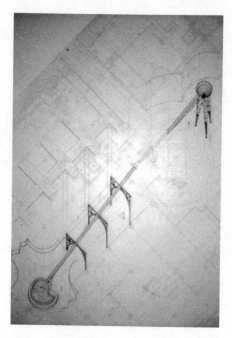

The proposal for an elevated aqueduct confounded the developers.

development. And they were not quite sure what to say to Hollis about it.

A few days later, Hollis showed the drawings to Scott Johnson. He, too, was silent for several minutes as he studied them. Finally he turned to the artist and said, "Doug, this is pretty invasive stuff."

Johnson had supported the choice of Hollis to execute a center-piece for the atrium. He admired his work and knew that he would create something special for the space, rather than just another rendi-tion of one of his other works. A well-executed piece, whatever its nature, would make the space more exciting. But the water trough struck him as a major distraction, something that called attention to itself and detracted from its environment. This was not what Johnson had in mind when he thought about a unifying concept for the project.

A silence settled over the whole matter. For days and days, Hollis did not hear a word from the developers. Finally, Topping telephoned him and said that they had decided to conduct some limited inter-views with a few artists just to get a couple other ideas. He said the interviews would be with Hollis, with an environmental artist from

New York named Ellen Zimmerman, and with Joan Brown, a prominent San Francisco artist who specialized in obelisks. "By the way," Topping added, "you should come up with a new concept. And, ah, confine it to the atrium."

Angered by the total lack of response to his water trough, Hollis thought of dropping out entirely. But he decided to give it one more try. In the meantime, he telephoned Zimmerman, a friend, and said, "I'm not trying to discourage you, but I think this is a complete nest of snakes. I'm trying to save you time out of courtesy. I'm not trying to win this thing by default."

Zimmerman came anyway and all three artists were interviewed separately. This time Hollis offered a far vaguer concept, simply indicating that he would like to create some sort of water curtain in the center of the atrium. The next day, Topping telephoned Hollis and said they would like to give him the commission. Would he mind coming up with a fuller concept?

"Fine, I'll do a new proposal," he said. "It'll cost you $16,000 this time." Hollis figured that if he wasn't going to get any respect, he would at least be well paid for his trouble. Topping agreed and told him he should get together with Scott Johnson and Richard Haas to coordinate their efforts. He also said they wanted to move as quickly as possible.

A few days later, Hollis was on an airplane to New York for a meeting with Haas and Johnson in the muralist's studio. He had not come up with a new concept and carried only a series of photographs of a large study model of the atrium that had been taken earlier as part of a study of light and shadows on the atrium. The photos were striking because they showed how sunlight was expected to stream into the area through the glass skylight. What he saw were big squares of sunlight coming down through the grid of the coffered ceiling. Hollis thought to himself that the sunlight pattern was natural and beautiful, that he could work it into his concept somehow.

"This idea just popped into my head," he recalled later. "What about a column of water drops? I thought about that and I thought it would be really beautiful to have these water drops coming all the way from the top of the atrium, with the sunlight pouring through them."

He stayed in a friend's apartment that night. Using a toothbrush dipped in ink, he made a series of little splatters representing a screen of water drops in a strong vertical pattern. He vaguely sketched in the atrium as a background. When he showed his crude sketch to Haas and Johnson the next day they thought it was terrific. It was one of those rare ideas that everyone looked at and said instinctively, "Yeah, it works." The tricky part was finding a way to present the concept to Mancini in a way that he would accept it. Hollis did not want a repeat of the last fiasco.

When he got back to San Francisco, Hollis had the photos of the atrium model with the sunlight streaming in blown up to three feet by four feet. He airbrushed the column of water drops onto the sunlight and assembled them into a series of poster-size images. The presentation was held at Pereira's Los Angeles office and was attended by Johnson, Mancini, Topping, Tamara Thomas, and Haas, who had come to present some of his own sketches for the murals. As he walked around the conference room sticking his large photographs on the walls, Hollis thought to himself, "Well, here goes nothing."

When he was done, there was silence again. But before the artist could protest, Mancini smiled broadly and said, "Yeah, yeah. That's great. That's really great." With an instinct that Hollis had not given him credit for possessing, Mancini had immediately grasped the daring and uniqueness of the water column. Here was a water event that appealed greatly to Mancini, and he could see that it would bring drama and individuality to the atrium and the entire project. As Mancini and the others circled the room admiring the photographs, the same crucial question was on the minds of everyone. Would it work? No one had seen a free-falling, eighty-five-foot indoor waterfall.

"Is this possible?" asked Mancini. "What happens if it splashes?"

"That's a good question," said Hollis. "Why don't I build a prototype and we'll see?"

Here was a concern that Hollis could deal with. He would build a large-scale model of his water column to find out whether it would splash or not, to find out whether the drops would fall in the elegant uniformity depicted by his airbrush. He would have to figure out how to get the water up to the ceiling and down to the ground again.

There was yet another modeling process under way in connection with Rincon Center. In two small buildings in an industrial park in

Culver City, a small community near Los Angeles International Airport, computer-driven milling machines were cutting out thousands of tiny pieces of plastic that would go into the presentation model for the development.

The fascination with smallness starts very young. Children spend hours lying on the floor playing with toy dolls and soldiers, building little houses and forts out of plastic blocks. Adults retain this love of miniatures and express it in many ways. A boat owner has a replica of his yacht on his desk at work. The airline executive displays models of his fleet on a shelf in his office. A visitor to an architect's design studio is drawn invariably to the study models scattered around the room.

But such architectural study models are crude structures, designed to provide only a sense of scale and massing. A presentation model is a leasing tool meant to show prospective tenants exactly what the final building will look like. The dimensions of a presentation model are accurate to within a ten-thousandth of an inch. The glass, stone, marble, and other materials that will go into the final product are mimicked precisely in texture and color. These elaborate, technically perfect models are the centerpieces of marketing centers for major commercial and big residential developments. Industry folklore credits developer Gerald Hines with being the first to employ sophisticated, highly visual marketing centers to attract tenants before a building is completed. Now, such marketing centers are routine in any big-time development.

A presentation model also provides the developer and architect with a chance to look at the building while changes can still be made, especially in areas such as the color and texture of exterior materials. These elaborate creations are useful as well in winning approval of designs from community organizations and public agencies. They can dazzle at the same time they evoke that childhood fascination with miniatures. Recent photographic advances even allow a photograph of a model to be seamlessly imposed on the building's proposed site. In a very real sense, the model maker is the first builder of the building.

In the case of Rincon Center, the model maker was Leonard Stern, the young president of Dimensional Presentations, Inc., or DPI, a leading architectural model fabricator. From his shop in Culver City, Stern had built models of major skyscrapers and developments around the world, from Fox Plaza and Home Savings Tower in Los Angeles to Metropolitan Square in St. Louis, Northwestern Terminal in Chicago, Park Tower in New York City, Canary Wharf in London, and the new mosques in the Saudi Arabian holy cities of Mecca and Medina.

Prices range from $20,000 to $250,000, and it takes a month to three months to complete most models. The results are often works of art themselves. Elevator doors open and close, lights work, and details are so incredibly precise that only their size gives them away. Indeed, developers often use tiny cameras to film the inside of a model and the results seem as real as a full-size building. Though he does little Hollywood work because his models are finer than most productions require, Stern built a replica of the hospital setting used in the television series "St. Elsewhere" that included details as tiny as handprints on the walls. It cost $22,000 and was used for about twenty seconds in a single episode.

The models for Mecca and Medina were commissioned by King Fahd of Saudi Arabia. They were the most elaborate and expensive ever created by DPI. Crews worked twenty-four hours a day in two shifts for ten weeks to complete models of the Prophet's Mosque in Medina and the Grand Mosque in Mecca. The Prophet's Mosque model covered an area twenty feet wide and twenty-five feet long; the one for Mecca was only slightly smaller. Their combined cost was $500,000. Stern loves to joke about the irony of a Jew fabricating models for a place he would never even be allowed to enter.

Stern, a college dropout, started building models for his father, an architect who designed many of the casinos in Las Vegas. As model making moved out of garages and into shops, the business grew more sophisticated and more competitive. (Stern once obtained a court injunction barring a former employee who left to start a rival business from contacting Stern's customers.) Stern built his business into a leader by developing and adapting the most modern techniques. For instance, in the early 1980s, aerospace firms were using computerized milling machines to cut tiny parts out of aluminum, metal, and nylon. Stern adapted the technique to cutting and etching the plastics used in model making. To replicate the mirrored glass popular on curtain walls, he hired a Hughes Aircraft engineer to develop a vacuum metalizing coating machine that matches the look called for by the design.

As more and more architects have converted to computer-aided design, known as CAD, Stern developed the programs that transfer the architect's dimensions and design directly onto the most sophisticated piece of equipment in his shop, a computer-aided manufacturing system, or CAM. If an architect does not use CAD, a technician at DPI will translate the design documents into corresponding numbers and program them into the CAM. The CAM then designs the shape of each of the thousands of model parts mathematically and the information is transferred to a separate computer system that drives four separate milling machines. The milling machines cut the pieces from sheets of clear acrylic plastic that have been planed to a tolerance of less than one five-thousandth of an inch, about the width of three strands of hair. A single piece may require 1,000 or more cuts, and a single model will have 10,000 or more of these tiny pieces.

The next steps are performed by hand. The first is assembling the parts of the model's inner core by gluing them together on special level-tested granite tabletops that ensure proper alignment. Other clear parts are painted to resemble whatever exterior skin the architect has selected. Stern's painters mix their own paints to match the colors and textures required by the design. They can replicate virtually any material, from pink granite to marble. To ensure that painted pieces are done exactly as required, special masking tape is applied along tiny "score" lines etched on the pieces of the milling machine. The exterior pieces are then assembled and added to the core using microfine industrial tape.

These elaborate little worlds come with many real-life accoutrements. Stern has people on his staff who do nothing but make trees. They can replicate an oak tree, a pine, or a palm using primarily steel wool and wire. Others specialize in creating water fountains and sidewalks. Tiny lights, fed by threadlike fiber optics, illuminate perfectly detailed interiors.

When Harry Topping first discussed the presentation model for Rincon Center with Stern, he said he wanted two models. One would cover the entire project and the other would be just the atrium, in a larger scale. Topping saw the atrium as a major leasing point and he wanted to be able to show potential tenants what it would be like in as much detail as possible.

Stern is as excitable and energetic as the exotic Lamborghini and Ferrari automobiles he owns. The prospect of doing the atrium on a big scale got his juices running. "We'll blow people away," he told Topping. "I'll hire an artist to handpaint the Haas murals at scale. It'll be incredible."

And Stern had done some incredible things with models. A $60,000 model for the Simon Wiesenthal Center in Beverly Hills recreated the museum's exhibits on the holocaust. A specialized "snorkle" videotape camera, with a flexible lens the size of a drinking straw, was inserted into the model and provided tape of a walking tour of the planned museum that viewers swore had to be the real thing. An $80,000 structure for a residential development contained 10,000 trees on 75 separate lots, with 8 different model homes. Again, a tiny camera was used to film the model and each of the model homes and homesites. A prospective buyer could walk into the marketing center, punch in a lot number and select a model, and watch as the film followed winding streets up to the door of the house and then inside.

"It's art," Stern insists. "We're like glorified renderers to architects, but we're really so much more. Developers ask me if their building is any good. Lots of times they're skeptical of their architect. We develop reality before it is reality."

But the cost of doing two models was more reality than the Rincon budget would stand. The decision was made to build a single model to cover the entire development. A bite would be taken out of the roof to provide a view of the atrium. It would be constructed at a relatively small scale for such a model; one-eighth inch would equal one foot. Still, the model would contain 10,000 parts and cost $43,000.

At the outset, Stern expected the trickiest part of this fabrication would be replicating the glass for the curtain wall on the new towers. But he soon found another problem. While developers often build their models before they start construction, the schedule on Rincon meant that construction had already started by the time the design documents got to DPI. That meant that the developers were in a rush to have the model completed in order to get a jump start for their leasing program. More important, however, it created a miniature version of a fast track. The fabrication work would start while the design was still undergoing major changes. The material for the atrium storefronts had not been selected. The colors of the glass for the curtain wall on the new towers had not been chosen. The shape of the exterior courtyard was undetermined. Just as Scott Johnson's team had had to redesign various elements of the project, so, too, did Stern's technicians have to make changes as the model's construction proceeded.

Over the weeks, the decisions were made on Rincon and passed on to the fabricators. Late in the process, twelve-inch squares of the actual glass for the curtain wall were brought into Stern's shop, along with samples of the various paving and flooring materials. Using the specialized coating machine, Stern's technicians re-created the precise shades of the exterior glass and the tiny pieces were taped to the exterior of the tower assemblies.

The resulting model, which was about six feet long and three feet wide, was loaded onto a truck in special packing and driven to San Francisco, where it was installed in Perini's offices in the Alcoa Building. Once a place was ready in the post office, it would be transferred there. Stern flew to San Francisco for the installation and he was there when Jay Mancini got his first look at the completed model. The developer was disturbed by the curtain wall on the towers. It was two shades of gray, as had finally been decided. But it seemed dull and monochromatic.

"Did you guys use the right glass?" asked Mancini.

"This is it," replied Stern. "This is the real thing."

Leonard Stern had created hundreds of skyscraper models. He knew he had re-created the grays in the exact tones of the samples. What he was wondering was whether the developer and the architect had picked the right glass.

18

TRICKY AS
A THREE-YEAR-OLD

If Leonard Stern had known the history behind selecting the color of the glass for the curtain wall, he might have kept his mouth shut and just nodded. To principal players on the development side of the project, the laborious process stood as an unpleasant symbol of the difficulties and delays involved in dealing with the staff of the San Francisco Redevelopment Agency. Ultimately, the developers had resorted to political muscle to make an end run around the staff and take the issue directly to the commissioners.

The debate over the color of glass dragged on for months, not only with the public agency but within the development team itself. Scott Johnson had originally designed the towers with light green glass panels. It was a cool, soft color that Johnson felt would work well in the overcast sunlight of San Francisco. But Jay Mancini had expressed reservations about the green, at least in part because of Randy Verrue's opposition to the color. Harry Topping also seemed to be aligned on the side that was against the green. He had once referred to the color Johnson had proposed as "Santa Monica green."

When Johnson asked what that meant, Topping said: "Oh, you know, that sort of mossy, pastel, cool, eighties kind of green that you see in Santa Monica all the time. The way the graphics world picks up the image of the beach and the ocean and all those greens in David Hockney paintings of swimming pools."

"I hadn't thought of it that way," Johnson said.

But in the internal discussions afterwards, the green was always referred to as "Santa Monica green." Johnson could see that the fashionable nickname itself was the kiss of death for his first choice. So he began to study other ranges of color, examining blues, blacks, bronzes, and grays. At one point, he favored a light bronze. But then he settled on two shades of light gray and proposed this color scheme to the developers. Mancini and Verrue both supported the gray, which they thought added class to the project. But the redevelopment staff, after overcoming their original opposition to glass of any shade, had seen Johnson's early drawings using light green glass and decided that, if they had to have glass, they liked the green. "We'd like to see the building in green," Frank Cannizzaro of redevelopment said at a session with the developers in late 1985.

The thought crossed Mancini's mind that his architect was trying to undermine him, that he had enlisted the redevelopment staff on his side in an attempt to resurrect his original green. Johnson in fact had never discussed the color with the staff, outside of the regular meetings, which were also attended by Mancini or Topping or both.

"No, we really don't think green is what we want," Mancini said at the meeting. "Can't we do something more neutral? Like maybe gray."

The main concern of the redevelopment staff was avoiding a building dominated by glass. But very light green tints had worked well on a number of buildings in the city. The city's purest example of the International Style, the twenty-story Crown Zellerbach Building, had an elegant curtain wall of green glass. At the same time, the new downtown plan was encouraging buildings that stood out on the skyline, with spires, sculpted tops, and, in some cases, glass curtain walls. A raffish example of this type of building was being constructed just a few blocks west on Mission Street in another area controlled by the redevelopment agency. It was the San Francisco Marriott Hotel, a forty-story mass with a skin of GFRC, the lightweight substitute for pre-cast concrete, and reflective glass rising to an all-glass crown. It was a brash design that had evoked comparisons to a jukebox and to Las Vegas casinos. But it also promised to enliven the city's skyline.

When Mancini proposed gray instead of green, the redevelopment staff began to worry that Rincon Center would turn out to be too dark and austere. Johnson's design stitched his glass panels together with horizontal and vertical aluminum mullions, which separated alternating panels of two-toned opaque glass. The result was a patterned look that avoided any large monolithic expanses of glass. Why not add color to the mullions if the glass was to be gray? suggested Walter Yanagita of redevelopment. The gray glass could be framed in red and green mullions. That would enliven the skin.

"Wait a minute," said Johnson. "What is this? Christmas or something?"

The discussions had reached an impasse back in December of 1985, when the redevelopment staff had agreed to sign the final design documents so construction could start before year's end. The decision on glass would be postponed. Plans to hold a mock-up of the various samples of glass had been delayed several times since then while the two sides continued to wrangle over colors and the pattern of the skin.

By mid-summer 1986, the situation was reaching a crisis point. The redevelopment staff had backed away from green and the Christmas mullions, but they were refusing to give a final okay to gray. They kept saying that they were afraid it would make the building too dark. A manufacturer requires several months to produce the thousands of square feet of custom-made glass required by a project the size of Rincon. Mancini was worried that he was going to blow another big hole in his schedule if the glass was not ordered soon. So in the middle of July, he asked Janet Roche, his housing consultant, to drop by for a visit.

Roche had helped lobby the executive director of the redevelopment staff, Wilbur Hamilton, on some early issues. And she was still working on a plan for the affordable-housing component that the redevelopment staff would have to approve. But Mancini had not yet asked her to use her ultimate clout. He had not asked her to intervene on his behalf with her uncle, Leroy King, the president of the redevelopment commission.

On this particular day, however, Mancini explained to Roche that the staff was refusing to give them the final okay for the color they wanted. He said he was afraid the project was threatened with a potentially expensive delay unless the issue was resolved very soon. "We want gray," he said. "It's up to date. It's a marketable color. But we can't get past the staff, and I'm afraid this could have a serious impact on the success of the project."

Mancini said he wanted to take the unusual step of inviting all seven members of the redevelopment commission to the mock-up. He felt that they would examine the various shades of gray under consideration and would surely realize that the color would work for the building and the skyline. Once they understood that, Mancini was sure the commissioners would agree that the final decision belonged to the owners of the building. The trick would be getting them to come.

During years of involvement in government and the private sector, mostly in public housing issues, Janet Roche had evolved from an idealogue into what might be called an idealistic realist. She had grappled with the relationship between the public and private sectors while working for the San Francisco Redevelopment Agency, its counterpart in Oakland, as director of housing and development in Berkeley, and as a private consultant.

Always she had been an advocate of affordable public housing. But her experiences on both sides of the battle had led her to the conclusion that a balance had to be struck between the public goals and private profits if such housing was to be built. Developers would not build buildings if they could not earn a profit. It was all right for the public to extract some common good from these projects. The question was, how much should be extracted out of the private sector to reach public goals?

"I'm a pragmatist in terms of the private sector," Roche explained at one point in the development of Rincon. "It provides most of the housing stock and it is important not to scare it away from the housing market with restrictions that are too onerous." She did not see a conflict with public goals if the developer got to choose the skin color for a building that he thought offered the best chance of financial success.

To Mancini that day in July she said: "The staff has never been in the business world and they do not understand business developments. They have laudable ideals, but they have no idea what their ideals may wind up costing you."

It was never any secret that Roche was Leroy King's niece. He kissed her when they met at public meetings and, when she was involved in a project, he always announced it before he voted on the development. At the same time, Roche knew enough about bureaucrats to realize that there were dangers in going directly to King. "I don't go over the staff's heads too often," she told Mancini. "I can't afford to alienate them and neither can you. They do have power."

This time, however, Roche agreed that the issue was important enough to warrant the end run. She telephoned her uncle Leroy, explained the problem to him, and invited him to a demonstration of the various examples of glass on the roof of the post office building on Wednesday, July 23. She said the developers would be pleased if the other commissioners and Wilbur Hamilton would come, too.

On the afternoon of July 23, half a dozen large glass panels were set up on the roof of the post office. Each measured two feet by five feet. The shades were all gray, varying from extremely light to medium-dark. The issue was whether the gray was too dark.

There were two basic kinds of glass: the darker panels were opaque and called spandrel glass; the lighter shades were lightly tinted, semitransparent vision glass. Both types would be used on the skin, and there would be at least two shades of the spandrel glass. Vision and spandrel glass start out the same. To create a spandrel panel, the glass manufacturer enamels a ceramic substance, called frit, onto the back of the glass so that vision is obscured. The color of the frit and the tint of the glass itself determine the color or shading of the glass.

When a building has an all-glass skin, or even a mostly glass skin, the architect can use vision glass above the floorline for windows and other open areas. Spandrel glass is used on the areas where the architect wants to conceal what is behind the glass, such as the space between floors where the floor structure, plumbing, and mechanical ducts run, or the positioning of a column.

Johnson's design for the glass skin of the Rincon towers, however, planned to use spandrel glass over some vision areas, too, in order to recompose the surface of the towers with alternating spandrels of different darkness. There were, however, no red and green mullions on the palette that day. Johnson had convinced the staff that, for the purposes of adding interest, the colored accents were a very bad idea. Instead, he had proposed increasing the prominence of the aluminum elements of the skin and the two-toned spandrel as ways of highlighting the tower facades, though in a more subdued manner.

Five of the seven members of the redevelopment board had shown up, led by Leroy King. The executive director, Wilbur Hamilton, had come, too, along with several members of the agency staff. Scott

Johnson had flown up from Los Angeles and he spent a long time explaining why he wanted the shades of gray and how they would be patterned to add interest to the towers. Coupled with the pre-cast concrete cladding on the lower levels and along the sides and balconies, the glass would lead an onlooker's eyes up the facade of the building to the spires.

The chief concern of the commissioners was that the skin be as light as possible. "I don't see what it hurts to have it gray, if that's what these guys want," King said, motioning to Johnson and Mancini.

The decision was as good as made. King's words were enough to assure approval of the gray glass sought by the developers. Several thousand dollars had been spent buying glass for the demonstration and setting it up on the roof of the old post office. But the results had gone the right way, and Johnson had played his part seriously. However, the process struck him as a bit of a joke. "Glass," he is fond of saying, "is the trickiest thing in the world, next to three-year-olds."

A sample of stone or cement will be basically the same color no matter how much sunlight there is on any given day. Glass, on the other hand, is semitransparent and semireflective, so that even absolutely clear glass reflects some light. Tinted glass, particularly the opaque panels, would change daily or hourly with the weather. On an overcast day, when the sky is white, a gray panel may look almost black. On a blue-sky day, it will reflect enough of the sky to appear to have a bluish tint. That is one of the reasons that glass is among the most complicated construction materials an architect deals with, and one of the reasons the redevelopment commissioners could not hope to make an informed decision. They had seen only a single piece of a giant jigsaw at one moment in time, in one weather condition. And yet they had insisted on the mock-up.

Whatever doubts Johnson had harbored about the gray glass were gone by this time. Looking back months later, he would say that the gray glass was a fine substitute for green, although the strongest endorsement he could muster was relatively mild. "It is perfectly all right," he said one evening in his office.

Perhaps it was simply a matter of not second-guessing the decision on a material that plays such a major role in the face his building presents to the public. "Once you make a decision like that, then you knit all the other details into it," he explained. "If it were green glass, a lot of things would be different. The skylight over the atrium would be different [it is tinted with the slightest gray]. The color palette for concrete might be different because it wouldn't make sense to have warm gray concrete with green glass."

Johnson was not always so sanguine in recalling the hazard-strewn process by which significant design decisions were made on Rincon Center. And he was not always so accommodating. For instance, later in 1986 he held off an assault on what he viewed as critical plans for the outdoor courtyard. The young architect drew a line around his concept and he was adamant that it not be crossed.

The dispute involved the shape of the courtyard between the old and new buildings. Johnson had conceived a formal space, a parterre that was integral to the flow between the old structure and the new one. There would be retail stores running the length of the Spear Street and Steuart Street sides of the plaza. Rather than a straight line of storefronts, however, Johnson had arranged them in a circling, baroque pattern. It broke the courtyard into a series of spaces that drew the eye around and through the space while simultaneously breaking down a potentially large rectangular space into more intimate sections of storefront. For Johnson, the design had character and formality. It was the antithesis of modern retail thinking.

From the first day he sketched his own vision of the development's retail space on a napkin, Bob Carey had wanted control over the layout of the courtyard between the buildings. He envisioned it as something along the lines of the channel gardens at Rockefeller Center, with storefronts arrayed in even lines around the perimeter and landscaping in the center. He objected to Johnson's staggered storefronts, complaining that they would not all be equally visible to someone entering the courtyard from the post office or from one of the two midblock entrances. He wanted a more egalitarian plan, with each storefront receiving roughly the same exposure. And again, he objected to what seemed insufficient room for signs. The width of the courtyard itself might be a problem unless a series of planters was installed right down the middle to divide the space. "I want to get a sense that you are surrounded by good retailing," he said.

The debate had dragged on for weeks, with Johnson and Carey

making their separate pitches to Mancini and the developer unable to decide between them or work out any compromise. Time was running out. The plans had to be finalized so the presentation model could be finished. Final design approvals from city agencies were hanging on this decision.

One weekend in the fall of 1986, Scott Johnson and his wife, Meg Bates, were in San Francisco on a brief holiday. Johnson got a call at his hotel from Mancini. The decision had to be made on the shape of the courtyard. They were having a meeting on Sunday morning at the Alcoa Building and Johnson needed to come. Bob Carey and Harry Topping would also be there.

When he arrived, Johnson heard more of the same from Carey. "The moment I enter the courtyard, I want to see all the storefronts," said Carey. "It is very important that I know where I am going to. I want to maximize the storefronts that I can see. When I walk into the courtyard from any entrance, I want to be able to see every vendor that is there." Carey picked up a piece of paper and began to sketch his plan, saying, "When I come in off of Spear Street and I'm standing there, I want to see every glass line possible and see every front door."

To Johnson, Carey was an isolationist. He was only concerned with his theory of what constituted good retail space. He had no background in architecture and seemed to have no concept of the urban space as a whole and the courtyard's place in the overall scheme of the design.

"Well of course you don't see these from here and these from here," Johnson said, pointing to storefronts on his own plan. "But as soon as you walk in you see them. People move through space. They don't stand still. They are liquid."

"No, I want a straight line," said Carey.

A few minutes later, after more of the same back and forth, Carey excused himself from the meeting. He had to catch a plane to New York at eleven o'clock that morning. Scott Johnson was livid as Carey walked out the door, but his tone was even and calm, even if the words were not.

"Jay, there is no way this will work. I consider this a deal breaker," he said, using some of Mancini's developer lingo. "There is no way this will work Carey's way."

Mancini said he would take the matter under advisement. He was not ready to make a decision on the spot. He never seemed to be, from Johnson's perspective. But Mancini confronted a real dilemma. He had faith in Bob Carey. He felt that Carey had accomplished a lot at Embarcadero Center and in restructuring the retail space at Rockefeller Center. If he was good enough for David Rockefeller, he was sure good enough for Jay Mancini. Here was his architect bucking the guy who knew about retail, the lifeblood of the project. Further, it was his own boss Randy Verrue who had suggested he hire Carey in the first place. On the other hand, Johnson seemed particularly adamant about his position. While Mancini did not think his architect would walk off the job, he respected him and wanted to give his views the consideration they deserved. It was a serious fight.

A few days later, Mancini telephoned Johnson in Los Angeles. He said that he had decided to go with Scott's plan for the courtyard. It was one of the toughest decisions that Jay Mancini made on a design question, and he crossed his fingers and hoped that it was the right one.

In late 1986, Randy Verrue was struggling with his own difficult decisions. The Perini Corporation board of directors had rejected the alternative proposal by the Boston Financial Group to raise money with an offering to smaller investors. The board felt that they would be sacrificing too much of the potential profits while risking a substantial amount of their own money. Instead, Verrue had been instructed to persuade Citibank to increase the loan on the project while a permanent solution to the financing bind was worked out. Verrue and Bob Mayer at Citibank had discussed the financial problems many times in recent weeks and Verrue's pitch was straightforward. He wanted an increase in the loan until part of the project could be sold to an insurance company or some other arrangement was made by Perini Corporation.

"Bob, if I have to fund 100 percent of the cost, I will do that," he said one day near the end of the year. "But I don't really want to do that. I'd like for the bank to find it within itself to come up with some more money. You recognize the ultimate value of this project. The bank will come out whole because we are creating value here."

Mayer faced a true dilemma. Here was his best account pleading for more money for a project facing uncertain costs and without any real equity contribution from the developers. The uncertainty over the construction costs was particularly troubling to Mayer. Sure, he knew that Perini Corporation was wealthy enough to make up the money lost when the syndication collapsed. But he also knew that they would do so only as a last resort. Leverage was the name of the game in big-time real estate development, finding a way to avoid sinking millions of dollars of your own money into a project. Plenty of developers in the 1980s were walking away from projects, leaving their lenders stuck with uncompleted office buildings, apartment complexes, and residential developments. Perini had never done anything of the sort, and Mayer did not expect them to do so now. But he was paid by Citibank to be a skeptic.

As part of the construction loan agreement, the bank had required Perini to come up with $25 million in cash before the bank would allow the developers to draw more than $25 million on the loan. As a result of the collapse of the syndication, that deadline had come and gone. But Citibank had kept funding the construction so work would not be halted. If that happened, the bank might never get its money back. Word travels fast when a major development is stopped. The project acquires a taint that can affect future leasing agreements and any number of other issues. For Rincon Center to have a real shot at succeeding, the money had to be found to finish the project without delay.

Bob Mayer was a good man for the situation. He understood the difficulties facing the Perini people. After all, he was facing the same problem himself, though on a bit smaller scale.

Mayer, a former architect, had bought a two-family duplex on Russian Hill in San Francisco. He had then taken out a large personal loan to cover the costs of a major renovation of the entire building. The plan was to sell half of the building to pay off the renovation loan and live in the other half. But there had been unforeseen costs, and Mayer had run out of money before the contractor finished the renovation. He could not find a buyer for the uncompleted half and faced the real prospect of declaring personal bankruptcy. Finally, he persuaded the bank to increase his loan so the contractor could finish the project and he could sell half the building.

His bosses, Mayer sensed, were a little anxious about extending additional financing on Rincon Center. This amount of money required contact with the home office, and there had been grumblings in New York. Along with the substantial amount of business Perini and Citibank did on the West Coast, however, the New York financial institution was a principal banker for the parent company on the East Coast. The long history and good relations between the two companies played a big role in the bank's decision to continue financing Rincon Center. The loan would not be increased, at least not at the moment. But the developers could continue to draw on the total amount. In exchange, Mayer required that Perini agree to begin putting their own cash into the project at a rate of $1 million a month until they found another way to finance their equity in the development.

With the new year, a new source for their equity was not the only problem that Mayer believed was confronting the developers. The guaranteed maximum price—the GMP for which the general contractor had promised to do the job—had not been signed yet, although Verrue kept promising that the document would be completed any day. Its delay meant to Mayer that, two and a half years after planning had begun, the developers still did not know how much the construction was going to cost. That in turn meant problems. The GMP was important to the banker because it marked the line at which, if it was exceeded, the developer would stop paying and the general contractor would have to start.

There also was the matter of the concrete budget. Ben Wang was Citibank's construction superintendent. His job was monitoring the progress and budgets of the major projects to which the bank had made loans. He was a veteran at spotting problems before they surfaced, and he had been concerned about the amount allocated for concrete on Rincon Center from the start. Wang had first told Mayer back in June that he did not believe that the $8.4 million allocated for concrete by Tutor-Saliba would be enough for such a complex project. When the shoring gave way later in the year and required a thicker concrete floor and larger caps above some of the clusters of pilings, it meant using more concrete. Wang's concerns grew.

In March, Wang felt the situation was serious enough to raise the issue again with Mayer. Each month, the contractors and the bank representatives gathered to decide how much progress had been made on the construction and determine the amount of the loan that would be funded. At these monthly draw meetings, Wang had watched as the concrete budget rose at a rate that far exceeded the progress on the building. At first, Mayer dismissed Wang's worries. There is always something out of whack in a construction budget. By the spring of 1987, however, the project was four months behind schedule. Only the two underground parking levels and the first floor of the office building had been completed. Yet 30 percent of the concrete budget had been spent.

"I expected overruns," Mayer would say later. "This was a very complex project. I wasn't surprised and I wasn't worried at that point." He was concerned enough, however, to telephone Verrue and alert him to what Wang had said.

"We think there is something seriously out of whack on concrete," Mayer told Verrue.

Verrue was surprised. He had not heard anything about concrete problems. In fact, he doubted that there were any problems. He figured that Mayer was just nervous because Perini still had not lined up additional financing or put the required cash into the project.

"Okay, we're going to take a look at this," he said. "But don't worry. I'm sure it's fine."

19

AN A OR AN F?

Early on, Scott Johnson had compared designing Rincon Center to a space shot. Thousands of calculations and decisions go into planning a major urban development. But the number is multiplied many times in a mixed-use development, where different functions compete for space on the same site or in the same building and where the solution to one dilemma is likely to lead to another somewhere else. Such was the case with the two residential towers.

Late in April, the thick concrete columns for the first floor had been poured into wood forms. In a matter of days, they were linked together by a network of concrete beams poured in forms erected between the columns. Then the concrete trucks, huge drums turning, extended in a line around the block as they waited to unload. High-pressure pumps were connected to outlets on the trucks and the concrete flowed into the forms built for the first floor of the building. Forty or fifty workers, using rakes, trowels, and shovels, rushed to push the concrete into place before it hardened. The depth had to be a uniform eight inches. While the concrete was still wet, it was polished smooth. Concrete requires twenty-eight days to harden or "cure" to almost its full strength. But hardening agents mixed into modern concrete accelerate the strength curve so that the material reaches 75 percent of its strength within a matter of days. Though the concrete cannot accept the full weight of the building, this allows work to proceed on and around the concrete long before the end of twenty-eight days.

As a result, in his pitch for concrete over steel, Ron Tutor had promised the developers that he could complete two floors a week, right up to the top of the towers. In Tutor's experience, this did not seem to be an unreasonable timetable. Tutor-Saliba has a fine record for concrete work. But the firm is best known for its heavy construction projects, such as Los Angeles International Airport, the long-delayed Los Angeles subway system, and other government projects. These projects are less refined and, in some ways, less demanding than a high-quality, mixed-use development.

The initial phase of the new building at Rincon Center seemed straightforward enough to allow Tutor to meet his schedule. The first six stories would be a conventional rectangle, with two arms extending on either side of the courtyard. Columns and girders would be installed along regular grids to create the appropriate dimensions for the offices. The next seventeen stories, however, would be trickier. The two residential towers were designed as curves to sit on top of the six-story podium. These curved towers were not chosen out of architectural whim. Their shape was central to renting the apartments at premium rates. As two curves, the towers provided maximum views of the bay bridge and the city, rather than into each other.

The redevelopment agency had restricted both the square footage and the height of the residential towers. To extract the most revenue possible from that space, Randy Verrue and Jay Mancini had specified a design that would squeeze in as many apartments as possible. That had been one argument for choosing concrete over steel for the construction; the shorter distances between floors in a concrete building had allowed the addition of an extra floor. Creating a maximum number of units on those floors meant that the apartments would be small. The largest two-bedroom, two-bath units had originally been designed to be about 1,100 square feet. But the narrowing of the towers in response to the redevelopment staff's desire for a more slender building profile had cut them to about 1,000 square feet. Some of the studios would be as small as 428 square feet, barely 20 by 20. Since Manhattan and Tokyo are the only cities on earth where people are willing to pay huge sums to live in such small spaces, the developers needed another attraction to charge high rents in San Francisco.

The obvious solution was to emphasize the spectacular views, particularly the southern views of the bay and the bridge. The height restriction stopped them from going higher to expand the views. But Scott Johnson came up with another way to offer the maximum view space possible. He designed the curved towers, with the wide part of the arc opening up the premium southern views like a fan. Coupled with plans for a high level of services, including a concierge and a doorman in the lobby, the apartments were expected to command the upper-bracket rents sought by the developers.

There was nothing exotic about curving the towers from an architectural or engineering standpoint. When it came to the actual construction, however, the curves added a new layer of complications. This was because of the choice of reinforced concrete over steel. Rincon Center would be the tallest concrete building in San Francisco, so the engineers at Chin & Hensolt had devised a system to make the concrete behave more like steel than normal reinforced concrete. This state-of-the-art system is called a moment-resisting ductile concrete frame. Although it is an extremely sophisticated design that was created on a computer, its essential ingredient can be summed up simply: it involves adding more steel rebar than is found in reinforced concrete. Using a computer program to calculate vertical and lateral loads, the engineers determined how much rebar would be necessary to achieve the necessary ductility in each of the nearly 5,000 girders and columns in the building. The computer also turned out specifications for the precise location of each piece of rebar.

Normally, concrete is reinforced by pouring it around long vertical lengths of steel rebar. The ductile-frame concept augments those vertical lengths with dozens of horizontal wraps of rebar for girders and columns. The width between the wraps starts out at about one foot near the center and the gap narrows as the girder or column gets closer to the end. This provides the most flexibility at the intersections or joints, where structural elements are joined and a building must give to withstand an earthquake. By the end of a column or girder, steel rebar as thick as a man's finger was spaced a little less than four inches apart.

"The key to the design is the horizontal ties, which make the system work as a ductile frame," explained P. Q. Chin. "Without the horizontal ties, the vertical rebar will buckle in an earthquake and the column collapses."

All of the concrete columns and girders for Rincon Center were manufactured at the construction site using this method. Welders bent and twisted the rebar into cages to match the specifications in the engineering plans. Carpenters then built plywood forms to enclose the cages and the concrete was poured into the forms. For girders, shoring was built to support the forms until the concrete hardened enough to allow the removal of the supports.

Concrete structural elements are usually created on location. But the additional rebar required by this system made the job tougher than usual. Achieving maximum strength in concrete requires an even flow of the material when it is being poured so there are no gaps to leave weak spots. The amount of rebar in the concrete structural elements for Rincon hindered this uniform flow because it was hard to get the concrete to flow around and between so much steel. Some of this had been anticipated, so a plasticizer had been added to the concrete to improve the flow by making it more liquid. But workers still found themselves spending a lot of extra time constantly pushing and prodding the concrete into the spaces around the narrowest wraps of rebar.

These problems only got worse when it came to forming the curved beams for the towers. The engineering calculations showed that curved beams required even more rebar in order to be as strong as a straight beam, so there were more narrow spaces into which concrete had to be pushed. Additionally, building the wood forms for the curved beams took the carpenters longer than constructing the straight forms. The problems were compounded in turn by the changing shape of the building as it moved upward. In a more conventionally designed building, each floor frequently is a carbon copy of the one below it. This allows the forms to be re-used on successive floors, which saves time and money. But as Rincon's shape curved and then narrowed with a series of setbacks, new forms were required at fairly regular intervals.

The shape of the towers presented another construction complication. The easiest buildings to erect are rectangles. The weight of the structure can be brought straight down to the foundation through a series of vertical columns, augmented by horizontal beams to ensure lateral stability. In perhaps the clearest example of this, most of the weight of the sixty-two-story AT&T Gateway Tower in Seattle is supported by four corner columns, which are nine-foot-wide steel tubes filled with high-strength concrete. The horizontal beams and other bracing are strung neatly between these giant pillars.

The structural system was more complicated with Rincon Center. The combination of the rectangular office building for the first six stories and the curved residential towers above necessitated a more complex system of columns and beams because the weight could not be brought straight down to the foundation. Instead, an intricate maze of columns and beams was poured one floor at a time, and they were tied together by thick pieces of overlapping rebar. Where the rectangle and the curve met, between the sixth and seventh floors, the columns and framing of the towers turned 45 degrees from the rectangular framing below. This required an extra network of columns and beams to transfer the weight of the towers to the lower building and on down to the foundation. At the points where the towers stepped back to reduce the floor areas and create a more slender profile, additional beams were necessary to transfer the vertical load.

Although the stepbacks were mandated by the redevelopment agency, the basic structural demands of the ductile-frame system and the two different building shapes were present in theory by the time the architect's design development documents were translated into working drawings for the actual construction. But this type of frame had been tried only once before in San Francisco. P. Q. Chin said later that he knew of no other place where such a ductile-frame system had been used. So when it came time to transfer the theory to practice, delays were considerable and unexpected by the general contractor.

"Ron Tutor had promised us that he would finish two floors a week, but it wasn't long until that had been reversed and he was completing a floor every two weeks," said Harry Topping. And sometimes it wasn't even that fast.

Delays were not the only problem. The building was requiring more concrete than Tutor had expected. Part of this was traceable to the early problems in the hole, which required extra concrete for the caps and the thicker foundation mat. But the complexity of the columns and beams also was requiring additional concrete. Plus, the ductile-frame system's appetite for rebar was more voracious than the original calculations, and the budget for that material was clearly going to be inadequate.

"It looks like this thing is being built in some Third World country where labor is cheap and time is of no essence," Ken Tardy said to Harry Topping one day as they looked at the construction site. A skeptic about concrete from the start, Topping believed that the delays were inevitable because it was such a "low-tech" construction method. The mistaken choice was symbolized for Topping by the new Marriott Hotel, a steel-frame building a few blocks west on Mission Street. Construction started on the hotel shortly after Rincon began, but the building rose its full forty stories before Rincon was completed.

Topping and Mancini did not have even a glimmer of how far out of line costs were getting on the project at this point because there was no one really keeping an eye on the day-to-day expenses for them. Most big projects employ at least one accountant full time to monitor expenditures in all major categories. This serves the dual purpose of spotting potential problems early and keeping a lid on overall expenses. If things get out of hand in one area, cuts can be made in another section of the budget to offset the extra expenses and keep the entire project within budget. Rincon's developers, however, were relying on Ron Tutor to keep costs down, since he was not only the general contractor but a part owner. It had seemed like a good idea at the time.

"It was not a matter of trying to shave administrative costs by not having a monitoring staff of our own," explained Randy Verrue. "But here our partners were the structural engineer and the contractor. Chin and Tutor were the last guys on the equity share. I presumed they were going to have a sharp eye on costs."

Not surprisingly, Mancini had adopted the same philosophy. "I had no idea we were going over on the concrete and rebar budgets before Wang brought it up," he said. "We didn't have a very good control budget. We were relying on the contractor and we kept getting assurances that everything was going to be okay or that there would be minor overruns. I thought we could do it with a few good men."

When Bob Mayer had first telephoned Verrue about the bank's concerns over the concrete costs earlier in April, Verrue had contacted

Tutor and asked about it. Tutor's response had been sharp and to the point. "The bank doesn't know what it's talking about," he insisted. "The whole process will be streamlined as it goes on. These first floors just establish the routine. And the offices are taking more concrete than the residential floors will."

Verrue relayed the response to Mayer, who said, "Okay. But track it, Randy. We don't see it working. You're going to run out of money before you top out."

"Well," replied Verrue, "we've got a guaranteed maximum price and Tutor is going to complete the job at that price. If they come in a couple million over on concrete, it comes out of his pocket. I'm not gonna cry over it."

Indeed, in March the contract establishing the guaranteed maximum price had been signed. Unless Tutor could prove any costs over the GMP were caused by design changes or other factors over which he had no control, he was obligated to finish the construction at that price.

The final cost of the construction for the post office and new building had been set at $63.8 million. The figure was, in some ways, a daring gamble. Tutor's last estimate of the construction costs had come in at $65 million. But the general contractor remained confident that he could complete the construction under that amount by cutting back on expensive material in some areas and, quite surprisingly to some involved in the project, by spending less than budgeted for concrete and rebar.

When the GMP contract was signed in March, the full budget impact of the excavation difficulties was not in. But enough was known for everyone to be certain the final price tag was going to exceed the GMP. Those overruns, however, such as the cost of the excavation, were associated with work performed by others and would not be charged against Tutor's $63.8 million guarantee. There were other costs that were rising to levels beyond the budget that would not be charged to Tutor, too. For instance, the redesigns of the atrium had added substantially to the architectural fees, as had the extra assignments given to Ken Tardy, Bob Carey, and some other consultants. As a result, the budget for architects and consultants had risen to $5.5 million in the spring of 1987, up $1.3 million over the past year. The concrete and rebar were another matter. Along with being the general contractor, Tutor was an expert in concrete work.

He would have a hard time convincing Randy Verrue or anyone else associated with the project that he was not to blame if his estimates in those two categories proved to be too low, regardless of the innovative design.

Bob Mayer was less sanguine than Verrue over what would happen if the concrete costs kept going up. If the concrete money ran out before the work was done, he envisioned a major fight between the developers and Tutor, something that would be good for no one, something that could slow or even stop the project. At that point, the people with the most financial risk would be Citibank. Perini still had not found a financial partner for the development, so the bank was funding the construction along with a million a month out of Perini's pocket.

In July, when the new office structure was three stories up, Ben Wang brought Mayer the latest numbers on the concrete. Sixty percent of the money had been drawn. The percentage was about the same in the rebar budget. Again, Mayer called Randy Verrue and raised the issue. He said he would not reduce the funding yet, but he wanted Verrue to take a very serious look at the concrete numbers.

In August, Verrue sent John Costello to Los Angeles to examine all of the design documents for the project. He was to estimate the amounts of concrete and rebar required to finish the job, based on the drawings. Steve Sabo, the construction foreman for Tutor-Saliba, did an estimate, too. Both men calculated that there was enough money left to pay for both materials. However, they said the full $8.4 million allocated for concrete would be needed. This projection contradicted the estimates made by Tutor in the GMP a few months earlier, in March. It meant that much of Tutor's projected savings were gone, but there still should be enough in the concrete and rebar budgets to finish the job. Ben Wang was less confident, and Mayer trusted him. Each month, as the concrete draw grew and the building did not keep pace, Mayer raised the issue with Tutor. Each time he was told not to worry. The columns and girders get narrower as the building goes up because there is less weight to support, the contractor said, so we will be using less concrete.

The original completion dates had been July 1987 for the post office renovation and January 1988 for the new building and towers. Both had been long buried beneath the blizzard of design changes, disputes with the redevelopment agency, excavation problems, slow concrete work, new shear walls in the post office, and many other factors.

And even as these dates came and went without completion, design disputes continued. One such was over the material that would be used for the storefronts in the atrium. This long-standing dispute centered on Scott Johnson's plan for metal and glass facades; Jay Mancini had favored wood all along. Now, in the summer of 1987, Richard Altoona, another consultant hired by Mancini, had sided with Bob Carey, both agreeing with Mancini that at least half of the storefronts should be done in wood to create the rich atmosphere the developers wanted. Mancini's only reservation was that the wood be obtained at the cost of metal and glass, materials that normally run about 50 percent cheaper. More redesigns were required throughout the summer, along with a search for an inexpensive wood that would not look cheap. Here again, Mancini's eyes were bigger than his stomach: the wood that he finally selected was solid cherry. It was indeed a rich look, and also an expensive one, which added to the bulging budget.

Another design dispute had concerned the atrium floor. Randy Verrue had wanted granite, but Mancini had convinced him that marble was the only material that would make it look right. "Marble is used in all good retail environments," he had argued at several points in late 1986 and early 1987. "Marble in fleshy tones will add warmth and make people look better." Verrue finally had agreed to marble, but the strained construction budget would not handle the cost. Instead, they had decided to use a less expensive agglomerate of crushed marble.

It was not until the fall of 1987 that these sorts of design disputes were finally resolved for the atrium and most of the material selected. While the renovation of the post office had proceeded without many of the final decisions being made, the construction was still far behind schedule. The earliest anyone could imagine opening that phase was late spring of 1988. But the pressure to complete the renovation sooner was enormous. A tenant had finally been located for most of the space.

Cushman & Wakefield, the large commercial real estate management firm handling the leasing, had spent months trying to find a major tenant for the post office. The appeal of the back-office space ran counter to the trend in the city, however. Most firms were following the Bank of America, Chevron, and other major employers and moving their clerical and computer staffs to the suburbs for lower rents and larger floorplates. The delay in completing the first phase also made it tough because a major selling point was the atrium and its interior views. The presentation model had been set up and provided a detailed vision of what the space would look like. But the leasing agents and Mancini were having trouble getting people to make the imaginative leap from model to reality. They did not seem to understand that the atrium would be a major amenity.

At one point, a national leasing agent for Peat Marwick came in for a tour. The big accounting firm was thinking about relocating its San Francisco office. Two senior partners from the local office had come through earlier, shaking their heads as they tried to imagine what the space would look like. Mancini showed the national representative the model, pointed out the atrium and the wonderful interior views. He led him through the building and tried to convey the excitement that would eventually be centered there. As they were walking out, the leasing agent turned to Mancini and said, "You know, Jay, this is either going to be an A or an F. I can't tell which until it's built." Mancini smiled politely and said he was sure it would be an A, but he added that he understood the reluctance. To himself, Mancini thought: "Accountants are not risk takers. Accountants are not where it's going to be at. We need some creative thinkers. Maybe an advertising agency."

It was not just the inability to lease the office space that was causing worries. A domino effect was at play, too. Until a major tenant was signed up, the leasing for the retail stores and restaurants was almost at a standstill. Nobody wanted to commit to renting space in a building that might wind up empty or half full at best. There were some heated exchanges between the Cushman & Wakefield leasing agents and Mancini, with the agents accusing the developer of not spending enough on marketing and advertising and Mancini firing back that they were not aggressive enough.

The dissension evaporated, at least temporarily, in late August when a subsidiary of Pacific Bell Telephone Company signed a lease for 150,000 square feet in the post office, more than two-thirds of the office space in the building. The subsidiary was the Pacific Bell

Directory, which publishes the company's telephone directories and Yellow Pages and conducts a few related operations. The company was the perfect back-office business for the space, with lots of clerical and administrative employees. At the same time, Rincon Center offered enough pizzazz to satisfy its desire to establish its own identity as an information company.

At the time, the subsidiary had more than 700 employees scattered at five locations around San Francisco. They wanted to consolidate the operation. Rincon Center had not been on the original list of possible locations because delays in finishing the renovation had pushed the completion date beyond the time when Pacific Bell needed space for its first workers. But the building fit so many of the needs described by the company employees that it was decided to see if at least a portion of the renovation could be completed in time for the first wave of workers. That was not an unusual request, particularly when it came from such a prize catch as a subsidiary of the phone company. What was unusual was the process by which Pacific Bell selected Rincon Center.

When the directory division decided to consolidate its operations, Michael Boulton, a San Francisco architect, was hired to help determine the kind of space that was needed and to select the location. Boulton and his staff conducted a series of meetings with company executives, employee representatives, and focus groups of employees. Out of those meetings grew a list of criteria that the new location should meet, ranging from proximity to transportation and appropriately priced restaurants to big floorplates and notable architecture.

"They also were concerned about the size of the building itself," said Boulton. "They did not want to be two hundred thousand square feet in a three-million-square-foot building. They would just disappear. Neither did they want to be the only tenant. They wanted a balance, with a lot of uniqueness and ambience. Once we looked at Rincon Center, everything we needed was there, if they could just complete it on time and the right financials could be negotiated."

Jay Mancini and Randy Verrue were eager to accommodate Pacific Bell. They promised to move workers from the new construction on the other end of the site so that enough space would be finished by January 1, 1988, to house the first Pac Bell employees. The issue of rent was a bit tougher. Pac Bell did not want to pay the $23 a square foot asking price. Randy Verrue's fears and Bob Mayer's predictions had come true: commercial rents in San Francisco, once as high as $35 a square foot for prime space, were dropping as a result of an over-supply of office space. Naturally, Pac Bell's negotiators argued that $23 a square foot was too much in the current market, and they pointed to a handful of other locations where rents were below $20. Verrue countered that the economic forecasts done for Perini by Cushman & Wakefield showed that commercial rents would begin rising once the full impact of the downtown plan's restrictions on new building kicked in. Locking in a long-term lease at $23 now would assure the company of beating the increase later, he argued.

Despite the near-desperation to sign a major tenant and Pac Bell's status as a prestige company, the developers were reluctant to give up on the rent. Naturally, they wanted to get as much as they could for the space, but there was added pressure to lease a substantial amount of space at a good rent so that they could attract potential buyers or investors to help bail out Perini from its deteriorating financial position.

Since early in the year, Perini had been paying $1 million a month into the project to keep it going until a partner could be found and a bailout arranged. Citibank had been patient, allowing the developers to continue spending their loan money without contributing the full share of equity. But Perini and the bank were both growing impatient with the inability to come up with a permanent solution to the financing problem. Perini's initial feelers among major institutional investors had received a cool reception. No one wanted to buy an uncompleted, unleased real estate development in a soft market.

So, while Perini was reluctant to give up rent, the company also needed to land Pac Bell as the first step in solving the much larger problem. Later no one would remember exactly whose idea it was, but someone came up with the notion of throwing the investment tax credits into the pot. Tax reform had nearly wiped out the tax incentives associated with the development; one of the only survivors of the massacre was the $7 million to $8 million worth of direct tax credits associated with the historic renovation. Perhaps they could be passed on directly to Pac Bell or maybe the lease could be structured to reflect their value. Maybe this crippled incentive could provide a helping hand after all.

The deal that was worked out essentially applied the tax credits to the rent payments that would come in from Pac Bell. The net effect would be to reduce the lease payments during the first three years while the credits were being used up. After that, the rent would go up to the market value. Pac Bell signed an initial lease for 150,000 square feet of the 220,000 square feet of office space available in the building. A short time later, they decided to take another 60,000 square feet. The net rent was set at $12 to $13 a square foot the first two years and $15 a square foot the third year. Then, when the tax credits were used up, the rent would rise over the next two years to $23 a square foot for the remainder of the ten-year lease.

The oversupply of office space, however, was forcing developers across the city to offer additional incentives to tenants. Perini had originally expected to give major tenants three months' free rent, a typical amount for a long-term lease. As the market softened, they had moved the figure to six months. But with Pac Bell, Perini was forced to add nine months' free rent to a package that already included the tax credits. In addition, the developers agreed to pay for nearly $1 million in extra tenant improvements, such as extensive additional electrical wiring to accommodate the computers used by the clerical staff. (This was one of many factors pushing the budget for tenant improvements well beyond the original $13.5 million estimate.) It was a stiff price for Perini. But it was a great coup, too. Virtually all of the commercial space in the building had been rented under a ten-year lease to a tenant with a solid financial background. There would be no questions about the phone company taking a hike when the rent came due.

The phone company employees were slated to start moving into some of the offices as early as January 1, and that created a sudden new interest in renting space for the restaurants and shops in the atrium. Unfortunately for Cushman & Wakefield, they would not benefit from this new interest. Jay Mancini had long felt that the real estate firm was not devoting enough attention to Rincon. He had clashed on occasion with Kirk Usher, the Cushman & Wakefield senior vice-president supervising the Rincon leasing. Now that a major tenant had been landed, he was worried that the big firm would be even less interested in lining up the twenty or so smaller tenants for the critical 40,000 square feet of retail space in the development. Securing the right mix of restaurants and small shops for the ground floor of the post office and the new building would be vital to the success of the project.

"Cushman was the right choice for the first deal," Mancini said. "We needed someone with access to all of the major businesses. But now we needed someone to devote 100 percent of their time to the project. For the harder slugging, we wanted somebody out there for us full time."

A few weeks earlier, a real estate agent named John Chamberlain had approached Mancini and Randy Verrue about the possibility of trying to lease some of the Rincon space for them. Chamberlain had sold space for Verrue on an earlier project while he was with a big firm, Grubb & Ellis. But he and another agent, Bill Rosetti, had recently formed a new operation, called TRI Realtors. TRI was leasing residential space in several downtown developments. Chamberlain offered to set up a new commercial real estate operation that would be devoted exclusively to marketing the retail and office space at Rincon Center. So, the same day that a congratulatory advertisement appeared in the San Francisco newspapers welcoming Pacific Bell Directory as the first major tenant at Rincon Center, Mancini removed Cushman & Wakefield and turned over the next phase of the leasing to Chamberlain and Rosetti.

Harry Topping, for one, thought Cushman & Wakefield got a raw deal. More to the point as far as the future of the project was concerned, he thought the change sent the wrong signal to San Francisco's close-knit business community. Despite the negotiations over rent and other financial aspects of a lease, the choice of where to rent a major chunk of space is a subjective decision. Peat Marwick had taken a pass on Rincon because an official could not be sure the atrium would work. Pac Bell had signed up in large part because they had faith that it would. Topping was worried that firing one of the city's biggest real estate firms right after they landed a major tenant would look bad to the corporate bosses, who would be the ones deciding whether to rent offices in the new phase of Rincon Center.

20

A ROGUE ELEPHANT

One morning shortly after the Pac Bell lease was signed, Jay Mancini was sitting in his office, examining his revised timetable for finishing the renovation. Mancini knew he would never make the January 1 move-in date for the first tenants. However, if things went smoothly for a change, enough of the work could be done to provide some usable space soon after the deadline. The work schedule would have to be speeded up, final decisions made and implemented in a hurry, workers shifted from other jobs. And Mancini was going to make sure that he made every one of those final decisions. He hadn't come this far to relinquish control now.

A couple of years before he had been hired by Perini L&D, Mancini had been working on plans for a small mixed-use development for Campeau Corporation. Campeau's partner in the deal was to be the Rouse Company, the Boston-based developers who had been so successful in transforming that city's Faneuil Hall into a thriving marketplace. During a conversation with Mike Speer, the president of the Rouse Company, Mancini had asked who had been responsible for the success of Faneuil Hall, the developers or Ben Thompson, the Cambridge architect who had designed the project.

"You don't really understand," Speer said. "Anytime you see anything good in a development, the owner has been involved at every detail level."

Mancini had not fully understood what Speer was talking about.

The Rouse Company had years of retailing experience, particularly in transforming older historic structures into new mixed-use developments. It was not until Mancini had taken the helm of Rincon Center that he grasped the level of decision making involved in such a major undertaking. With the suddenness of revelation, he came to believe that his role as project manager required him not only to approve every decision but to be involved in the process of arriving at every decision. (The problem was that, unlike Speer's years of expertise, this was Mancini's first big project. He was further handicapped because Perini, while a major construction company, never had been the developer on a project the size and complexity of Rincon Center.)

Mancini liked to compare the decision making on Rincon to his days as a liberal arts student at Lawrence College in Appleton, Wisconsin. He described it in terms of an academic exercise in which he listened to the arguments and opinions of Harry Topping, the architects, and the growing ranks of consultants. Then, he said, he would dissect the arguments and come up with the right answer. "There are smart guys who have gotten through life without being too rigorous," said Mancini. "They can get by on brains alone in many cases. But a single flaw can be serious, and that won't happen if someone is rigorous, if you pay attention to every detail."

Few others involved in the project were willing to put such a positive gloss on the way decisions were made at Rincon. Scott Johnson, in particular, had grown critical of Mancini's methods. While Johnson applauded group decisions intellectually, he felt strongly that there was not always a "right" decision for every dilemma.

"What you do," said Johnson, "is weigh this thing and that thing carefully and apply the best experience and data available. After you have done that, and thought long and hard about the issues, you are still building something that has never been built before. At that point, you all get to the edge of the canyon and you hold hands and you jump off. A piece of architecture is new. If it is art and not some knockoff, it has never been done before. You can build scale models and ones with periscopes in the middle. You can ask a dozen people what they think. But in the end you have to trust instinct and talent and art and a little mystery."

Mystery eluded Jay Mancini. He saw the building as a product. He was in charge of quality control. He was the "captain of the team," and he often compared the job to his days as an officer leading a Marine reconnaissance platoon in Vietnam. This parallel became clear one day when Tutor-Saliba's foreman, Steve Sabo, wandered over to Mancini on the construction site. Like others, Sabo had seen the job taking its toll on the project manager and he remarked, "You know, Jay, do you agree that the stress level isn't far off Vietnam?"

"Oh yes. I know what you mean," replied Mancini.

Later, Mancini explained his sense of the parallels. The issue was not life or death as it had been for thirteen months in Vietnam. But the pressures were enormous, and he personalized and internalized all of them. He was running several miles a day to escape some of the pressure. He was losing weight. His divorce had been finalized and he had already ended a brief new romance with a woman he had hired as a consultant on the development. He was tired and the job was going poorly from almost every imaginable perspective.

"You are going over budget," he said. "You don't know what the project is going to look like. Maybe the Peat Marwick guy is right and the atrium will be an F. The project manager is out there on the edge by himself. He is the platoon leader leading his guys up the hill."

The exchange with Sabo occurred in the fall of 1987, as Mancini contemplated the new deadlines for phase one and the continuing difficulties associated with the new construction. By this point, a grimness had settled over these troops. The music had stopped in a game of musical chairs. There was no more joking or friendly banter with Randy Verrue, who was coming under pressure himself from the corporate executives and board of directors back in Framingham. The issue was raised at a number of board meetings. There was concern about the overruns, but also about the apparent inability of the on-site managers to provide an accurate assessment of how bad things were and how much it was going to cost to finish the job.

Verrue had never had significant cost overruns on one of his projects before. Tom Steele cautioned him: "Once the overruns start, you cannot stop them directly in terms of money. But you can mitigate their impact financially by establishing options for what to do. What we need to know back here, as early as possible, is what the ultimate outcome is going to be so we can begin preparations that give us the most options possible." But Verrue, dependent on the optimistic Ron Tutor for all of his numbers, was unable to predict where costs were headed. So each new bump up in the estimate created new uncertainty in Framingham.

For Mancini, the matter was more personal. He started losing control of his temper more often. One day he blew up at Topping over a small matter and chewed him out in his best Marine Corps language. Topping, who is several inches taller and fifty or sixty pounds heavier than the compact Mancini, shot back: "Don't mess with me like this, Jay. You are yelling at the wrong guy. I've worked the hardest for you on this project and I've always had your best interests in mind." Mancini apologized and never again lost his temper with Topping.

But the pressures continued. Mancini would find himself writing a report to Verrue on cost overruns or why the cherrywood for the storefronts was running four times the cost of metal and glass, and he would suddenly plunge into a deep depression. This was when he began to walk to his apartment a few blocks away over lunch hour every day and take a noontime run along the waterfront to clear his head.

"It was profoundly demoralizing," he explained later. "I had a great sense of personal failure. I wasn't able to predict events, much less control them. I had this image of Rincon as a rogue elephant and I'm the mahout and the elephant is off in the bush and I'm running after him. All I could do was the best I could do.

"I knew Randy was getting pressures from the home office. I had the feeling that the Perini executives thought, 'Who are these yahoos?' You get a sense no one believes in you. There is a time when no one can see how good it is going to be and the numbers are all going the wrong way. You begin to doubt the value of the project yourself. You can't quit. That's not cricket. Either they fire you or you complete the project."

What he needed was a victory. And finally he got it.

Near the middle of November, Mancini and the other principal participants in the Rincon project gathered at the Exploratorium, an offbeat science museum in the Marina District. They were there to test the centerpiece of the five-story atrium, the water column. As Mancini got out of a taxi and walked toward the museum entrance, he believed that more was at stake than artistic design. He needed something that would restore the confidence of his employers, demonstrate that the project was on track, save his job. Mancini needed the atrium's water column to work.

Doug Hollis had spent weeks working on the mechanics necessary to execute his plan for a giant but elegant shower in the middle of the atrium. He had begun calling it a rain column, and what he wanted was an even, steady flow of water from the skylight into a shallow basin on the floor. The trick was to make sure that the water did not splash when it hit the basin.

No one knew whether the rain column would work. Nothing like it had ever been tried before. And that generated understandable nervousness among everyone connected with the project. A fountain in Rincon's atrium would not have raised an eyebrow. But water falling eighty-five feet in a column? The idea was exciting and, if it worked, it would be something that would draw people to the development. But Mancini's first question after Hollis had unveiled it months earlier was still unanswered: Will it work?

If drops sprayed when they hit, the shallow pool containing the water would have to be enlarged. And that would mean intruding on the available room for pedestrian flow and for the tables of the fast-food restaurants called for in the plan. Instead of an open, pleasant area where people gathered for food and conversation, the atrium would feel cramped, jammed. People would not be drawn there for lunch or to grab a drink. And if an atrium did not attract people, the restaurants and shops would suffer. But since Rincon Center was a mixed-use project, there would be a ripple effect because the activity generated by the shops and restaurants was one of the big draws in the plans to lease the offices and rent the apartments.

Hollis had rigged up a half-scale test at the Exploratorium for a Monday, when the museum was closed to the public. He had once been an artist-in-residence at the museum and had chosen it as the test site for a couple of reasons. First, it was one of the few places with a ceiling high enough, forty-five feet, to test the column. Second, as a center for experimentation in science and art, the Exploratorium was one of the few places that would let an artist run a hose up to the roof and spray water down at the floor.

To help translate his vision into something workable, Hollis had turned to Ned Kahn, a friend who creates exhibits at the Exploratorium. They had assembled a primitive mock-up earlier that day. A Plexiglas tray measuring four feet on each side and perforated with 2,000 holes had been hoisted to the ceiling. A garden hose had been strung up to the Plexiglas and a satellite dish had been upended on the floor beneath it to catch the water. Hollis and Kahn had calculated that the drops would reach maximum velocity from forty-five feet. So the additional forty-foot drop in the atrium should not affect the splashing of the real thing.

While the garden hose and satellite dish were crude, weeks of planning had gone into the test. Hollis wanted the drops to fall out of the panel like rain, steadily but randomly. He and Kahn had tried various patterns for holes in a search for the perfect flow. Along with the pattern, the distance between the holes was important. The waterfall could not be too dense, but it had to be heavy enough to create the sound effects that were a critical part of the piece. They eventually decided on a grid pattern within a circle inside the square panel. Two thousand holes were drilled an inch apart across the circle.

As he walked into the cavernous museum that day, Jay Mancini heard the sound of falling water before he could see the column itself. It was a pleasing sound. But it told him nothing of the central question. Before Mancini reached the mock-up, Hollis had turned off the water. He wanted to wait until everyone was assembled to demonstrate his rain column.

Mancini was the first to arrive. He was soon joined by Harry Topping, Scott Johnson, Randy Verrue, Bob Carey, and a couple of the new leasing agents. As they looked on, Hollis turned the spigot and the water began pouring through the Plexiglas pan. It fell in a soft, even flow. When it reached the satellite dish, the sound was indeed pleasing and musical. Even more pleasing, the dish contained the splashes.

As Hollis watched the onlookers, he had the sense that they were mesmerized. "It was like all of a sudden these little wheels started to spin and they understood what a good thing it was," he said. "They were knocked out by it. I was knocked out by it. It was beautiful and it was great to see that it actually worked."

Scott Johnson was not quite mesmerized, but he was quite satisfied. The rain column would be a good addition to the atrium. It was the final major detail and finally it had been settled. Randy Verrue liked it. The drama reminded him of the soaring atriums that had become the trademark of the successful Hyatt Hotel chain, an effect Verrue had long hoped to imitate at Rincon Center. And the sound would fulfill what he had seen as the device's primary function, providing white noise to muffle the conversations of the diners, add energy to the public space, and turn the balconies on the upper floors into space that could be used by the office workers—and hence, added to the square footage when the rent was calculated.

To Jay Mancini, the rain column was nothing less than magical. He had wanted a piece of art that would focus attention on the center of the atrium. But here was something more, something riveting and delightful. He closed his eyes and imagined the sound tumbling through an atrium crowded with people. He left the Exploratorium uplifted. If his troubles were not all behind him, as he knew they were not, at least this major piece of work had gone right.

The euphoria of success, unfortunately, was short lived. About two weeks in this case.

21

A MOMENT OF DECISION

The regular monthly draw meeting for Rincon Center at Citibank was held on December 2. Ron Tutor wanted more money for concrete and rebar. If his request was approved, 90 percent of the two budgets would be spent. Yet Ben Wang had told Bob Mayer that the towers were only up ten stories. Wang's estimate was that the job was only 50 percent complete, so far as the concrete and rebar were concerned. So Mayer refused to loan the project more money for concrete. His intent was never to stop the project. He was not even overly concerned about the costs in general. He was confident that Perini was going to perform. But he needed to draw attention to the problem with the concrete and rebar so that a solution would be devised. The earlier assurances from the developers had not been sufficient, as the current problems proved. "As a banker, you sometimes have to force customers to come to grips with an issue," he said.

But his action did threaten the project's future. Cutting off the concrete money meant Tutor would not be paid for additional concrete work. He in turn would stop paying the concrete suppliers and other subcontractors involved in that aspect of the project. The impact would ripple through the development and threaten to bring the whole effort to a halt.

A few days after Mayer's drastic action, Tutor submitted a huge change order to Randy Verrue. He wanted $3 million more for the concrete and rebar budgets. He blamed the overruns on changes in the design of the building since the GMP had been signed and on overdesigning in the concrete columns and girders. None of it was his fault, Tutor said, so he would not pay the costs.

Verrue faced a crisis. Approve the change order and he would have to persuade Mayer to unfreeze the concrete budget or Perini would foot the bill for the extra costs. Demand that Tutor honor the GMP and the contractor could shut the job down and mothball the project until a court settled the dispute. He managed to buy a little time by promising Tutor that he would work out a solution. For a few weeks, Tutor continued to work. But he did not pay the suppliers of steel and concrete. And some subcontractors went unpaid as well. He and Verrue engaged in heated encounters during those weeks, with Tutor threatening to walk off the site and Verrue promising to haul him into court if he did not fulfill the contract.

For Verrue, it came to a head in February, when Tutor wrote him a letter which said that Perini Land & Development, as the general partner, would either renegotiate the GMP contract or Tutor would shut the job down. As he had in the earlier discussions, Tutor argued that design changes and other factors outside his control were responsible for the additional concrete and rebar. Verrue responded with a letter of his own, repeating that Tutor had a contract specifying the amount allocated for the concrete and rebar work and he had better honor it.

But Verrue knew the situation was more complicated than that. Enforcing the contract meant shutting down the entire project, since Tutor's role extended to the renovation, too. Pacific Bell had started moving employees into the unfinished post office building in February, a month later than planned but not late enough to upset the deal. However, if the project was mothballed now, they would surely pack up and cancel the lease. Then the developers would have to wait until a judge decided whether the developer or the general contractor was responsible for paying for the extra concrete and rebar. Alternatively, simply firing Tutor-Saliba and bringing in another contractor would mean long delays while the job was bid again and the new personnel got up to speed. And there was a chance that Tutor could go to court and win a restraining order stopping work until the issue was re-solved.

In the meantime, whether awaiting a court decision or getting out new bids, Perini would still face interest costs in excess of $40,000 a day. The bank could decide not to wait for the outcome and foreclose, taking back the project and turning it over to another developer for completion. Perini could lose every penny it had put into the project.

Another potential cost of stopping the project and going to court was hidden, but just as real. Even if the issue was resolved in a matter of months, a record time considering the crowded court docket in San Francisco and every other major city, Rincon Center would restart with a stigma. Brokers would have stopped trying to lease space. Its niche in the market might have been lost. Potential tenants would always wonder what really caused the shutdown, why Pacific Bell had moved out, whether corners had been cut to cope with the budget problems or work had been shoddy.

"No matter what the contract says, the practical matter is that you don't stop construction," said Verrue.

His conversations with Perini executives in Framingham convinced Verrue that they shared his sentiment. Tom Steele said later: "It is never a pleasant trade-off, and there were some pretty serious disputes here. But in the final analysis, and this happens often in big projects, you have to make a decision about what is the most practical way to proceed with respect to your dispute with the contractor. Because the project was so far along and there were so many dollars riding on it, any kind of a slowdown, let alone a stoppage, was going to be enormously expensive. We felt that the most rational economic decision was to get the project done. Once you are that far into a project, you have to get it done. Any delays will just absolutely kill the economics. That's the way the numbers work."

The GMP contract had turned out to be worthless. Or, as Bob Mayer summed up the agreement: "It wasn't a contract. It was a piece of garbage."

Although there have been instances in which developers have fired contractors midproject, they are extremely unusual. Practical considerations almost always override the legal ones. "Litigation," says Tom Steele, "is rarely satisfactory to anyone but the lawyers."

The contract with Tutor would be renegotiated and, in the meantime, Citibank agreed to free up additional money so work could continue. In February, Tutor came over to Verrue's office and sat down with Verrue, Mancini, and John Costello. Verrue's assistants were trying to explain the magnitude of the financial problems to him and Tutor kept interrupting to denigrate Costello and Mancini.

His language was extremely harsh and personal. While Randy Verrue is tough and frequently uses strong language, he does not swear in public. He refused to sit quietly as Tutor berated his staff, so he stood up at the conference table and said simply and loudly, "This meeting is over." With that, he walked out of the room, followed by the surprised Mancini and Costello.

Verrue decided that he would conduct the remaining talks with Tutor by himself. In the meantime, he told Mancini and Costello to prepare an overview of the budget to see how far out of line costs had got. He wanted a preliminary report in his hands before he sat down again with Tutor.

The updated budget numbers were not good. Tutor's request to increase the budget for concrete and rebar by $3 million was probably on the optimistic side. Other costs, such as those related to the excavation and the "soft costs" for architects and consultants, were also well over budget. Delays had pushed the timetable back at least six months, and Costello acknowledged that further delays seemed likely because the concrete process was taking so long. The building was beginning to look more like a $74 million job than a $64 million one.

Verrue and Tutor held several sessions and, as Verrue recalled it later, most of them involved heated exchanges and ended with Ron Tutor shouting about one thing or another. The point the general contractor continued to hammer on was that the working documents had not been completed when the GMP was reached. And, he claimed, even since the drawings had been completed, there were changes almost weekly that were affecting his costs and his ability to keep his schedule. He was particularly insistent that the revised drawings called for more rebar than the original documents. Verrue was unsympathetic. He said the working drawings were 95 percent done when the contract was signed. Tutor was an experienced contractor, he said, and should have known what he was getting into.

After three weeks without a settlement, Verrue decided that they needed a mediator to help resolve the dispute. The logical choice was David Perini, the chairman of Perini Corporation and an astute and reasonable businessman. Perini also had a long relationship with Tutor. But the tangled corporate relationships in Rincon Center put David Perini in an awkward position. Not only was Tutor the general contractor and a part owner, Tutor-Saliba and Perini Construction were partners on the construction contract for the job. Some of the responsibility for the overruns and delays might actually be the responsibility of the Perini affiliate. That placed Perini Land & Development, as general partner in Rincon Center Associates, on one side of the bargaining table and Perini Construction on the other. David Perini could not involve himself in talks with one foot on each side of the divide.

In his place, Perini appointed Jack Chiaverini, the western division construction manager for Perini and the man who had persuaded Verrue to take a second look at Rincon four years earlier. Both Verrue and Tutor respected Chiaverini and within days he had found a middle ground between the two men. By the middle of March, a letter of understanding was negotiated that amounted to a cost-plus contract for Tutor-Saliba. The developers would pay the entire cost of construction and Tutor would receive a flat fee. But there was a sting in the deal for Tutor, too. His original arrangement was for a fee of 3.5 percent over the construction costs. At the GMP, the fee was worth more than $2.3 million. With construction costs headed toward $75 million or more, the fee would rise to more than $2.5 million. But the new deal reduced Tutor's take to a flat $2 million. And rather than pay him in the normal manner, as work progressed, he would not receive the first $1 million until a year after completion of the project. The second million would be withheld until two years after the job was finished.

"What that allowed us to do was hold the money to help pay for the overruns and generate money from the completed project before we paid his fee," explained Verrue later.

The episode contributed to the sense shared by many people associated with the project that Rincon Center's new buildings never should have been built out of concrete. The design demands for a concrete building in a seismic area erased the cost advantages over steel. The complicated nature of the construction slowed a process that was probably never going to go as fast as Ron Tutor had expected. Scott Johnson believed that Tutor had underestimated the complexity and costs because he was unaccustomed to building this sort of premium mixed-use project.

For all his detractors, there was validity to Tutor's claims. Design changes had affected the construction schedule. The ductile-frame system required more concrete and steel rebar than anyone had anticipated. If he was unaccustomed to dealing with a project of this complexity, so too were the architect and the developers. The space shot, as Johnson had termed it, had created unforeseen problems for everyone associated with Rincon.

Indeed, some of the design problems and changes that Tutor complained about involved the layouts for the apartments. Plumbing systems had not lined up properly and expensive modifications were required as construction progressed. Beams had been moved to improve the floor plans, requiring additional costs and time. Those were problems that Ron Tutor had to cope with, but they were not problems he had created.

Harry Topping had first expressed concern about the apartment floor plans in April 1986. At the time, he was examining the residential layout of both towers in an attempt to find the least expensive way of fulfilling the developer's agreement to provide apartments at below-market rates to low- and moderate-income tenants.

The original development agreement with the redevelopment agency specified that 20 percent of Rincon's apartments be rented at below-market rates, called BMR units. However, in negotiating for the $36 million in tax-exempt bonds, the developer had agreed to increase that figure to 50 percent of the 320 apartments. Like most housing subsidies, the agreement had a time limit. In this case, the rent controls would expire ten years after the first 10 percent of the units were occupied. If the towers were turned into condominiums before the time was up, roughly one-quarter of the units had to be sold to qualified low- and moderate-income people. If there were not enough qualified buyers in those categories, the redevelopment agency would have an option to buy 50 percent of the unsold low- and moderate-income units at 15 percent over the developer's cost of construction.

The BMRs were divided into three categories, based on a rising percentage of the city's median income: low income, moderate income, and affordable. The low-income units, which would make up 20 percent of the apartments, were expected to rent for $599 a month. They had to be "reasonably distributed" throughout the towers and they had to reflect the same general mix of the building. In other words, if half the apartments were one-bedroom units, then roughly half the low-income units would be one-bedroom units. (The developer did succeed in exempting the development's premium units, the two-bedroom, two-bath apartments, from the rent-control program.) The rents in the other categories were expected to average $804 a month for moderate-income units and $1,050 a month for affordable units. These were not exactly poverty levels, but they were still well under the average rents for similar housing in the city at the time. The only restriction on the other two categories was that not all of them be located on the same floor.

These factors play a long-term role in the economics of a project and there is a tension between developers and public agencies on several fronts. Not the least of them is the location of the apartments. The developer wanted to concentrate the BMR units in the apartments that would fetch the cheapest price anyway, namely the studios on the lower floors. Locating the BMRs on a few lower floors also would meet a need that no one was willing to say out loud: the professionals who could afford the full rents would not have to rub shoulders with the lower-income tenants. But the redevelopment agency was after economic integration as well as badly needed affordable housing. They did not want to create a mini-ghetto within the project. So the agreement set out some broad parameters aimed at mixing the units throughout both towers.

These guidelines gave Topping and the development's housing consultant, Janet Roche, considerable latitude in deciding which units would fall under the rental guidelines. For instance, the low-income units might have to be spread "reasonably" throughout the building, but Topping came up with a plan to keep the apartments with the best views outside the rent restrictions. While the moderate-income and affordable units could not be grouped on a single floor, Roche devised a plan to concentrate them on the lower floors. Also, since there was no regulation on the mix of units for these two categories, she restricted them to the smaller units.

"Harry and I went floor by floor for days," said Roche. "We wanted to gang up the moderate and affordable units on the lower floors and in the one-bedroom and studio apartments." The resulting housing chart distributed the sixty-four low-income units evenly throughout the building and by size. There were twenty-one studios, thirty-three one-bedrooms, and ten two-bedrooms, and they were located all the way to the 22nd floor, which was the top residential floor since the 23rd and 24th floors contained mechanical equipment. But the story was different for the other two categories. Sixty of the ninety-six units were studios; the remainder were one-bedrooms. None was above the 15th floor.

When the redevelopment agency staff got their first look at the chart in late August of 1986, they objected strenuously. They complained that the units had to be distributed evenly throughout the building. Roche pulled out the agreement and flipped to the pages where she had underlined the guidelines, which were much more vague. The staff still objected, accusing the developers of violating the spirit of the agreement. But Topping and Roche, who had gone over the chart with the project's lawyers, knew they were on firm ground. When they refused to budge, the staff had no choice but to relent and approve the housing plan.

Because Topping had gone over the floor plans so thoroughly to isolate the BMR apartments, he had been the first person on the developer's team to examine the units closely. Jay Mancini's insistence on smaller units back in 1985 had been a cost-saving measure. But now Topping was worried that the ceilings, down to seven feet in some places, were too low and that some of the rooms seemed too small for furniture. The marketing plan for the apartments would emphasize view, convenient location, and such amenities as a concierge. But you had to be able to fit a bed into a bedroom in even the fanciest building. Some of the beams also bothered him. It was one thing to have a beam drop low along a wall or in front of a window. It was another, less acceptable situation when a low beam sliced diagonally across the living room.

Yet these were the floor plans that the architects had come up with in response to Mancini's space restrictions and, contrary to later assertions by some, the room sizes and ceiling heights met the building codes. What Topping was about to embark on was a major redesign of the apartment space at an extremely late date in the project in an attempt to come up with units that he thought would be easier to rent.

By June 1986, Topping had got Mancini's okay to have an outside architect examine the designs to see if the apartments would be marketable. Topping then telephoned Bruce Ross, a partner at the San Francisco firm of Backen, Arrigoni and Ross, which had started out in 1966 as specialists in designing high-density, multifamily housing. While their work had branched out laterally into most other areas of architecture, the firm still retained a reputation as one of the leading housing-design shops in the city. Topping sent over drawings for the apartments and asked Ross to critique the plans from a marketability standpoint.

A few days later, Ross telephoned Topping and said: "Harry, the problem is not marketability. These things don't even work. There are master bedrooms where, once you put the bed in the room, you can't open the door. It looks to me like nobody thought about furniture."

Topping was receptive when Ross said that the plans were so bad that the best way to proceed was for Ross to make drawings to alter the floor plans in simple ways that would make them workable. He did a series of overlay sketches, adjusting room sizes and locations in minor ways, presented them to Topping, and then flew down to Los Angeles to meet for the only time with the architects at Pereira Associates. Scott Johnson did not attend the meeting, and said later that he never even knew that Bruce Ross was reworking his plans.

Ross was in an uncomfortable position. He did not like to be reworking the designs of another architect. But he believed a housing specialist should have been involved from the start of design work on the project because of the complications in stacking so many different uses on top of each other in one structure. He thought that the architects at Pereira had had their hands full with other matters and had not devoted enough time or expertise to laying out the apartments.

"If you don't do housing, you take these things for granted," Ross explained to Topping. "You draw a kitchen, a square. There are counters and a place for the stove and the refrigerator. But a good kitchen is like a watch. The pieces need to fit nicely and work, especially when you are talking about production housing—that is, housing with lots of units. You want cabinets to be standard and spaces for refrigerators to be standard so you can use the same types in every unit. You draw a bedroom, fine. But every bedroom must have a bed wall, a space large enough to accommodate a bed and still allow the door to the hall to open into the room."

The uses of the new building, from the garage to the retail stores through the offices to the apartments, had created a jumbled grid of columns and beams. By the time the jumble reached the apartments, it created a mess of diagonal beams and overlarge columns. Larger units would have given the planners room to work around such things as a three-foot-square column protruding through the kitchen. Taller floor-to-ceiling heights would have allowed dropped ceilings to conceal the obtrusive beams. No such flexibility existed at Rincon. The space between floors had been kept to the minimum to allow the greatest number of floors possible within the city's height restriction. The units were small at the developer's insistence, designed to rent for view and service, not space. And the odd shapes were dictated by the stepbacks and curves of the exterior design, which in turn was a product of many forces. These conditions necessitated careful planning by experienced hands to make the apartments work. And, as Ross explained the situation to Topping, he felt that that had not happened.

At the meeting in Los Angeles with the young architects and Chuck Grein, the senior supervising architect on the project for Pereira, Ross tried to keep as low a profile as possible, and Topping did the talking. He explained that the floor plans needed to be reworked to make sure that every bedroom accommodated a bed, that ceilings were a comfortable and legal height. Topping sensed a level of hostility among the younger architects, but he found Grein to be a pro, accommodating and eager to resolve the problems. Grein promised personally to supervise a reworking, and he took the sketches Ross had done as a starting point.

During this period, Topping and Johnson had several conversations about the changes that Topping wanted in the apartment layouts. In those talks, Johnson never recalled that Topping had told him Bruce Ross was doing new floor plans. (Johnson said he would definitely have remembered Ross since he had considered applying to the firm after he graduated from Berkeley because he admired its work. Rather, Johnson said, he was simply informed that the changes were being requested by "Perini rental marketing people.")

When the new plans came back a few weeks later, Topping was still not satisfied. Calling Ross over to look at the changes, Topping said: "They're not making it. They are trying to put on Band-Aids." At Topping's urging, Ross agreed to become more deeply involved. He would examine the residential floor plans in detail, studying whether corridors, columns, and beams could be altered to cure some of the continuing ills. He also had an idea for a major change that could be a real plus for marketing.

Much of the building's pattern, of course, could not be changed. The so-called footprint, or shape of the building, had been determined over months of designing and negotiations with the redevelopment agency. The structural engineers had translated the design into a system of columns and beams to support the building. Unfortunately, the engineering specifications required columns and beams that were so big they impinged on the apartments. In an office building, this would not have been as much of a problem. But in housing, when you start subdividing the space into rooms, you get smaller pieces to work with and the problems become significant. This late in the game, the basic structure of the building could not be altered in a major way. That is part of the reason the first solutions offered by the Pereira architects seemed like Band-Aids to Topping. But Ross took a fresh look at the floor plans, discussed with the engineers the possibility of moving some particularly offensive beams, and started refining the floor plans for the units.

Some beams were moved in the drawings when there was no alternative means of allowing ceilings to be raised to eight feet. Where beams appeared in strange places and could not be moved, Ross looked for ways to expose them as part of the decoration, enclose them to create a different level of ceiling, or incorporate them into a closet by rearranging the room. Bathrooms had to be moved because they had been located too far from the main vertical plumbing cores, called chases, that ran through the building. Appliance locations were rearranged in many of the kitchens so that the small spaces flowed better.

One of the major changes made by Ross was motivated more by marketing than design considerations. The largest apartment in the plans was a two-bedroom, two-bath unit. The Pereira architects had placed the bedrooms side by side, a conventional pattern that permitted the economy of shared plumbing for the bathrooms. Ross split the bedrooms, creating two master bedrooms and bathrooms on either side of the living room. Dividing the bedrooms made them more private and would enhance the appeal of the apartments to two groups of prospective tenants: corporations looking for short-term space for unrelated employees and people forced to share an apartment with someone else in the expensive San Francisco housing market.

These alterations occurred over a period of many weeks. Plans were passed back and forth between Ross and the Pereira architects through Topping. The engineers from Chin & Hensolt also were involved in okaying the changes. Completion of the final plans dragged into 1987, after construction had begun on the new phase of the project.

From these layout changes, others hung. Moving even sixty or so beams rippled down through the structure, causing additional changes in column and beam grids. Shifting one of the bathrooms in the two-bedroom layout to the other side of the apartment required reworking the plumbing lines to the vertical core of pipes.

This eleventh-hour reprogramming of the entire residential space reflected many of the problems that afflicted the Rincon development. The original plans had been approved by Jay Mancini, probably without sufficient consideration of how well the resulting units would rent. Once the potential problems were discovered, albeit inadvertently, Harry Topping had brought in an outside architect to rework Johnson's designs, adding more costs and delays. This is part of what Ron Tutor was complaining about and, though they denied it, perhaps was part of the reason for the developer's decision to negotiate a new construction contract with the contractor rather than confront a judge. Coupled with the fears over mothballing the project and losing the multimillion-dollar lease with Pacific Bell, Verrue may have felt he had no choice but to negotiate the best arrangement possible with Tutor to keep the project going.

22

THE CHRYSLER
BAILOUT

By the spring of 1988, Perini had been paying a million a month out of its own pocket for a year, and the tab would soon triple to $3 million a month to cope with rising overruns. Perini Corporation was not exactly reeling from the costs, but nobody was happy. There was pressure from the corporate offices in Framingham, and Jay Mancini and Randy Verrue were beginning to wonder whether Rincon Center would cost them their jobs.

For Verrue, undertaking Rincon was an attempt to move Perini into the big league of development on the West Coast. While he often pointed to the Golden Gateway Commons as a comparable mixed-use project accomplished by Perini, in fact it was not as complex and Perini's role had been more limited. By this juncture, Tom Steele and some of the board members back in Massachusetts had begun to wonder if Verrue and the rest of his team had moved too quickly on a project of the complexity and magnitude of Rincon. Questions about the cost overruns and delays were now coming up at every board meeting. When Verrue and Perini's other regional managers assembled in Framingham every three months to compare notes on their projects, the problems at Rincon Center were the subject of lengthy discussions. For the first time in nearly a decade with Perini, Verrue found himself in the uncomfortable position of defending the red ink in which the biggest project of his career was drowning. And that did not bode well for his future with the company.

Mancini had even more at stake. Unlike his boss, he did not have a track record of successes that would cushion him from the fallout of a disastrous project. He also lacked Verrue's self-confidence, and the financial pressures rekindled Mancini's fear that he would be fired. Mancini, who had thought the rain column's successful test at the Exploratorium had got him out from under the dark clouds, began confiding in his closest friends that he wouldn't be surprised to find himself out of a job. Much like the development company itself, Mancini had seen Rincon Center as a chance to leapfrog up from suburban office parks to big-time downtown projects. Now it seemed as though he might find himself selling warehouses with his father again.

Even Scott Johnson was not immune from the financial problems besetting Rincon. He had staked a substantial amount of his future and that of his firm on completing a trophy development in downtown San Francisco. It was his way of signaling the birth of the new Pereira Associates in a town that was home to Bill Pereira's most famous building. If Rincon Center got shut down, or became known as a giant white elephant in real estate and architectural circles, then Johnson would suffer the consequences, too. And it would come at a delicate stage in his career.

While the ultimate success of the development itself would not be known for years, the fates of Verrue, Mancini, and, to a lesser extent, Johnson were a much more short-term affair. By the spring of 1988, all bets seemed to be riding on whether a financial partner could be found to shoulder enough of the financial burden to ease the pressure from Framingham and Citibank long enough to complete Rincon Center.

As Bob Mayer had expected, Perini had the financial resources and the corporate integrity to come up with the money to cover the ballooning costs. But as the overruns rose, so did the pressure for a permanent solution. No one had done more than kick the tires when the prospective deal involved selling a share of the entire project. After all, it was unfinished and even a cursory look at the books showed that it was beset with financial problems. So, if they couldn't sell a stake in the entire development, the decision was made to concentrate on selling the nearly completed renovation. "It was really the only piece of the property that could carry a deal," said John Schwarz, the chief financial officer of Perini Land & Development.

Limiting the sale to the renovated building also would extract maximum value from the Pac Bell lease, since an investor was far more likely to buy an occupied building with a reliable revenue stream. Perini hoped to sell it for enough to pay off the portion of the Citibank loan covering that phase of the project and finance the overruns on the second phase. But, like so many other things associated with Rincon Center, there was a twist. It would not be an outright sale. Perini still wanted to maintain as much control as possible over the entire project, and the Postal Service might balk at anything less.

The plan was to sell phase one to an institutional investor who would lease the building back to the developers so they could still operate the entire project. This type of transaction, called a sale-leaseback, is really an inexpensive loan structured to look like a sale in order to satisfy the tax code. It's all perfectly legal. The 1986 tax reform had knocked out tax shelters for wealthy investors, but the law still allowed corporations to write off their investments in new plants and facilities. The write-off took the form of long-term depreciation, and it was designed to encourage businesses to make capital investments to create jobs and stimulate the economy. It seemed a sound theory and, under the proper circumstances, a major corporation could use the depreciation allowances associated with these expenditures to shelter operating income.

If Verrue and the others could find a way to make this sale work, perhaps the project and their careers would be salvaged. If not, Perini would keep pouring in more money to complete the project, and that was a prospect that did not bode well for the job future of anyone connected with the development.

Once Perini began to offer only the renovated, newly leased building for sale, there was interest from several corporations. Preliminary talks were held with three or four. The best offer seemed to come from Chrysler Corporation through a unit called Chrysler-McNally, a subsidiary of its credit division. The idea of Chrysler bailing out anyone would have been laughable a decade earlier, when it was the recipient of a huge federal bailout. But the company was posting record earnings by 1988 and the depreciation advantages looked good to its financial experts.

Here is the way the multistep transaction was designed to work after several weeks of negotiations: the price was to be $63.5 million.

Chrysler-McNally would pay Perini $7.5 million in cash and get a permanent loan of its own for the remaining $56 million. Perini would arrange the loan and guarantee to pay all of the costs to complete the renovation. Perini would retain the master lease on the space in the building, which meant the rent money would flow to the developers and then be used to pay Chrysler's loan payments. In addition, Perini guaranteed Chrysler a 7 percent return on its investment. The $56 million loan would be used to pay off the $54 million of the Citibank construction loan associated with the renovation and cover some of the overruns to date. Perini would be able to use the $7.5 million cash to offset some of what it paid in as equity and some of the overruns on the second phase.

The transaction also provided Perini with an option to repurchase the property at the original sale price at intervals of ten, fifteen, and twenty years after the deal was closed. This aspect of the deal really turned it into a cheap loan for Perini. The buyback gave Perini the option of returning Chrysler's principal after paying what amounted to 7 percent interest in the interval. This resulted in a considerable savings at a time when interest rates were 11 percent and higher for a conventional construction loan.

This interest-rate margin was one reason Perini chose to sell the renovation phase rather than secure a take-out loan on its own for that portion of the project. The sale also was expected to net more money. Even if a bank had agreed to make a long-term loan on the first phase, the rule of thumb was that the loan not exceed 75 percent of the value. At $63.5 million, that would have totaled only $47.25 million. And that presumes a bank would have agreed the renovation was worth that much in the first place, which turned out to be quite a presumption. In exploring a potential deal soon after the Pac Bell lease was signed, Perini found that it could borrow only $47 million from an insurance-company pension fund in a conventional loan arrangement and that plan was dropped.

What Perini had here was another form of a tax-driven deal. The depreciation credits made the deal work from Chrysler's end, and the repurchase agreement was critical from Perini's perspective. However, changes in accounting regulations scheduled to go into effect June 30 would wipe out the repurchase option in depreciation-driven deals and make other, damaging changes in the way the deal could be recorded on the books of both Chrysler and Perini, so there was a rush to complete the transaction.

When Randy Verrue brought this complicated deal to Bob Mayer near the end of April, he wanted desperately for Citibank to make the loan to Chrysler and haul his project out of the fire. The bank knew the project and was most likely to provide the quick approval needed to make the deal work before the end of June. But again there was a hitch that threatened to scuttle the transaction: Mayer thought the figures were out of line. He calculated the value of the completed phase at only $54 million, the amount of the outstanding construction loan assigned to that phase. The maximum he would loan Chrysler was $43 million, slightly more than 75 percent of the estimated value.

"I don't think you can get $56 million," the banker told Verrue. "I don't think you can get more than $43 million."

"I think I can get it," Verrue said confidently. "I think Wells Fargo will do this loan for us."

On June 15, with just two weeks remaining under the deadline, Verrue was back at Citibank. He had not had the time to bring Wells Fargo up to date on the history and prospects of the project, so the bank had declined to make the loan within the time frame. Time was running out on the Chrysler bailout deal and Verrue knew it. This trip he said upfront that he would settle for $43 million on the new loan if the bank would transfer the remaining $11 million it was owed to the new phase of the project. Verrue had to wait two agonizing days, with the clock ticking, to hear back from his friend. After talks with his bosses, Mayer agreed to the $54 million transaction, but he wanted two additional commitments from Perini.

First, the second phase of the project would be used as additional security for the entire $54 million loan, not just the $11 million. Second, Perini had to put $5 million in an escrow account as additional security on phase one. Chrysler was paying Perini $7.5 million in cash. After closing costs and fees to obtain the new loan for Chrysler, Perini would net about $5 million. Perini had planned to use that money to help defray the overruns on phase two. Mayer wanted it locked up in an escrow account until the entire project was completed or all Citibank's loans were repaid. Randy Verrue was forced to agree to both demands. There was really no choice.

But it was not all "take" and no "give" on the bank's part. Shortly after the deal was concluded on June 30, Citibank agreed to increase the construction loan on the second phase to $28 million. The additional $17 million was to allow Perini to pay the tab for the mounting overruns and recover some of the money it had put into both projects.

The Chrysler sale-leaseback was less profitable for Perini and its partners in the short term than the syndication would have been. There were other problems from the developers' standpoint, too. For one thing, Chrysler would be the owner of the renovated portion of the project, so Perini's control over that phase would be limited. For instance, if the market took a dramatic upswing, Perini would be unable to sell the entire development and cash out at a handsome profit. But the transaction was clearly preferable to the alternative of Perini winding up with the whole tab for a project that was exceeding $70 million in construction costs by this time. And, for Verrue and Mancini, if the deal wasn't a miracle, it sure seemed to be close enough. They had the breathing room they needed to get the rest of the job done and cope with the still-rising construction costs.

The forces driving up the cost of the building were diverse. Even as the towers rose toward their full height, the amount of concrete and rebar required to build them was not slowing down as had been predicted. Instead of meeting Ron Tutor's early expectations for saving millions of dollars by building with concrete, the costs were going to exceed the budget by several million dollars. Delays had increased the carrying costs of the loans. The excavation problems had added $6 million to the cost of the project. The soft costs associated with hiring so many consultants and having so many aspects designed over and over had now skyrocketed to close to $8 million from the original $4.2 million and the revised $5.5 million of just a year before. A large part of the increase was associated with the extra work done by Ken Tardy's firm. Tardy's work had been budgeted at $250,000 for consulting work on the commercial floor plans. As Tardy became a sounding board and redesign center for Mancini, the fee had ballooned to almost $2 million. A fight also was brewing with Scott Johnson's Pereira Associates over the size of their bill for additional services, which was almost $1 million on top of the $2.4 million they were to receive on the base contract.

And there were still other additional expenses, some incurred through choice, not necessity.

Most people enter the renovated building through the historic lobby and pass on through a transition area leading to the atrium. So do most workers on their way to offices in the former post office. Scott Johnson had seen this as the visitor's introduction to the new interior, and he had designed a contemporary Plexiglas ceiling to conceal overhead lighting and, for the walls, a complex latticework of metal tubes. The stone in the floor had been carried partway up the wall to form a wainscoting. But around April, when the cherrywood was being added to the storefronts around the atrium, Mancini decided he did not like the transitional lobby. He told Scott Johnson that it seemed too cold and harsh. He really liked the rich tone of the cherry and, he wondered aloud to Johnson, "Couldn't we get some of that in this front lobby?"

Mancini ordered the latticework torn out of the lobby. And, since the wood was so rich, he wanted a new ceiling to reflect the new atmosphere. Johnson was given Richard Altoona's drawings for the storefronts and a sample of the cherrywood, and asked to adapt them to a new lobby scheme. The result was a new lobby design, with rich cherry walls and a sculpted ceiling with modern chandeliers. Mancini was pleased. He thought it made a far more dignified entry, particularly for the office workers. The price tag for the instant renovation: an additional $150,000, not counting the architects.

Not even the water column was immune from money problems. These costs were not enough to bring down the empire, or even dampen the enthusiasm for the piece. Rather, it demonstrated how the money problems seemed to have gained their own momentum and were rolling over everything connected with the project, soaking up a few hundred thousand here, a couple million there.

Doug Hollis knew the rain column had to be more than a garden hose and an upturned satellite dish. He also knew that he could not figure out every aspect of a more sophisticated system. To help implement his vision, he returned to the Exploratorium and engaged the services of Allen Wilson, a researcher there who had made a specialty of water. Mostly through Wilson's efforts, they designed a recirculating pumping system that would put fifty-five gallons of water a minute onto the Plexiglas panel. Water from the pool on the floor would drain to a small reservoir in the basement, where it would be pumped back to the skylight through pipes concealed in a wall of the atrium. The pipe leading out to the Plexiglas panel could be hidden in a piece of the frame supporting the skylight. While Wilson was not an engineer, he illustrated the plans in intricate drawings.

Creating the actual piece for the atrium involved essentially doubling the size of everything from the test model. The Plexiglas panel onto which the water would flow grew into a square measuring eight feet on each side, twice the size of the prototype. The holes were two inches apart, instead of one. The thickness, however, posed a dilemma. Hollis wanted the Plexiglas to be as thin as possible, hanging by thin cables and virtually invisible against the skylight. But the panel also had to be strong enough to support the water flow without bending. The Plexiglas for the prototype had been a quarter-inch thick. But the atrium version would be larger and more prone to twisting out of shape under the additional water pressure. After trying several thicknesses, Hollis and Wilson decided that three-eighths inch was the thinnest panel that would work.

The original assumption was that the water would fall into a pool surrounded by a short border or curb on which people could sit. But as Hollis worked on the full-scale version, he began doing sketches that showed the border growing smaller and smaller. Eventually, it disappeared entirely and the pool was flush with the floor of the atrium. Instead of flowing into a center drain, the pool would be shaped so the water would flow to a channel cut around the perimeter of the pool. The concept enhanced the image of the rain column falling into a pond in the country, particularly when coupled with the abstract wave pattern that Hollis was designing for the terrazzo floor around the basin. When Hollis described the idea for a pool flush with the floor to Mancini early in 1988, he was pleased by its immediate acceptance.

Where Mancini had trouble was with the plan for the plumbing. Wilson's drawings were not the sort of documents that a plumber could follow to actually build the recirculating pumping system. As he had many times in the past, Mancini turned to the ever-pragmatic Ken Tardy with the request to translate the vision into a workable reality.

Tardy, who is always blunt, described his role with the rain column this way: "This artist guy had done water features of a more pedestrian nature. But he has this designer-plumber, which is a pretty funny thing. But that guy is really brilliant. I had never received a set of plumbing working drawings that were done in perspective. It was actually kind of interesting. But whoa, there was a ways to go between interesting and making it work and comply with the various building and fire codes."

Along with translating the drawings into working documents for the plumbers, Tardy had to design a filter system for the recirculating water to keep it free of fungus and other bad elements. Where the pipes penetrated the concrete slab between the public space and the parking garage, he had to design elements to keep air and fire from coming through that space so that it met code. He had to find space in the parking level for the pumping room. The result was a twenty-page document and a fee to Tardy's firm of $45,000.

A total of $250,000 had been budgeted for the rain column, with $100,000 designated as the fee for Doug Hollis. But Mancini interpreted the fee to include the plans for getting the system up and working, so he wanted to take Tardy's $45,000 out of it. Hollis balked, they negotiated, and the artist wound up getting $65,000. The costs of actually installing the system also exceeded the estimate and the cost wound up at nearly $300,000.

The final system was installed in late March 1988. Hollis arranged with the plumbers to have a secret test on a Sunday afternoon, when the building was empty. He and Wilson met a plumber at the building and waited in the atrium while the plumber went down and turned on the system. As they stood there, eyes fixed on the panel eighty-five feet above them, the water burst through the wall about halfway up and sprayed down on them. Hollis raced down to the basement and told the plumber to shut off the system. When he examined it, the plumber discovered that he had left a valve closed in one of the riser pipes. The water pressure had built up where the valve was shut and burst the pipe.

At four o'clock on the following Friday afternoon, with office workers in the building, Hollis came back to the atrium with Jay Mancini for a second try at testing the system. The damaged wall had been repaired and the valves were all opened. As he had at the Exploratorium, Mancini believed an incredible amount was riding on the success or failure of the rain column. Even after the successful test of the model, Randy Verrue and others had asked him if he was sure the device was going to work at full scale. The sense that Mancini had developed was that his job was on the line once more. Randy Verrue would say later that Mancini had exaggerated the importance of the rain column on both occasions, that he had overdramatized the significance of the device and focused too many of his frustrations and hopes on it. But as he walked into the atrium for the test, Jay Mancini believed that nearly four years of work were on trial.

This time it worked. The water fell in an even pattern into the basin in the floor. It rippled out to the channeled edge and disappeared. The drops looked like rainfall on a pond. The sound filled the atrium, drawing workers from Pacific Bell out of their offices onto the balconies and decks. As Mancini looked up at the rain column and the workers, they began to applaud. One of the Pac Bell executives came into the atrium and walked up to Mancini. "How do you feel?" he asked. Mancini had only a one-word reply: "Vindicated."

The atrium walls were still being painted about the time of the rain column's successful debut. A few weeks earlier, a large sample of custom-blended paints had been tested on panels displayed at Richard Altoona's design studio in San Francisco. There, Altoona, Johnson, Mancini, and Topping had chosen the color, a light beige with darker speckles that they decided achieved the warmth and richness they were seeking. Mancini had then delegated oversight of the actual painting to Topping. As the chief painter began applying the paint to the actual atrium walls one day in March, Topping climbed onto the scaffolding and inspected the color. It seemed right to him, and so Topping called Mancini down for a look. He thought it was fine, too, just the right warmth and color.

The next day, Topping returned to the atrium to check on the progress. A team of painters was spraying on the paint. But it didn't look right to Topping. "This isn't the color we chose!" he shouted. "This isn't it. Oh, shit. Stop right now."

By this time, he and Mancini had moved to temporary offices on the 2nd floor of the post office. Topping ran to the offices and, out of breath, summoned Mancini. "They're painting it wrong. The color is wrong," he said. Together they hurried back to the atrium, with

Topping muttering that the painters must have somehow mixed up the blend. Just before they got there, Topping stopped cold and said: "But, you know, it looks more like sandstone. You might like it." Mancini examined the paint that had been applied and turned to Topping. "It is better, Harry. Let's paint the whole damn place this way. It's good somebody made a mistake." (Johnson later said he could see no difference in the final color and the original choice.)

In this last big push to finish the renovation, Mancini's instincts were telling him that the worst was behind him. The success of the rain column, finding a mistake in the paint that actually constituted an improvement, the financial relief provided by the Chrysler deal. It was "heavens are opening" kind of stuff for the beleagured project manager. Plenty of problems still lay ahead with the completion of the second phase. But Jay Mancini was buoyed. A measure of pride was restored. He stopped waking up with a sick sensation about his job.

By the spring of 1988, Scott Johnson's involvement with Rincon Center had tapered off. Mostly, it was a natural process. With the exception of the occasional flare-up, such as the transitional lobby, the design work was done. He had a solid enough staff now that he was comfortable relying on them to monitor the remaining work, with occasional consultations with him if a problem emerged. And partly it was the press of other business.

Through 1986 and much of 1987, Pereira Associates had struggled to stay alive. There was little work, except for Rincon, Fox Plaza, and Bill Fain's planning project in Hawaii. Dissension continued among the partners until, one by one, the remaining figures from the days of Bill Pereira resigned or retired. Roy Schmidt, who had served as president, and Allistair Laws, who had been replaced by Bill Fain as director of planning, had been the last to go, both retiring in early 1987.

Despite all the hopes he had initially for it, Rincon Center would not be finished in time to evoke the sort of publicity and attention that Johnson felt the firm needed to attract new commissions. Anyway, the new downtown plan in San Francisco had reduced the entire city to only 500,000 square feet of new office building a year, so there were few major commissions there. Los Angeles would be their primary market. So the bets for the future of the firm were riding chiefly on Fox Plaza, the thirty-four-story office tower that Johnson had designed for a knoll in Century City at the edge of the 20th Century-Fox movie lot. The building would be far more impressive than its thirty-four stories. First of all, the location was the corner of Avenue of the Stars and Olympic Boulevard, the focal point for commerce in the busy area on the west side of Los Angeles. Second, the building itself was a daring tower with a multifaceted crown that reflected light and seemed to revolve when seen from different angles. Amid its boxy and boring neighbors, Fox Plaza was flamboyant, with a skin of pink granite and gray tinted glass.

Even before its opening in the fall of 1987, the building had been honored by the Chamber of Commerce as the city's outstanding new commercial building. Although at $36 a square foot the rents were the highest ever charged in a West Los Angeles office building, Fox Plaza was 75 percent leased before it opened, and 100 percent of the space was taken within six months of the opening. A key element in the successful leasing: Johnson had designed the upper stories in a prism pattern that created sixteen prized corner offices per floor.

True to its location on one of the legendary studio lots, the building was even used as the setting for the Bruce Willis blockbuster movie *Die Hard*. It was a new experience for Johnson when he watched portions of the finished building destroyed and a model of it blown up during an early Hollywood screening of the film.

But that was the only discomfort associated with Fox Plaza for Johnson. The rest was all gain. On its heels came a stream of new commissions. The firm was hired to design a forty-story office building in Century City for JMB Realty, a major developer based in Chicago. They got the job of designing a twenty-story corporate headquarters building in nearby Glendale for the Carnation Company, and a new campus for the Otis Parsons School of Design in Los Angeles.

And there were projects that were destined to increase Johnson's profile and test his skills in other arenas of design. He landed the commission to design a state-of-the-art winery in the Napa Valley for a joint venture by California winemaker Robert Mondavi and the famous French vinter Baron Phillippe de Rothschild. Jerry Perenchio, a former partner of TV producer Norman Lear and a wealthy businessman in his own right, hired Johnson to oversee the restoration of a 30,000-square-foot mansion in Bel Air and the adjoining thirteen acres of formal gardens.

Late in the spring of 1988, the name of the firm had been changed to reflect the new reality. It became Johnson, Fain & Pereira Associates.

23

FINAL CEREMONIES

One cool, sunny September day in 1988, most of the people who had played a role in the renovation of the post office building, and several hundred who had not, came together for a party marking the official opening of that portion of the project. An hour before the party was to start, Scott Johnson had donned a white hard hat for a private tour of the construction still underway on the new building at the opposite end of the site. He had to ask a security guard for directions to find an entrance that was not locked or fenced and he laughed at himself when he could not find a stairway.

"I thought this space would have felt bigger," Johnson said as he walked through what was to become the main residential lobby on the Howard Street side of the building. The vaulted concrete ceiling was bare, displaying large heating and ventilation ducts and electrical wiring. The concrete floor was dusty and littered with Styrofoam coffee cups. "Ultimately there is nothing like standing in it," he said. "It's like doing a concert hall. You know, there is no scientific formula for acoustics. It is always a surprise, the way it turns out."

He climbed the stairs to the 7th floor, the start of the apartment levels, and slipped into a hallway. The apartments were far from finished, and the hallways were a repeat of the dirty concrete and exposed intestines of the building on the first floor. But a model apartment on the southeast corner had been decorated to entice early-bird renters, and Johnson wanted to get a look at it. The door was locked, so he stepped through the empty window opening of a neighboring unit and walked around the terrace to try an outside door. It was locked, too. But through the dirt-streaked windows, the interior of the apartment could be seen. It had been decorated in the style found in models everywhere, right down to magazines on the coffee table. The ceiling seemed low, but Johnson said that the oversized windows and the views from the inside counteract that sensation. Turning, he pointed to the bay and said, "See what I mean."

He turned back to his building and gestured up the facade of the tower, where much of the glass skin and four-by-five-foot pre-cast concrete panels had been attached to the metal trusses that would hold them in place. The pattern of the skin was hard to make out that close up, but Johnson described the way he had tried to scale down the mass of the towers into panels and planes that the eye could follow in a sequence up the facades.

As he started to leave, Johnson stopped and offered a summary of more than four years of involvement with Rincon Center: "This was the most exhaustive project I've ever undertaken. There are several reasons. One is the nature of doing a building in San Francisco in the eighties. Also there is the client. A project of this size and complexity was a new venture to them. I sometimes think I should have got a teaching fee in addition to an architectural fee. And this was the second major job I had after moving out to California from New York. I wasn't interested in giving up anything. I had fired the entire design team except one after coming out. I had to hoard almost every detail. If I had worked with these people for a long period, it would have been different. I am too busy today to come up every three or four days and make models with the junior architects. But on this one, I had to be there. Now, we have more experienced people. We can talk in abbreviated terms. But everything on this job had to be spelled out to everybody."

Johnson shook his head and smiled. "Let's go to the party," he said. "It should be interesting."

While the architect was touring the new phase of the development, an unusual ritual was being conducted in the renovated building. Despite the gala opening planned for later that day, Jay Mancini had never shaken the depression associated with the darkest days of the project. A deeply religious man, he had first decided that he would have a special blessing recited as part of the ceremonies that night. But on the morning of the celebration, he had changed his mind. That would not be good enough; it would not rid the project of what Mancini perceived as its taint. So he decided that he would try to purge these particular demons by having a priest conduct an exorcism in each and every room of the old post office.

For assistance, Mancini had called upon his closest friend, an Anglican Church bishop named John Cahoon. A robust and friendly man with a keen intellect, Cahoon had counseled Mancini for long hours during the collapse of his marriage and his profound anxieties over the development. So, if it would help his friend put this period behind him, Cahoon was happy to don his collar and deep burgundy vestments to rid the building of its evil spirits.

It took most of the afternoon. The two men would slip quietly into an office and Cahoon would flick a little holy water into the air and recite two psalms. Then, while the workers stared in puzzlement, the pair would leave and move to the next room. By the time the ritual was finished, Cahoon thought that his friend was noticeably cheered and ready for the party.

Naturally, the celebration was held in the atrium. A pianist, cellist, and violinist competed with the rain column to entertain the 700 or so guests as waiters in tuxedos passed among them with champagne and trays of food. The combination of sounds was pleasant: soft classical music, the falling water, and a steady burble of conversation and admiring comments about the building. The murals by Richard Haas caught the attention of one group of guests. Examining the panels depicting the modern history of San Francisco in muted pastels, they tried to pick out identifiable figures. The only person they could positively identify was A. W. Clausen, the chairman of Bank of America, in the panel commemorating the city's role as a financial center. The other figures seemed to be compilations, caricatures of the Silicon Valley computer expert, the educator, the poet, the athlete. Like these blurred identities, the murals themselves were fuzzy and almost indistinct in their softness. The colors were pinks, dove gray, and beige. The descriptive words they evoked were not dazzling, bold, or brave. They were corporate and safe.

"Yuppie murals," Doug Hollis said scathingly, champagne glass in hand. "I really respect Richard Haas. I really do. When he wants to, he can really pull it off. But his interest level was real low on this project, and the hassle level was real high. It was interior decorator thinking."

There was more rancor in Hollis's comments than the works deserved, but then he was in high dudgeon. He had entered the building an hour earlier through one of the Mission Street doors. He had heard the sound of his rain column and been pleased. But as he passed through the transitional lobby, his pleasure turned to shock.

"Holy shit," Hollis had said out loud. The reaction might have been mistaken for awe over the rain column. He might have been another guest seeing it for the first time, for all who did were truly stunned. But Hollis was stunned by something else. Arrayed around his pool were six clusters of large plants. Worse, much worse, was what was within the pool itself. Perched on black podiums were six dolphins carved out of ice. Hollis walked around and around the pool, cursing and muttering to himself about the disregard that had been demonstrated for his art. Sure, he and Jay Mancini had discussed the need for some sort of barrier around the edge of the pool several times in recent weeks, after at least two people had walked into the water and fallen while scouring the ceiling with their eyes for the source of the waterfall. Hollis had proposed an unobtrusive, eighteen-inch-high railing. Mancini had said he did not think that would be enough of a barrier.

Hollis knew Mancini had planned something else, but this was too much. He told himself that he could have tolerated the clusters of plants. They at least served a function. But the ice sculptures told him that the developers had just been paying lip service to his art all along. As the evening continued, Hollis drank more champagne and his mood grew blacker. At one point, Ken Tardy walked over, smiled, and said: "Well, Doug, looks pretty good. How you doing?"

"Well Ken, how did you enjoy drinking my blood?" came the sharp reply.

"Whoa," said the stunned Tardy. "Wait a minute. What the hell are you talking about?"

"You know what I'm talking about," said Hollis before he turned and walked away, his anger turned fleetingly on the portion of his fee that had gone to Tardy.

Hollis had invited several of his friends to see the rain column that night, including Diana Fuller, the San Francisco gallery owner who represented his work. They hatched a plot: each person would move around the pool to a spot beside one of the ice sculptures. On a cue from Hollis, they would push them all over and then blend back in with the crowd. As these rain-column guerrillas moved into position, Hollis got cold feet or began to sober up. He walked away and the moment passed. Fuller, however, still had to vent her rage. She stalked over to Jay Mancini, who was talking with a group of men and women, and pulled on one of his suitcoat lapels. "This is cultural vandalism!" she shouted at him. "Cultural vandalism!" Then she stormed off without further comment, leaving Mancini dumbfounded in her wake. He had no idea who the woman was or what in the hell she was talking about. After a few minutes, he returned to the conversation. Nothing could dampen his mood that night; his demons were gone.

With a broad smile, Mancini resumed working the crowd, clapping people on the back, thanking them for coming, praising their contributions to the project, urging them to come down for lunch once the restaurants began opening. When he saw a tall black man enter the atrium, Mancini rushed over and embraced him.

"We just couldn't have done it without you. We really couldn't. You were always there for us," Mancini said to Leroy King, the president of the San Francisco Redevelopment Agency.

Scott Johnson hung back from the crowd, spending most of the evening standing on the edge of one of the seating platforms chatting with a few people. Yes, he told a woman, he liked the rain column. It was a positive addition to the space. And Johnson did like the rain column, although he was privately critical of what he considered a lack of elegance in its details. To him, it still looked too much like a Plexiglas pan suspended from the ceiling.

There were, of course, the obligatory speeches. Art Agnos, who had replaced Dianne Feinstein as mayor of San Francisco, praised the renovation as a bright light in the rejuvenated neighborhood and the salvation of a historic building. Tom Steele, as chairman and chief executive of Perini Land & Development, noted that the grand opening came almost exactly twenty-eight years after the company had been selected to redevelop a major section of the waterfront four blocks away, turning it into Golden Gateway Center. Randy Verrue delivered the "Academy Award" speech, thanking a long list of people associated with the project. He neglected to mention Scott Johnson.

Verrue later denied that the oversight had been intentional, and he praised Johnson's work on the project. But at the time of the grand opening of the renovated phase, the developers were locked in a bitter dispute with Johnson over the size of his bill for additional services. The figure had reached $1 million. Johnson could produce the time cards for his designers and account for enough of his own time to warrant the extra money. But Verrue and Mancini were arguing that much of the additional work had been caused by the architect's failure to do it right the first time. This was aggravated by the fact that the base fee for the architects, 4 percent of construction costs, had been pushed up by the overruns. There also had been some hot exchanges when the developer discovered that the architects had allowed their errors-and-omissions insurance coverage to drop to $2 million from the $5 million specified in the contract. This meant that if Perini decided to sue Pereira Associates over the fees, $2 million was probably the maximum they could hope to recover.

Once again, Mancini had enlisted Ken Tardy to help him find a solution. Not long before the opening party, Johnson and Bill Fain had asked Mancini to come down to Los Angeles to go over the papers that they felt supported their fee for additional services. Mancini had already asked Tardy to examine the list of extra items. When he mentioned that he was going to Los Angeles, Tardy was adamant that Mancini not go to them.

"Jay, you will lose the psychological control," insisted Tardy. "Make them come to you. And Jay, you kick their balls." Tardy had come to the conclusion that half of the additional fees were the result of mistakes by the architects that should have been corrected under the original fee.

The meeting was held in Perini's offices in San Francisco. When Johnson and Fain showed up, they were surprised to find Tardy sitting beside Mancini at the conference table. When Fain asked what he was doing there, Tardy said, "I'm here as ball buster." He had analyzed their list of additional services, he told them, and recommended cutting it by $750,000. A few minutes into the discussion, Fain asked to speak privately with Mancini. Tardy left the room and Fain, Johnson, and Mancini continued their negotiations without him. However, there was no resolution of the matter and it was still unresolved as Randy Verrue gave his thank-you speech.

The shift of workers to the renovation to complete it had pushed the completion of the new building back further. By September, the building had reached its full height and about half of the exterior had been covered with the skin of glass and pre-cast concrete panels. Over the remainder of the fall and early winter, interior walls were finished and most of the building was enclosed in skin.

On the Friday before Christmas, Scott Johnson was in San Francisco on other business and he stopped by the Rincon Center offices to look at two mock-ups for the new lobby in the residential section. One of the mock-ups used the elements from Johnson's plan, and the other had been designed by Debra Walker, an interior decorator and friend of Mancini's, who had been doing some consulting work for Mancini on various aspects of the project. It was she who had decorated the model apartments and put together a display in the historic post office lobby of artifacts recovered from the excavation at the site.

Mancini had told Johnson some weeks earlier that he was not satisfied with the design for the residential lobby. Johnson's design made extensive use of granite to give the large space a monumental atmosphere. The large concrete columns that pierced the space were to be clad in granite, and he had planned to use marble and a light gold carpet that picked up some of the flecks of color in the granite elsewhere in the lobby. But Mancini had been inspecting first-class apartment and condominium buildings around the city. The ones he liked best contained a lot of dark wood. It reminded him, he said, of the interior of the Bohemian Club. He had told Johnson that he had asked Debra Walker to come up with a new scheme for the lobby along these lines.

When Johnson walked into the lobby just before Christmas, he found the two examples side by side on one of the walls. Walker had used an oxblood carpet and deep walnut paneling for the walls. It struck Johnson as the interior of a men's club. But Mancini clearly favored her design, or at least elements of it.

"Jay, if you want to do this, fine, okay," said Johnson impassively. "But I don't want to be associated with it. It has no redeeming characteristics. Just count me out of the project."

Now, it was unclear what counting Johnson out would have meant at that stage. Certainly he did not want to disassociate himself from the entire project. He did not really want to let someone else redesign the lobby, either. Even he would later acknowledge that he had overreacted. That day Johnson stalked out. A week went by before Mancini called him and asked the architect to rework his design of the lobby to incorporate wood paneling and a deeper color for the carpet. Johnson agreed, having decided that it was better to do as much as he could to salvage his concept than abandon a trying project at this late juncture.

"Developers often have radar for things that are new and different about a project," he said in reaction to the incident. "They can look around a room and zero in on a wall that is a unique color or a detail that has never been tried before. To some, if it clearly works after examining it, they've got to have it. And to others, it's another thing to fear."

Jay Mancini offered this assessment of what happened: "It's my building. Not his. I have to live with it. So I'll make the final decisions."

At four minutes past five on the afternoon of October 17, 1989, just as the Oakland A's and San Francisco Giants were about to begin the third game of the World Series at Candlestick Park, an earthquake struck the San Francisco Bay Area. A long section of the double-decked Nimitz Freeway in Oakland collapsed when its concrete pillars buckled, causing the worst loss of life. Natural-gas lines ruptured and fires raged through San Francisco's Marina District. Old buildings, most of them stucco and unreinforced concrete and brick, all built on unstable soil, crumbled. Concrete fell from the huge columns holding up the two-level Embarcadero Freeway and it was quickly closed.

Andrea Hine, a Pacific Bell Directory employee, was in a rest room on the fourth floor of the former post office when the earthquake hit. "There was this rolling back and forth," she said. "The whole building seemed to roll for, what was it, eight seconds or so. It seemed longer."

There had been a practice fire drill the previous month, so there was calm and order as the hundreds of Pacific Bell employees made their way down the stairs and out of the building. When a few brave souls returned to their offices half an hour later, they found no damage at all.

Early in the morning on the day after the quake, P. Q. Chin got a telephone call at home. One of his clients wanted him to come downtown right away to inspect the damaged facade of a building a block from the Embarcadero. On his way, Chin could not resist stopping by Rincon Center first. The atrium had been fully leased by this time, and work had finally been completed on the new building and towers. Apartments had been leased. People were living in the tallest concrete building in San Francisco, though there were only a few and none were apparently home when the quake struck.

As he walked through the renovated portion, Chin saw no evidence of damage from the earthquake. The skylight was intact; the windows overlooking the atrium were undamaged. He crossed the courtyard and went into the new building. Again, there was no obvious evidence of any substantial damage. Looking closer, Chin saw that plaster had cracked in a handful of places near the intersections of major columns and girders, where the ductile-frame system was designed to absorb the lateral force of the earthquake. Very minor stuff. Chin was well satisfied that the building had withstood the quake.

On his way to inspect the nearby building for his client, Chin stopped to look at one of the huge concrete columns supporting a section of the Embarcadero Freeway about a block from Rincon. The force of the quake, which measured 6.9 on the Richter scale, had caused the column to buckle partially. Concrete had broken away from the column, exposing the steel reinforcing bars. All of the steel was vertical. The column, and many like it supporting the Embarcadero and Nimitz freeways, had failed largely because of the lack of horizontal rebars. Indeed, part of a program to upgrade California highways and bridges involves putting steel jackets and collars around such pillars, but it had not begun when the quake hit. Not long after Chin examined the column, workers erected temporary wood supports to ensure against the collapse of the Embarcadero Freeway, and the city re-opened a decades-old debate over whether to tear down the entire eyesore and free up that area of the waterfront for first-class development. In January 1991 the mayor announced the freeway would be demolished.

Well before the earthquake, the development team had broken up and each had gone his separate way. P. Q. Chin's business had gone through some rough periods, largely because the downtown plan had cooled the red-hot building market. When it picked up again, he landed a lot of jobs outside San Francisco, including the structural engineering for the nationwide chain of showrooms built by General Motors for its new line of Saturn cars. After twenty-five years in the same job, Dennis Oh left to form his own engineering firm after a dispute with Chin.

Bob Mayer left Citibank to form a real estate syndication and venture capital firm in San Francisco. Ken Tardy retired to a small estate outside Phoenix, where he planned to build other houses so that his grown children would be close to him.

Michael Blumenthal, the catalyst for the project, went to jail. He was convicted of making false statements to a bank and sentenced to a year in federal prison. He had apparently faked the amount of work completed on a construction project so he could draw down more of his loan than he should have. In a civil lawsuit connected with the incident, an attorney for the bank that lost the money tried to get Blumenthal to say some of the funds had been used to pay his share of the initial costs of forming the Rincon Center partnership. He denied it and the issue was dropped.

Harry Topping had left the Rincon team early in 1989, joining a developer in Los Angeles as project manager for a new downtown office building. With two architecture degrees and an MBA, Topping felt he had added another to his resume: a doctorate in real estate, the hard way.

Michael Praszker had suffered his jolt months before the earthquake. In January of 1989, the developers had filed a lawsuit against Praszker's company. The suit accused the firm of negligence in the testing of the soils and design of the shoring. The company denied any wrongdoing in court papers and in late 1990 Praszker's firm was dropped as a defendant. In Praszker's view, the suit was an unfair blot on his reputation from the start.

In the spring of 1989, a Hong Kong businessman approached Randy Verrue about the possibility of providing financing for some major developments on the West Coast. The businessman suggested that Perini Land & Development act as the general partner and he would be the bankroller. The idea appealed to Verrue, who was eager to embark on another large-scale development. But Perini officials in Framingham were less eager. Talks dragged on for weeks before Perini executives said they didn't really care to pursue another major West Coast development at the time. Rincon Center had left a bad taste back east. While no one was blaming Verrue for the cost problems, no one was eager to start another major project just then. Verrue did not relish returning to a string of smaller developments, and he had to wonder whether his star would ever again be on the rise at Perini Corporation. So he quit Perini and joined the Hong Kong financier in a new development company based in San Francisco.

On the same Saturday in July of 1989, Jay Mancini and Scott Johnson got on airplanes headed for the opposite ends of the world.

When he had found out that Verrue was leaving, Mancini's immediate reaction was that he would get the job as regional head of Perini Land & Development. Despite the difficulties of the past five years, such hopes were not without some foundation in Mancini's mind. In April of 1989, just after work was officially completed on the new phase, Perini Investment Properties, the subsidiary that had taken over management of Rincon Center, held its annual meeting in San Francisco. The directors and their wives had toured the development one afternoon. At dinner that night, Mancini was seated between David Perini, the chairman of Perini Corporation, and Dick Boushka, a director of Perini Investment. Boushka leaned over to Mancini and said, "You know, Jay, we're going to make a lot of money on this project." Mancini was certain it had been loud enough for Perini to hear, but the chairman of the board did not say anything.

"I really think I've earned Randy's job," Mancini told John Cahoon not long after that dinner. A few minutes later, he shook his head as if awakening from a dream and said, "No, John. I'll be lucky if they don't fire me."

As it turned out, Perini didn't fire Mancini, but neither did the company offer him the top spot. So he put out a few feelers for other positions. He considered an offer to become project manager for a major high-rise about to start construction in Seattle, but decided he didn't want to leave San Francisco. In early July, he became director of development in the Oakland office of another Canadian developer. He would supervise project managers on various medium-size developments around the Bay Area. It was not the jump up that Mancini had hoped for; it was a lateral move at best. But it wasn't selling warehouses, either. And Mancini still had his dreams. What he really wanted to do, he confided, was become a developer on his own, taking an equity position in major commercial buildings. That, he said, is where the real money is to be made.

Before starting his new job, Mancini returned to Lake Como in Italy, the spot where he had vacationed in 1984 before starting full time on Rincon. The trips stood as bookends to the most difficult period of his professional life. For reading on the plane to Italy, he had taken William H. Whyte's treatise on architecture and public space, *City: Rediscovering the Center*. Even now, he was looking for other opinions on Rincon Center.

Scott Johnson's plane that Saturday left Los Angeles International Airport for Tokyo. Instead of a book, Johnson carried a tube filled with drawings for a 3,000-acre development on the island of Guam that he and Bill Fain were designing for a Japanese corporation. It was a huge job, involving designs for an entire new resort community, from vacation homes to condominiums, hotels to retail shops and stores. New architects were being added to the staff again, and the office had expanded onto another floor at its new location on Wilshire Boulevard.

Johnson and the firm were busy and prospering. In the spring of 1990, Donald Trump hired Johnson to design what Trump said would be the tallest building in the world, a giant 145-story tower on the site of the old Ambassador Hotel in Los Angeles. The Trump building raised an immediate furor in Los Angeles. The city school district wanted to build a new school on the location and filed a lawsuit to block the project. Trump, of course, was having his own financial difficulties elsewhere, but he still managed to file his own lawsuit against the school district. It seemed possible that this might turn out to be a paper project.

Rincon Center had not turned out to be the career boost that Johnson had anticipated. Events interceded, mostly for the good. Fox Plaza had made his name and brought in a string of important new commissions in Los Angeles. But Rincon Center had been a learning experience for its architect, too. He had seen firsthand that making buildings involved far more than a brilliant concept, and he had used the lessons to reshape the staff at his office and hone his own skills in translating his designs into reality.

EPILOGUE

"A BIGGER CHECK"

In twelfth-century France, a convergence of cultural and political factors produced the Gothic cathedral, one of the greatest achievements in architectural history. They were magnificent and monumental structures, signs of a new prosperity that allowed so much wealth to be spent for spiritual purposes. Whether we like it or not, today's cathedrals are the soaring towers of glass and granite and concrete that have transformed the public spaces of America's great cities. They, too, are the result of a convergence of cultural and political factors. If they are less monumental than Chartres, they are no less a window on the priorities and prosperity of the age in which we live.

Rincon Center was an ambitious undertaking, tricky and complicated in one of the most regulated building environments in the United States. Unlike the master cathedral builders, whose labors on a single building could span generations, the builders of Rincon were under enormous pressure to move fast at every juncture. The bottom line here was not the glory of God, but the almighty dollar. When combined with the inexperience of some of the team members, mistakes were inevitable and costly. These factors are by no means unique to Rincon Center; dozens of major urban developments across the country face similar pressures. Perhaps understanding the challenges confronted in this particular project provides a better understanding of how these modern cathedrals are conceived and constructed everywhere. Whether we like it or not, this is the way it is done these days.

The final construction costs for Rincon Center remain something of a mystery. Randy Verrue and Jay Mancini had both promised to provide a full rundown of the costs. But Verrue had a change of heart near the end of the project and instructed Mancini not to disclose precise information about the final costs. Tom Steele sat in his office in Framingham one day not long after the earthquake and talked about many aspects of the project for hours. But he, too, refused to provide any details about the final construction costs. They were, he said, a confidential matter. Perhaps they were embarrassed by the scale of the overruns. Or perhaps Perini Corporation simply did not want to set a precedent; real estate developers are a secretive bunch when it comes to money.

The best estimate, gleaned from a variety of people associated with the project, put the cost of construction at somewhere between $83 million and $85 million. One of the key development team members said that $85 million was the most accurate figure. That would be an overrun in the neighborhood of 33 percent. Much of the additional costs were traceable to two factors: the collapse of the excavation and the costs of concrete and rebar. Indeed, according to the estimates, the costs of concrete and rebar turned out to be 50 percent higher than the original budget. Other factors pushed up the costs. Perhaps, as Dianna Wong and her young associates had predicted, Rincon Center was always an $85 million construction project. That would make the final price tag a testament to the complexity and quality of the building. But then, that would not account for the occasional collision of chaos and stupidity.

Other costs also wound up far over budget. The soft costs for architects, engineers, and other consultants were about double the original estimate of $4.2 million. Tenant improvements cost more than $20 million, far exceeding the projected $13.5 million. Each phase of the development was opened more than a year later than planned, and those delays pushed out the date at which the project began generating revenue and meant that the developers had to pay longer on their loans. And the loans themselves were larger than anticipated because of the failure of the real estate syndication and the cost overruns.

Until the fall of 1990, the 168,000 square feet of office space in the new phase of the project had stood virtually empty for a year and a half. The inability to fill it translated into about $4 million in lost revenue a year. Finally, the U.S. Court of Appeals for the Ninth Circuit signed a long-term lease for almost all of the office space in the building. Because the court includes a large legal library, the government wanted a building that would support the heavy load created by the books. It required rearranging some interior walls and other adjustments, but Rincon Center turned out to be one of the few places that would fit the bill. Like Pac Bell, the Court of Appeals was a prestigious major tenant. Also like Pac Bell, it was an expensive one. The developers had to commit millions in extra tenant improvements to snare the court.

When Randy Verrue first asked Bob Mayer and Citibank to finance Rincon Center, the projected total cost was $115 million. In the end, according to Mayer and others, it cost somewhere between $150 million and $160 million. But Perini Land & Development and its parent, Perini Corporation, never backed away from their commitment. As the costs rose and more cash came out of their corporate pockets, they stuck with the project. Ken Tardy phrased it best when he said: "If you have a problem, you write a check. If you have a bigger problem, you write a bigger check."

It is still too early to say for certain how the developers and their partners will fare in the long term with Rincon Center. The growth cap imposed by San Francisco's downtown plan will work in their favor. The city's decision to tear down the Embarcadero Freeway will be a great boon to the neighborhood and Rincon Center. The weak real estate market nationwide hurt all developers, but such markets have always been cyclical.

As for the public, Rincon Center seems to be a success. The atrium bustles with life as office workers, professionals, and laborers crowd in every workday at lunchtime. The rain column adds a delightful energy. Anton Refregier's murals are as colorful and lively as the day they were painted, and the best of Gilbert Stanley Underwood's building has been preserved. As public space, this must be counted a grand victory. The affordable housing is more of a mixed bag. Rather than serving the low-income people displaced by San Francisco's changing downtown and high rents, Rincon's below-market rents are being taken advantage of by office workers and young professionals on their way up. That does not make it wrong for them to live there. But it does seem to demonstrate the limitations inherent in this kind of development, if not also in our reliance on private interests in general to solve the problems of our cities.

The developers, engineers, and architects sought to accomplish a lot with Rincon Center. The result was certainly far more interesting than erecting another boxlike office building. And so was getting there.

ACKNOWLEDGMENTS

I owe an enormous debt of gratitude to dozens of people. This book would not exist if they had not taken the time to teach me about architecture, construction, banking, and real estate development. Not all of them are named in the text, nor could I list them here. I offer my regrets for the omissions. Those who read this book should realize that its characters do not form the complete cast of Rincon Center.

To Scott Johnson, who shared his vision and spent countless hours explaining the intricacies and artistry of architecture to me, I am forever grateful. Special thanks also to Jay Mancini, Bob Mayer, Ken Tardy, Harry Topping, and Tim Tosta, all of whom were generous with their time and knowledge. Any inaccuracies or misunderstandings here are not their fault.

The original idea for this book came from my agent, Dominick Abel. Once again, Marian Wood proved to be the editor every writer dreams of and few are fortunate enough to work with. I thank them both, and consider myself lucky to count them as my friends.

BIBLIOGRAPHY

American Institute of Architects. *AIA Firm Survey Report*. Washington, D.C.: American Institute of Architects, 1989.
_____.*AIA Firm Survey Report*. Washington, D.C.: American Institute of Architects, 1986.
Boston Financial Group. *Rincon Center: A Prospectus*. Boston: Boston Financial Group, 1986.
Camp, William Martin. *San Francisco: Port of Gold*. New York: Doubleday & Company, 1947.
Frieden, Bernard J., and Lynne B. Sagalyn. *Downtown, Inc.: How America Rebuilds Cities*. Cambridge: MIT Press, 1989.
Goldberger, Paul. *The Skyscraper.* New York: Alfred A. Knopf, 1982.
McCullough, David. *The Great Bridge*. New York: Simon and Schuster, 1972.
Ross, Steven S. *Construction Disasters: Design Failures, Causes, and Prevention*. New York: McGraw-Hill Book Company, 1984.
Rybczynski, Witold. *The Most Beautiful House in the World*. New York: Viking, 1989.
Salvadori, Mario. *Why Buildings Stand Up: The Strength of Architecture*. New York: W. W. Norton & Company, 1980.
San Francisco City Planning Commission, Redevelopment Agency of the City and County of San Francisco. *Rincon Point–South Beach Redevelopment Plan*. San Francisco: City of San Francisco, 1980.
Scully, Vincent. *American Architecture and Urbanism: New Revised Edition*. New York: Henry Holt & Company, 1988.
Whyte, William H. *City: Rediscovering the Center.* New York: Doubleday, 1988.

INDEX

Note: Buildings are in San Francisco unless otherwise noted.